DATE DUE

BRODART, CO.   Cat. No. 23-221-003

THE WIRE THAT FENCED THE WEST

THE
WIRE
THAT
FENCED
THE
WEST

By Henry D. and Frances T. McCallum

UNIVERSITY OF OKLAHOMA PRESS : NORMAN

Library of Congress Catalog Card Number: 65-11234

Copyright 1965 by the University of Oklahoma Press, Publishing Division of the University. Composed and printed at Norman, Oklahoma, U.S.A., by the University of Oklahoma Press. First edition, May, 1965; second printing, April, 1966.

Most people are of the opinion that all there is to be said on the subject of barbed wire could be put into one paragraph—or, more than likely, into one exclamation, such as, "Of all things to write a book about—barbed wire!" The average person knows little about the history of barbed wire and less about collections of it. Yet when the facts concerning the invention and development of this product are put together with actual samples of different types of early barbed-wire fencing, there is unfolded quite a story—of big stakes, high tempers, and patched fences—a story which in its sweep pervades the history of our nation.

It was through interest in making a collection of barbed wire samples that I was led to study and research for background information concerning barbed wire. In my profession as oil geologist, I worked for many years in the fields and along the country lanes of sections of the Southwest where there were miles of farm fences around or over which I was obliged to make my way, and scores of gaps and gates with which I had to wrestle. I saw some mighty strange and interesting kinds of fencing, and one day when I came on barbed wire made in links like a chain, I determined to take home a sample as a novelty. That was the beginning of my collection. Through the course of years, it has grown to more than one hundred different kinds of wire from all over the United States and from many foreign countries also.

Let me explain here and now that I do not take my samples

out of a man's good fence. After all, fence-cutting is still a felony in my native state of Texas, and I do not propose to lay myself open to this charge. From the surplus of old wire left dangling from deserted fence lines, or discarded in arroyos, or hanging in rolls on the posts where fencing has been replaced or repaired, I have found most of the wire in my collection. Also much has been acquired through exchange with fellow collectors—sometimes called "Barb-arians"—and through gifts sent to me from far and near, by friends and by strangers whose imaginations have been captured by the idea of a man making so curious a collection as—of all things, barbed wire.

One of the first bits of factual information I learned about barbed wire came to me from my mother, Jane Y. McCallum, who was an avid reader and an eager student of history. After I had started my collection, she saved clippings from anything she read that made even a mention of barbed wire, and she passed on to me this habit. Other members of the family have "put up" with my collection—of both barbed wire and materials dealing with it—but not without a lot of joshing! Friends in all walks of life have helped me and encouraged me to further the study of barbed wire —bosses, the chairman of a board of directors, the vice-president of an oil company, librarians, museum curators, collectors throughout the United States, teachers, farmers, old-time story-tellers, descendants of prominent early-day figures, secretaries (Estelle and Anne—and Gwynne); so many, many wonderful friends have given me of their time and their talents and their confidence—and their wire!—that I cannot begin to account for all of them. But two must be named specifically: my wife Frances, who has collaborated with me in the writing of this book on a subject which was distasteful to her in the beginning but from which she resignedly agreed she could not escape; and our friend and teacher, the late Walter Prescott Webb, to whom we are indebted not only for his reading of the manuscript of this book, but also for his opening the way to an understanding of barbed wire through his revelation of the importance of the Great Plains of America and the pioneering agricultural attachments thereto.

To these I offer my thanks—and to a providence which open-ed my eyes to the significance of what remained before me of old fences and old fence-builders. The men who can remember any-thing of early barbed-wire experiences are nearly all gone, and the fences are vanishing also. With the straightening and widen-ing of modern highways, fences are coming down every day, and with a new philosophy of enclosure which directs the owners of stock to keep their animals *in* rather than expect the tiller of the soil to keep them *out*, many fences will not be replaced. I was almost too late; if I have been able to capture the spirit of the story of barbed wire as well as to recount the history, it has been done just in time. Barbed-wire manufacture and marketing will go on and on, but barbed-wire collecting will soon become an impossibility. I am thankful that I have been privileged to take part in it.

Henry D. McCallum

It should be understood, I think, that in the matter of barbed-wire study and collecting, I am merely a helper—and sometimes a reluctant one. The subject is my husband's entirely, and I have been but an accessory to the study and research, a helpmeet in turning the crank—so to speak—to grind out not a strand of prick-ered wire such as Mrs. Glidden helped her husband to produce, but a whole sequence of events which make up the history of barbed wire.

Once while Henry and I were in the process of uncovering information filed away in the recesses of the Smithsonian Institu-tion, someone said to me jokingly, "Think of Mrs. Glidden pro-viding a coffee mill for making that first practical barbed wire. How much more helpful wives were in those days than now!" And at once the curator—a real gentleman, I would say—came back with, "Well, I don't know. Here is Mrs. McCallum helping her husband with barbed wire too." This remark—in addition to a desire to be a writer—has long sustained me, for if there has been nothing else accomplished in this work, it has been a pleasure and a benefit for us to do it together.

FRANCES T. McCALLUM

Tyler, Texas
February 2, 1965

ACKNOWLEDGMENTS

RESEARCH ON BARBED WIRE takes many forms. Much of it of course is dependent on books and other written matter, but most of it is slowly evolved through familiarity with barbed-wire fences and with the places where barbed-wire fences abound. In this respect, the work of compilation for a study such as has been undertaken here could not have been done by one man—nor even by one man and wife—alone. There had to be help along the way.

From the beginning there was an understanding and innately inquisitive mother who showed interest in the subject of barbed wire, or in the idea of a fellow's spending time studying such a subject. Always there has been someone who has helped keep alive the spirit of quest—which is, in truth, more lively than average research, more concrete than standard study.

Among those who have come forward at the turning points and have traveled with us to the next turn ahead, those named here are well remembered: in writing—Jane Y. McCallum, Walter Prescott Webb, and H. Bailey Carroll; in research—P. W. Bishop, Martin Wenger, Eleanor C. Bishop, Helen Hargrave, Lorene Ellerd, Gene M. Gressley, Frank D. Smith, Chas. B. Rayner, John W. Crudgington, Mattie Sue Mounce, Bill Garner and associates, M. P. Tixier, L. H. Skromme, Roy D. Holt, Boone McClure, Mrs. E. Perry Ellwood, I. L. Ellwood II, Mrs. Abel B. Pierce, Mrs. J. H. Bohlender, and R. N. Richardson; in collecting—R. G. Hart, Jack Morley, George Johnson, Bill Reiss, Ralph B. Lee, Tom Medder, R. M. Kleberg, Jr., Herbert Holmgreen, Frank Pennington,

Jacque Cauwe, Richard Holt, and especially Ben Peterson, Wilmer T. Swink, and Roy Winslow.

Furthermore, the final compilation of information could not have been conveyed to the reader in words alone; pictures of the actual wire were essential to full clarification. In this connection, William C. Ward's analytical drawings constitute not only a handsome addition to the book but also an important ingredient in the study. And the use of other illustrative material provided by several sources greatly enhances the work as a whole.

CONTENTS

PART THREE: Types of Barbed Wire

ILLUSTRATIONS

PART ONE
Barbed-Wire Fence-Makers

CHAPTER 1

THRESHOLD OF PROMISE

ACROSS HALF A CONTINENT the American settler of the nineteenth century made his way westward with tools of the forest. Leaving the rocky coast line of the Atlantic, he passed the great inland waterways and advanced through the virgin forests with the aid of equipment such as his forefathers had used to found a new world. But when he came out of the forest, suddenly removed from familiar environment and faced with conditions for which no previous experience had prepared him, he found that he was—in his own idiom—"not rightly outfitted" to go on. It was not a question of the quality of the axes and knives and spades and plows which had brought him through the wilderness of wooded lands onto the threshold of promise; it was a question of their suitability. The fact was, tools of the Eastern forests were not usable on Western plains and prairies. Change in scenery called for change and adaptation in provisions, and with the farm-minded pioneer, one of the features most radically in need of adaptation to the changing scene was fencing.

Because for long ages fencing had been made of native materials, because it had been a natural rather than an industrial development, no substitute for standard fencing was provided for use in the new lands of the West. Planters attempting to protect cultivation heretofore had used local substitutes for fences. Like men of other eras who had built barriers by lining up tree trunks where there were trees to be cut, and by erecting stone walls where there were stones to be dug, American colonists had put

[3]

into fences whatever surplus raw materials were left from the clearing of land. They had fenced with the by-products of agriculture—brush, trees, rocks, levees, whatever was corollary to the tilling of the soil—and descendants of the colonists had continued to do the same.

In New England there was a surplus of loose stones. The saying was that when a New England farmer bought one acre of land for plowing, he bought also a second acre to be used for piling up stones taken from the first.[1] Piled up stones gradually became rock walls, and rock walls became traditional in New England. Even in parts where there were both stones and trees to be disposed of, timber usually was reserved for the building of houses and for fuel, rather than for fences. Because of the abundance of stone in the area, this was one of the few sections of early settlement where wooden rails were not the predominant form of boundary markers. The "rock-ribbed" land came to be rock-bound as well.

In forested areas farther down the Atlantic seaboard where there were fewer stones to contend with, there was within the range of early settlement a seemingly inexhaustible supply of wood. Although there were many uses for the fine trees felled in opening up land in this region, there was excess timber for fences, most of which were made of rails split with mauls and wedges such as young Abe Lincoln was to immortalize. Combat with the forest was one of the constant tasks, and encroachment of the trees back into cultivated lands was one of the worrisome responsibilities for settlers of extensive regions of the continent. The raw materials derived from these natural conditions became, as a consequence, an integral part of daily living for most early Americans.

In the South, as far west as the Colorado River of Texas, for a distance of 150 miles inland from the Gulf of Mexico, rail fences, "worm" or "stake-and-rider" style, were prevalent. Rich coastal lands were cleared for planting tobacco, sugar, rice, and

[1] Rowland C. Robinson, "New England Fences," *Scribner's Monthly* (February, 1880), 502–11.

cotton, and lumber from the trees was put to good use as plantation fencing. Slaves—who had to be fed at any cost—provided man power for building fences in the South, and provided too the important follow-up workers needed for making the continual repairs which wooden fences required. After the Civil War, planters still could secure cheap labor to help with rebuilding, for it was said that a Negro freedman would split rails all week long for a jug of molasses or a side of bacon. Wherever timber had not been destroyed, Southerners went on using wooden fencing almost exclusively, repairing it almost constantly, and replacing with more wooden rails the sections carried away by indigents in search of fuel. So great was the burden that Southern landowners, even at the edge of timberlands, claimed they would welcome some other kind of fencing material.

In the Midwest and Southwest, conditions were far different. Out of the crowded seaboard states and beyond the farms of the Allegheny foothills was a different setting, and the farther it was explored, the stranger it was found to be. For the settler who came with family and family possessions, intending to make a permanent settlement, the strangeness many times caused him to falter.

Migration for the farm settler was meant to be final. It was a once-in-a-lifetime gamble—not a speculation for profit but an investment for existence. In most cases the settler had only his two hands and the help of his family to count on. In his "mover wagon" he brought the tools he leaned on for a living—a spade or shovel, buckets and ropes, occasionally a breaking plow, and a shotgun "which hung inside the wagon near the seat."[2] There was sometimes an extra horse tied alongside, or an extra yoke of oxen, and a dog "which followed behind or under the wagon where there was some shade from the sun."[3] As this kind of pioneer and his family passed mid-continent streams and rivers and came onto the margin of sparsely inhabited high plains, as they

[2] Ben Peterson, The Peterson Scrapbook, property of Mrs. Ben Peterson, Everson, Washington.
[3] *Ibid.*

[5]

looked off in the distance to see what lay beyond, they found reason to hesitate and, many times, reason to draw their wagons to a halt.

Ahead stretched mile after uninterrupted mile of tablelands, not entirely without trees, not entirely without loose stone, not entirely without water, but seriously affected by the scarcity of all three. The land was spread between the seasonal waters of meandering river-beds. Only brush or occasional canyon walls offered shelter or the wherewithall for building shelter. The climate was semiarid to arid, and insufficiency of moisture, coupled with characteristics of open terrain, limited the types of crops which could be grown. Because of these conditions, it would be necessary to plant more acreage than was needed in Eastern states, yet settlers could see that they would not be able to care for additional acres without suitable equipment—and the equipment they had was not suitable.

Farmers believed that food crops could be raised on the rolling prairie, and more than sustenance shares of feed and forage on the grass-covered plains, but they could not prove it unassisted. It was soon clear that if they were to move into the new West, farmers would require legislative provisions which allotted acreage in amounts adequate for homesteading on the plains and prairies, and industrial adjustments which provided equipment adapted to Western environment. As historian Walter Prescott Webb expressed it: ". . . the old technique of pioneering broke down, and an entirely new technique had to be evolved. . . ."[4] But until such time as new developments should catch up with the needs of the advancing agricultural front, many a wagon, once halted, never passed over the threshold of promise.

By the time the front had been drawn along the western edges of wooded lands, the farm settler could see that much of the change he must work out for himself. He was not likely to have direct help from the regions he had left, for men of the

---

[4] "The Frontier Machine," in Virginia Faulkner, comp., *Roundup: A Nebraska Reader,* 14. See also Webb's *The Great Plains.*

East did not understand his needs. From the regions toward which he was headed, he could expect no help at all, for he and his retinue were not made welcome by men of the West. His only recourse was to postpone settlement, and to use the interim of waiting as a period of adjustment.

Farmers were by tradition the fence-makers of the world. The historic function of the fence was to serve as defense. The word "fence," itself a contraction of "defense" or "defence," implied resistance against or protection from an outside foe. In ancient cultures across the earth the man who erected defense had been the tiller of the soil protecting the fruits of his labor, and the same was true on the frontier where nineteenth-century American settlers developed various protective devices for their own uses. In the states where they congregated along the edge of the prairie and plains, farmers experimented on their own initiative, adapting such equipment as they had and improvising what they did not have. Fence-wise, this was discouraging because there was not much to start with. But in independent ways they attempted to improve on whatever inadequate barricades they had, and many of their farm experiments proved to be forward-looking—some of them, patentable—inventions.

In the most barren regions, the simplest substitutes sometimes sufficed for fences. "Furrow fences" contained an area for a little while, and leaving stubble in the fields helped to hold soil in summer or snow in winter. In Kansas where much of the country was flat, guideposts were made by industrious Russo-German settlers who dug into the bedrock exposed in their fields. They uncovered an eight-inch stratum of limestone which they managed to break into slabs approximately eight inches wide and three feet long, and these they set up like the cornerstones of ancient Hebrew culture. This work was not often imitated in the West, however, because the tedious process of drilling holes into the limestone, then filling them with water to freeze in the winter or with water-soaked wooden pegs to swell in summer, could be carried through only by those peoples whose strong backs were

[7]

matched with strong wills, and then only in those places where beds of native limestone were to be found.[5] In parts of Nebraska the clay soil lent itself to the building of earthen ridges three feet and higher. "Ditching and embanking and surmounting the embankment with 3 rails" was possible where some wood was available, as in sections of Illinois, but it was generally said of such barriers that they "showed a woeful lack of ability to keep the farmer's hogs out of his own corn."[6] Sometimes hobbles and stakes were used to confine horses and mules; sometimes a few saplings or a pile of brush served as temporary corrals; but for protecting plowed fields, for surrounding them and defending them from depredation by unfettered livestock grazing at will, there was little material at hand.

In areas where native thorn bushes flourished or where they could be cultivated as hedges, hedge fencing gained popularity for a time. Some few farmers in less remote regions put up wire for horse lots and around small garden plots, but since the only kind of wire available in commercial quantities before 1874 was smooth wire—and usually of inferior quality—it was not satisfactory. Furthermore, labor to haul materials from a distance could not be spared from farm work, water transport was seldom within reach, and the cost of having goods brought by overland "freighters" was prohibitive. "Grass freight" brought by oxen grazing on native grasses was quoted at $.50 per hundred pounds, and the faster "corn freight" drawn by animals corn fed by hand along the way was as high as $2.50 per hundred.[7]

Lack of fencing for use on lands cultivated at great risk many times turned back the earliest settlers in the plains and prairies, and it became a problem of increasing importance as more and more farm families arrived in the edge-of-the-prairie states, and stayed on there. There were other problems, other needs, other

[5] Because of this unusual practice by the immigrants, the Kansas ledge rock was listed in early geologies of the region as "fence post rock." Cecil Howes in The Peterson Scrapbook, *loc. cit.*

[6] William V. Pooley, "The Settlement of Illinois from 1830 to 1850," University of Wisconsin *Bulletin No. 220* (May, 1908), 287–595.

[7] Laura V. Hamner, *Short Grass and Longhorns*, 12.

[8]

necessities required before the settler could pass into the promised land, but none more vital to the continuance of settlement than protection, in the form of dwelling places and in the form of fences. In an almost treeless land, with a scarcity of loose stones, and removed from navigable waterways, effective protection was hard to come by. No one knew it better than the homesteader, yet no one knew better than he that he must have protection—not only from the elements but from man and beast as well.

—III—III—III—III—III—III—

Throughout the plains country and on the prairie-plains, there already was established another kind of pioneer who had little sympathy for "intruders" in sway-back schooners coming to the new lands. This was a pioneer who had come empty-handed, unencumbered by family and family possessions, free to move across the great expanse of virgin territory as the seasons and nature's whims ordained. Partly he was the wanderer-herdsman of yore, the nomad; partly he was the adventurer—soldier of fortune, following upon the heels of Indians and in the footsteps of conquistadors. He was the American cowman.

The cowman had come early to the West. He had found a land which from the beginning was natural grazing ground. Much of it was covered with short grass upon which herds of buffalo and wild cattle fed, and although tall grass flourishing in certain portions suggested the ultimate raising of small grains and grain sorghums, such a possibility was still remote. Experiences of men like the trader who turned his oxen out to die in the winter on the high plains, but found in the spring that they were "not only alive but in better condition than when he had turned them loose," encouraged herding and grazing even in northern areas. But the possibility of widespread developments of other kinds seemed remote because the character of the land itself was discouraging to permanent settlement. The cowman saw it as land without enough rainfall to support farming of standard crops, without enough trees to provide fuel or building material, without enough streams to invite the founding of towns and cities. He saw it as natural range-land and he used it as such. He took upon himself the tending of great herds. He marshaled cattle from natural grasslands to natural water. He turned to the lonely life of the keeper of stock, guarding his animals against wolves and Indians, fire and drought, shadeless heat and driving cold. The land which he had found open and free for range cattle, he maintained open and free for range cattlemen; he kept it intact. But he came to regard it early in its history as his own domain.

The beginnings of the cowman's regime dated back a long time, but it was during the years following the close of the Civil War that the marketing of his livestock became an important business. He already controlled the cattle and the grazing lands when, at the end of the war, an upsurge in demand for meat to feed a hungry nation quickly grew to undreamed-of proportions. In the late 1860's government emphasis on deploying military units to end the Indian troubles meant that large quantities of fresh meat were needed for soldiers stationed at government forts in the West, and attention was drawn to the supply of both buffalo and beef available close at hand, on the plains and prairies. First the great wild herds of buffalo were attacked. Hunters came in a rush which was said to be "second only to the rush to the California gold fields some twenty years before," and because of the excitement of the times and the novelty of the situation, buffalo which should have been taken only for meat were slaughtered for hides and even for sport.[8] By 1870 they were all but exterminated. There remained in their place, however, herds of beef cattle. Native cattle, untended during war years, had multiplied by natural increase and by the admixture of domesticated stock that strayed from areas neglected or laid waste in the fighting. Herds of cattle ranged like the buffalo over vast stretches of low-growing nutritious grasses, and when the buffalo were gone, they were supplanted by mature cattle—scrawny and tough, but in enormous supply and ready for market. Texas Longhorns, which heretofore had been looked upon as nearly worthless, suddenly were

[8] Edward Everett Dale, *The Range Cattle Industry*, 43.

of great value, and the men who controlled the ranges suddenly were in position to gain great benefit.

In this setting cowmen built their empire. In this setting, by a sort of feudalistic arrangement of their own, they formulated rules governing the use of the range, and they worked out customs which were, by their hierarchy, the equivalent of law. Within their code were regulations to which every cowman was committed—but which other men sometimes found importunate.

The rule which seemed most unwarranted to contemporaries, and which was the source of most contention between cowmen and farmers, was the Law of the Open Range. Few cowmen owned their ranges. Few individuals could finance the purchase and maintenance of the immense amounts of acreage needed to support both summer and winter grazing. Few made any pretext of ownership or any practice of leasing. Free use of unoccupied government lands was the foundation of the range cattle industry. The Law of the Open Range was the unwritten rule of free access to grass and water. By implication it gave notice that open terrain in the West was not to be broken into by settlement. Newcomers were thereby forewarned not to stand in the cowman's route to the ranges, not to block his way with towns and fields and—of all things—fences.

Cowmen regarded settlers with hostility and with derision also. Even the names used between them reflected the cowman's position of superiority. "Granger," referring to Midwest and Northwest farm organizations under the Grange movement of a later period, was innocuous enough, except that it was sounded with a snort. And "nester" was a term used mainly in the Southwest, where cowmen literally looked down on places where farmers chose to settle. "Viewed from some ridge," the explanation goes, "the early nester's home, as he cleared his little patch of brush and stacked it in a circular form to protect his first feed patch from range cattle, looked like a giant bird's nest."[9] The occupant of the nest was dubbed "nester." Cowmen kept their distance from him, and watched with unconcealed scorn his efforts

[9] Ramon F. Adams, *Western Words*, 104.

[11]

to work out necessary change and adaptation. But they watched also with growing apprehension.

Farmers realized that if they were to homestead the unclaimed lands beyond the fringes of established settlement, they must arm themselves with fencing to withstand assault by unruly cattle. There was no other way to safeguard cultivation. The Law of the Open Range, providing free grazing, was in direct contrast to the Herd Law under which stockmen built barriers to confine their cattle. In the West the philosophy of fencing had reverted to the ancient custom of enclosing fields to keep livestock *out*, rather than enclosing pastures to keep livestock *in*. It was incumbent on the tiller of the soil again to be fence-maker, to put up his own defenses—and since he had not the raw materials for building, he was confronted with a problem of major importance.

In the early part of the 1880's, innovations in fencing had come mainly from the farm sectors of Ohio and Pennsylvania. During the period from 1790 through 1873 there had been 652 United States patents issued on fencing in general. Although few marked changes had emerged, variations from plain "Fence" through "Fence, flexible" to "Fence, wood"—alphabetically arranged with an assortment of related gadgets—had been listed by the United States Patent Office, and much of the list gave credit to inventors in Eastern states.[10] But as agricultural settlement moved westward, preoccupation with agricultural equipment moved also, and in the last decades of the century, mid-continent states—dominated by Illinois—led all other groups in patented fence patterns.

Illinois in the 1870's was situated on the border between city and prairie, between consumer and producer; it looked to the East and to the West, to the old and to the new. It was of the frontier and yet not the frontier, a meeting ground for the past and the future. Because of its location, it was at the heart of agitation over agricultural problems.

[10] *Subject Matter Index of Patents for Inventions issued by U.S. Patent Office from 1790 to 1873, Inclusive,* I, 508–16.

A tide of prairie settlement had washed past Illinois as early as 1825. Some settlers had passed on many miles farther, to the Far West where parts of California and Oregon beckoned, and to the wildernesses of Utah grown green under the hands of the Mormons. Others, though, had chosen to remain in the Midwest, and by the 1870's a sprinkling of small towns dotted an area from the valley of the upper Mississippi River to the big bend of the Missouri. Here prosperous farms had been established, and here, along an imaginary north-south line approximating the ninety-seventh meridian, covered wagons stopped for reconditioning of men and materials bound for the open prairie and plains. Here many new settlers stayed, and here they experimented in developing, among other things, practical fencing for the West.

The number of fence patents from this area increased steadily, and after a series of events which caught the public attention in 1874, the number grew rapidly. By the end of the century, nearly half of the fencing devices qualified for patent were attributed to citizens of Illinois alone.[11] And, remarkably enough, a large percentage of these inventors were residents of one county, concentrated in or around one town—the otherwise unremarkable farm community of De Kalb, in De Kalb County, Illinois.

[11] Earl W. Hayter, "Barbed Wire Fencing—A Prairie Invention," *Agricultural History* (October, 1939), 190 n.

CHAPTER 2

PRELUDE TO 1874

Even in the west, where the need to improvise fences was greatest and the inclination to acknowledge innovations strongest, the influence of established customs concerning fencing held sway through several decades. Settlers on the edge of the prairie were not long enough or far enough removed from ample supplies of natural materials to accept immediately the inevitability of man-made substitutes. Standard fences of wood were preferred above all others, in the Midwest as in other regions.

The use of wire for fencing, though seen as a possibility, was generally rejected. Smooth-strand wire had been tried and reported in a number of farm areas across the country since early in the nineteenth century. In open plains and prairies, however, only token cases were attempted, and these were recorded in wholly disparaging terms. Plain, smooth wire was far from adequate for Western fencing. Because of inferior quality, the early forms were given to contracting in winter and expanding in summer, and frequently when strung between posts spaced at sixteen-to eighteen-foot intervals, gave the impression of complete ineffectuality. Wherever an occasional newcomer to Western lands tried to "make do" with a single strand of "imported" wire sagging between wide-apart, hard-to-get posts, the sight was, as a rule, thoroughly disheartening. It was only a pretext of protection, captioned as "the early settlers' fence of one wire and a dog."[1] Poor results obtained from poor construction with poor products re-

[1] Edward Everett Dale, *Cow Country.*

duced the introduction of smooth wire for Western fencing to failure, and delayed its acceptance in other areas also. Wire was not counted as a replacement for wood and stone on a wide scale in any area, even though its adaptation to other uses had been accomplished long before.

The process of hammering metal and passing it through draw-plates to make it into wire was an art performed by the ancients. Wire work has been ranked with "the oldest of known industries, the roots of its beginnings reaching practically to the dawn of civilization."[2] First copper, gold, and silver were drawn into thin strands for making ornaments, and then during the Middle Ages in Europe wire was utilized mainly in the making of chain-mail armor for defense. Technical methods were gradually improved as the difficulties of working with crude equipment were overcome.[3] In the nineteenth century Bessemer furnaces and Bedson rolling processes, developed in comparatively quick succession, brought about unprecedented growth and expansion of the industry. In America a number of unrelated happenings which served to accelerate wire production throughout the nation converged, as it were, with special force on a small New England workshop founded in the early 1800's by a descendant of William Bradford, governor of Plymouth Colony.

Because a friend needed iron drawn small enough to use in making screws, a certain Ichabod Washburn was prompted to set up a small wire-manufacturing establishment near Worcester, Massachusetts, in the year 1831. As use of wire increased, the six-man force was enlarged by degrees so that by 1846, "23 men and 1 boy" were employed.[4] In 1850 the Yankee firm was approached by one Jonas Chickering and asked to make fine piano wire. The vogue for hoop skirts, bulwarked with wire, created another call for wire products and consequent expansion of the Worcester plant. By 1852, Ichabod Washburn had tested his own secret system of wire-drawing which he felt produced as good a wire as

[2] Arthur G. Warren, "The Wire Industry" (1928), American Steel & Wire Company Records, American Steel & Wire Company of New Jersey.
[3] Louis H. Winkler, *Mordia Memorial Lecture of 1942.*
[4] Warren, "The Wire Industry," AS&W Records, *loc. cit.*

the English made, yet he held back notice of his invention because, he said, it would not yet "admit of competition."[5] By the time Morse's telegraph appeared, Ichabod (then in partnership with his son-in-law Phillip Moen) was in a position to become one of the chief suppliers of telegraph wire, and his company, Washburn & Moen, was on the way to becoming the most important wire-drawing factory in the country. When Mr. Washburn and Mr. Bedson became friends and the two began working together on the new rolling processes, Ichabod's company attained such importance as to be considered a leader in world production of steel wire.[6]

During this interim of close to fifty years, various members of the Washburn family who were engaged in manufacturing projects in and around Worcester were in and out of partnership with Ichabod and with each other, and through their combined efforts they made a number of important contributions to the industrial progress of New England. But it was the I. Washburn & Moen Company (originally known as Worcester Wire Works, Ichabod Washburn & Company—Ichabod Washburn and Phillip E. Moen —Proprietors in 1865)) which in 1873 was making the wire used in small amounts—for sectioning off feed lots or small gardens—in and around the Midwest town of De Kalb, Illinois. It was Ichabod's kinsman (son of Ichabod's twin brother Charles), Charles Francis Washburn, who made a special investigation of the unusual circumstances at De Kalb which indicated to him that there might be in 1874 another sudden upsurge in demand for wire. As a result of these accumulative developments, in 1876, when adoption of the Bessemer system in American plants created renewed activity in the wire business, Mr. Washburn went in person to De Kalb on a mission which placed the Worcester firm in a position to step forward and assume control of the latest de-

[5] Photograph of a document in Ichabod Washburn's handwriting whereby he bound an employee named Garfield to keep secret the method used in the Washburn plant where Garfield worked. AS&W Interior Views, American Steel & Wire Company of New Jersey, Plate #138.

[6] "People, Products and Progress," a review of 125 years of wire-making, delivered as a speech by the president of the United States Steel Corporation (February, 1956).

The Fence Rider
From an oil painting by Peter Hurd

The Fence Cutters
From an oil painting by Joe Grandee

velopment in steel products—i.e., an improvement in wire for fencing.

Mr. Charles F. Washburn, then vice-president of the Worcester firm, recognized the fact that a very small part of the company's output of wire was sold for fencing material. Wire for fences had been tried intermittently for many years but only on a small scale. White & Hazard Company of Pennsylvania, for example, had reported in 1816 that the combination of "rails of wire and posts of living trees" had provided a good type of barricade at reasonable cost. In 1821 the *American Farmer of Baltimore,* and in 1823 the *New England Farmer,* urged experiments with wire for fences. In 1845 a Mr. Edward Clark secured his place with posterity by asserting in a speech before the New York State Agricultural Society that he had seen a wire fence "check a furious Bull." And by 1847 this same Society was sanctioning the proposition that wire fencing was cheaper than wood.[7] During the 1850's, publications in Massachusetts, Illinois, Kansas, and New York made similar reports.[8]

Despite these experiences, however, smooth-wire fencing was not a success. Though ratified in theory, it was never utilized in fact—and for good reasons. Charles F. Washburn himself, in later years reviewing the beginnings of the business, read from an early text which gave the following summary:

> It is estimated that 350,000 miles of plain galvanized wire was used for fencing purposes in the 20 years preceding 1870. It was cheap, easily transported, easily erected . . . [yet] farmers and herders were never thoroughly happy in its use. The fence of plain and single wire was susceptible to all changes of temperature. It snapped in cold and sagged in heat. It had no terrors for cattle. They pressed up to the boundaries of the pasture, and easily lunched [*sic*] through the fence on the adjacent crop. Growing more resolute, they broke bounds altogether, or contentedly

[7] John Gedge and William Boley, "History of the Manufacture of Barbed Wire," I, 10–12. "Cost of a common fence for 100 acres for fifty years, $3,080; cost of a Wire Fence for the same period, $1,751, leaving a profit of $1,329.— (*Transactions,* Philadelphia Agricultural Society, 1816)."

[8] "Statement of Washburn & Moen Manufacturing Company to Legislature of New Hampshire" (July 12, 1881), AS&W Records, *loc. cit.*

sawed their itching necks, or polls, on the smooth wire, in the acme of creature satisfaction, until the fence gave way.[9]

The plain wire fence was plainly not the answer to the serious fencing problems arising with expansion. Preference for native materials persisted throughout three-quarters of the century, while farmers went right on sectioning off their properties as they had done for ages past, with ridges and ditches, rocks and sod, brush and stumps, mounds and moats, trees and hedges—whichever could be improvised from the resources of the earth—and in America the predilection for wood and stone continued.

There were, of course, known advantages to the use of native materials. The lasting qualities of stone walls, built of the earth's natural matter and conforming to the earth's natural contours, are even now unsurpassed. There are in existence in the New World today remnants of stone walls said to have been built by Indians of Arizona one thousand years ago.[10] But stone walls take up space which might otherwise be put into cultivation. Unless expertly chinked, they provide refuge for vermin. Unless constructed to comply with drainage needs, they constitute an erosion hazard. Moreover, the building of stone walls was a prodigious task, and slow of completion. Time and raw materials at hand were the two prerequisites for working with stone, and men attempting to provide protection for pioneer settlement of the West were short on both. Most people still hoped for and looked for wooden fencing, though this too was at a premium. As a rule, the immediacy of the fencing needs, coupled with the scarcity of "rocks and rails," dominated the Western scene to such an extent that had there been better wire fencing available at an early date, its advantages with respect to saving time alone well might have outweighed all other considerations.[11]

[9] *Ibid.*

[10] Roy Bedichek, *Adventures of a Texas Naturalist,* 9.

[11] There were some instances of satisfactory use of stone walls in parts of the West, of course. For example, farmers sometimes managed to enclose small fields in rocky areas such as the hill country of central Texas where sheep-raising was prevalent; but even so, no plan of enclosing the sheep could have been attempted. As Roy D. Holt described it: "The German settlers . . . erected countless miles of rock fences, a monument today to their energy and perse-

[18]

There were, of course, disadvantages to wood also. One of the main sources of fear to settlers was the prairie fire, and when structures were made of wood, the fear was compounded. As has been said, with good effect, "Nothing else, not even Indians, was dreaded as much as the plume of smoke that indicated that a prairie was on fire."[12] Life itself was then at stake. Prairie fires not only consumed wood fences built at great cost, but they also destroyed the supply from which to replace the fences. Farm publications of the day wrote of serious losses "on the new prairie pasture lands" when the annual burning of grass took place. The same periodicals noted also that wood harbored insects sometimes more than stone walls did, and that wooden rails constructed in the form of zigzag fences took up more space. A report from Ohio in 1877 stated: "If we had to buy the fence material at this time and if the fences were to be of the old Virginia rail pattern, the fences would cost as much as the land."[13] It was said—whether in exaggeration or not—that such structures, along with their projecting stakes, "could occupy a strip of land at least twelve feet wide, occasioning a loss of land equal to their breadth, on two sides of every arable field—or half a rod more than is occasioned by a straight boundary."[14]

In addition to these complaints, there were others concerning the tendency of wood to require much mending and expensive rebuilding. An Iowa agricultural report of 1859 stated that "present fences are rotting down," and in 1873 the report renounced worm fences as "costly, not very lasting, and [requiring] renewal every few years, besides their liability to destruction."[15] The United States Department of Agriculture Report of 1871 estimated that where the cost of fencing in thirty-seven states had amounted to $1,747,549,091, the annual cost of repairs in the

verance . . . [but] usually the fields alone were enclosed and livestock were allowed to range outside." "Net-Wire Fences Changed Sheep Raising," *The Sheep and Goat Raiser* (March, 1951), 22–26.

[12] Lewis Nordyke, *Cattle Empire*, 45.

[13] C. W. Marsh, comp., *The De Kalb County Manufacturer*, 15.

[14] "Statement of Washburn & Moen Manufacturing Company to Legislature of New Hampshire," 6, AS&W Records, *loc. cit.*

[15] Marsh, *The De Kalb County Manufacturer*, 15.

same era had reached $93,963,187, so that the expense of upkeep was in many places considered to be more than the gross intake by farmers.

Wood was sadly lacking in permanence, though there were some types less subject to decay than others. *Bois d'arc* was one of the most durable, lasting sometimes thirty years; locust lasted twenty-four years; red cedar, twenty; bur oak, fifteen, etc.[16] Although it tended to split when nails and staples were driven into it, *bois d'arc* properly used as posts for wire fencing gave exceptionally good service, lasting in one known instance for sixty to seventy years.[17] Heart of pine, untreated, was known to serve an average of eleven years, and specimens of the oaks stood up with less attention than many other types of fence posts. For making section corners, *bois d'arc* posts were preferred in many places, and especially in Missouri and adjoining areas where the plant flourished.[18] If hard woods were not obtainable, most zigzag, post, stake-and-rider, or board fences were made of chestnut, walnut, hickory, and yellow pine, but these were chosen for lack of something better and could not be expected to last long. The most widely utilized of all was yellow pine. Even in Gulf states where cypress was available and in California where in 1880 redwood was used for posts, pine boards often served as fencing.[19] From the Atlantic Coast to the Mississippi River, "broad, brush-inviting" pine board fences were in most common usage. They became so much a part of the landscape that they were sometimes put into service for advertisement purposes. One farmer

[16] Henry Giese, *Farm Fence Handbook*, 43.

[17] This case was recounted by W. H. Hudson, Jr., vice-president of the St. Louis Southwestern Railway Company, who reported also that near Sherman, Texas, there were railroad ties of *bois d'arc* made in 1888 and used for over sixty-five years.

[18] In Missouri where once the Osage Indians lived, *bois d'arc* was often called the "Osage orange." But the name *"bois d'arc"* came indirectly from Indian lore also.

Indians had long appreciated the durability of the *bois d'arc's* yellow wood and had used it for making bows, when Frenchmen, fraternizing with Indians along the rivers leading to Louisiana and the Gulf, gave the native plant its French name, *"bois d'arc"*—"wood of the bow."

[19] Clara M. Love, "History of the Cattle Industry," *Southwestern Historical Quarterly* (April, 1916), 379.

wrote that he decided "to turn the tables on the impudent advertisers . . . of patent nostrums" by knocking the boards off and then nailing them on again with the letters facing the fields. "The cattle stared a little at first at Ridgeway's Ready Restorative," the farmer said, "but [they] never took any."[20] But beyond the ready reach of the pineries of the upper Mississippi, on the plains of the West, few such placid sights were seen.

Wood fences at their best, perhaps, would have availed little against half-wild cattle, foraging Indians, or even snow which was driven by the wind for enormously great distances over the plains. Standard rail and board would not have sufficed as controls for ranging herds. The elements would have played havoc with any conventional form of wood fences put up in the open country. In all probability timber could not have satisfied the requirements of Western expansion, had it been obtainable. But it would have helped! The chief drawback to universal use of wood was lack of universal supply. Scarcity of wood was second only to scarcity of water as a factor affecting settlement of the so-called American desert.

In the late 1860's and throughout most of the 1870's a revival of hedge-planting was attempted in farm districts of the borderline states, and from it arose some of the interesting sidelights which left marks still to be seen on the landscape as well as in the agricultural histories of these regions.

The hedge fence had long been respected in various parts of Europe, where it had been used for many generations. American colonists settling the eastern seaboard had not completely neglected the hedge fence, but because of the nature of the land and the life it generated, neither had they adopted hedging generally. Hedges and stone walls had in common the advantage of longevity, but they had also certain common disadvantages, and usually it was not considered expedient to depend on these two materials except in places where there was a natural supply. Few people tried raising plants in one region to be transplanted for

[20] Robinson, "New England Fences," *loc. cit.*

hedges in another. When it was found, though, that in some sections of the West, and particularly in the Southwest, there were native bushes of thorn which were suitable for hedge fences, and when it was decided that these could be grown in other sections where wood and stone were wanting, there was a renewal of interest, and, for a time, it was said that hedge fences held out the brightest hope farmers had known since they had ventured onto the plains and prairies.

Experiments were made with the marketing and planting of a number of different kinds of plants. Along the banks of waterways and in boggy places, willow stakes were driven into the ground at an angle and planted so close together that they grew into a close-set mass. Such thorny plants as honey locusts, thorn locusts, Pyrocantha, rose, pomegranate, mesquite, and cactus were tried; but the most widely used were the *bois d'arc* (Osage orange) and briar (Cherokee rose). These two plants grew strong and dense when cropped into hedges, and were, in addition, provided by nature with a profusion of stout thorns. Closely planted rows of this type of spiked growth served to break the sweep of snow and wind across the plains, and these "live fences" also presented a front decidedly discouraging to stray livestock.

Thorny hedges fitting these dimensions seemed to fit the new land and to blend in with the setting. Farmers began to take up the refrain of one old-timer who said: "The Almighty never would have made such a country . . . without furnishing a hedge plant to go with it."[21] So great was the interest shown that the marketing of hedge plants and seeds came to be a business in which people from many localities speculated.

In De Kalb, Illinois, a German lumber dealer—for one—experimented with *bois d'arc* for hedge fences, selling the seeds for planting on farms around De Kalb. The lumberman said, in his "Reminiscent Chapter from the Unwritten History of Barb Wire," that at the time when he was attempting to discover a good substitute fence material, he had *bois d'arc* much in his thoughts. Reviewing the matter at a later date, he wrote:

[21] Webb, *The Great Plains*, 293.

[22]

Some of you may remember that in the late 6os and early 7os, the planting of willow slips and osage orange seed was at a fever heat. I had received a consignment of osage orange seed from Texas, supplying some of my customers with the same at $5.00 per pound . . . . It was in my mind [at one time] to plant osage orange seed and when of suitable growth cut and weave it into plain wire and board fences, using the thorns as a safeguard against the encroachment of stock.[22]

By so saying, Jacob Haish set himself up as a man of vision, for the prickered hedges of such thorny plants as the Osage orange proved to be one of the strongest deterrents tried against cattle grown half-wild during war years. And although he was writing at a date when the benefits of hindsight gave him the appearance of wisdom, it might be granted that whether from foresight or daring, the shrewd Illinois lumberman was one of the early exponents of *bois d'arc* hedge fencing.

Few people went so far as to imagine entwining prickly branches around the smooth wire fences as Haish suggested, but many people did find the matted growth of *bois d'arc* hedges useful. Although the Cherokee or Macartney rose was the favorite in some regions—particularly in the Texas Gulf Coast plains— and although it proved hardy and persistent to the point of becoming uncontrollable in these regions, across the nation as a whole the rose hedges were not as numerous as the Osage orange. It was this rank treelike shrub which was acclaimed with most enthusiasm. Farmers in the prairie states did not ask of each other, "What is the best fence to use?" so much as they asked, "What is the best hedge?" And in a great blackland belt stretching lengthwise from the sparsely wooded Illinois prairie into central Texas, the answer was *"Bois d'arc."*

Hedges of *bois d'arc* could be propagated by seeds, sprouts, and cuttings. The usual method was through use of seeds grown in nursery-like fashion, mainly in Texas and Arkansas, and de-

[22] Jacob Haish, "A Reminiscent Chapter from the Unwritten History of Barb Wire Prior to and Immediately Following the Celebrated Decision of Judge Blodgett, December 15, 1881," 3. (Hereinafter this work will be referred to as "A Reminiscent History.")

livered on order to other areas. The price of seeds in Texas was $25.00 per bushel, but in Illinois seeds sold for as much as Haish's $5.00 per pound, and $80.00 per bushel. It was said that in some instances one quart of seeds would produce "about 5 thousand plants."[23] The demand was so great that at one stage the gathering, cutting, washing, drying, and shipping of *bois d'arc* seeds became a thriving little industry. Advertisements went out across the plains states with the news that *bois d'arc* hedges provided the "horse high, bull strong, and pig tight" dimensions needed for keeping livestock out of farmers' fields. And so long as no mention was made of the time required for the plants to reach these proportions (about four years), the claims were true.

In processing seeds for market, the knobby green "hedge apples" or "horse apples," as the fruit of the *bois d'arc* was called, were handled as follows:

> In about the year 1870 nearly everyone was trying to get bois d'arc seed either to speculate on or to plant for hedges. The apples first had to be gathered and put in piles and let lie until rotten. Then the four sides were cut away with knives and the core was ready to grind up in a small wooden mill with a horse hitched to it.
>
> Then they were put in a trough with holes bored in the bottom. The seed had to be washed through three or four waters, and then put on a scaffold to dry. It was necessary to stir the seed to keep them from moulding.
>
> It took about one thousand apples to make a bushel of seed. Four or five good hands could get out ten bushels a day. The apples were bought at $1.50 per thousand, and the seed sold at $25.00 per bushel.
>
> I learned all I know about bois d'arc or Osage Orange seed while living five miles from Ladonia, Fannin County. The market for seed was Bonham, Texas.[24]

[23] "The Bois d'Arc of the Creoles called Osage Orange, or malclura, by the Americans, is never attacked by worms. The tree is sturdy, vigorous, and long-lived, covered with branches, and endures trimming very well. It is provided with large thorns, and its glossy leaves, which have the appearance of being varnished, give it a luxuriant . . . appearance. It grows in almost any soil, and soon forms an impenetrable hedge." Viktor Bracht, *Texas in 1848.*

[24] From the statement of W. H. Harper in Webb, *The Great Plains,* 292.

Bois d'arc could be grown to much more than "horse high" measurements, even to thirty-five to forty feet, and in this form the trees served as windbreaks as well as boundaries. Generally, though, the plants were kept cut back to five- to ten-foot height. In Kansas in 1867, the state offered a bounty for hedge fences meeting the minimum requirements of four and one-half feet in height and eighteen inches in thickness.[25] Such specifications could be attained only by frequent pruning to limit natural top growth and force additional branching at the base of the plant. Farmers used at first a homemade "hedge knife" with a long curved blade of iron on a wooden handle, yet they managed to produce thickets so compact as to be actually "bull strong and pig tight," and at times cattle could see little more than light and dark through the mass of dense growth.

The hedges, once grown, remained despite wind, weather, and lack of ample moisture. When farmers later tried to kill them out or to cut down the trees for posts, remnants of the plants left standing in rows along property lines were sometimes put to use again as fencing. In Texas and Arkansas the thorny trees spread and multiplied wherever left in uncultivated land. At Garland City, near where the two states meet, on a large ranch-plantation belonging to one family for six successive generations, *bois d'arc* left to grow wild in the pastures provided in time a good supply of posts for fences, fuel for "field hands," windbreaks for crops, and shelter for wild game. When unwanted stumps, which refused to rot or to give way to digging and pulling, finally were destroyed by fire, smoke from their burning drifted for many miles across the countryside. In most places where *bois d'arc* had served for hedging, it continued to be as tenacious in its decline as it had been hardy in its prime. The plants were as rough and tough as the West itself, and in the undeveloped prairie-plains, they provided for a time the best thing settlers yet had found to deter stray animals moving uninhibited from range to range.

But for all their prickles and semipermanence, hedges could supply only temporary relief from the predicament afflicting

[25] The Peterson Scrapbook, *loc. cit.*

[25]

America immediately before and soon after mid-century. Hedges could not provide a quick and adequate solution. Hedges were too slow of growth, too seldom found ready-grown in the places where they were needed. They took up space, harbored rodents, and were acknowledged to be generally unwieldly and inflexible. Said the Iowa State Agricultural Society on the subject of hedge fences in 1857:

> Prairie fires were disastrous to shrubs; small animals as well as sheep ate the bark and leaves; it was impossible to move them [hedge fences] in case of faulty surveying; they served as nurseries for weeds and vermin as well as snow; they cast shade; and they required from three to five years for a good growth.[26]

It was clear that settlers moving with increased momentum to the level land of prairie-plains had need of something more than hedge-rows to serve as fencing. There was no use wishing for wood or digging for stone or compromising with hedges. The need was critical for another material, and it was becoming evident that the material should meet not only the problems of the West but situations arising in other parts of the country also.

The United States Department of Agriculture *Report* of 1869 indicated that fencing was a problem of the times, since "some sort of fence [was] usually necessary to guard against intruders or to designate ownership." It was suggested that in Eastern states where large herds of cattle were seldom found, and where the chief concern of landowners with a cow or two was the separation of field from meadow or house from garden, wire fences might be halfheartedly recommended; but "for the southern states where a somewhat formidable fence is desired," Osage orange and honey locust were in order. It was noted that most innovations in fencing were "portable rail-and-panel fences" on which patents already could be counted "by the hundreds."[27] In

---

[26] *Annual Report* (1857), cited by Earl W. Hayter, "An Iowa Farmer's Protective Association," *Iowa Journal of History and Politics* (October, 1939), 332 n.

[27] United States Department of Agriculture Report, 1869, 332. Elsewhere

1871 a similar government report dealt with the subject in a more urgent vein, for each intervening year increased rather than alleviated the pressing problem of fencing.

In the first seventy-five years of the nineteenth century, there had been approximately 1,200 United States patents for farm and field fences of all types, more than two-thirds of them issued after 1865. Moreover, "in the three years 1866, 1867, and 1868, *three hundred and sixty-eight* fence patents were issued."[28] Obviously the search was on. Reports showed rising concern in all regions, as the great urgency of the problem in the West focused attention on fencing elsewhere. In states most interested in farming, fencing was serious business; and it was everywhere, even at its best, costly business.

From New England, with plenty of both rock and rails, came the statement that "gentlemen present" at a special agricultural meeting in New Hampshire offered to sell their farms for the cost of the fencing.[29] At the other extremity, on the farthest outskirts of Western settlement, the expense of protective fencing was said to be more than new settlers could bear. And between East and West, farmers who had built their fences many years before, now were faced with high cost of repairs and replacement. The editor of *North East Farmer,* speaking for agriculturists of the seventies, was quoted as saying: "It takes on the average for the whole country $1.74 worth of fences to keep $1.65 worth of stock from eating up $2.45 worth of crops."[30] In the West, agitation mounted so that by the decade 1870–80, according to historian Webb, "questions pertaining to fencing occupied more space in the public prints in the prairie and plains states than any other issue—political, military, or economic."[31]

in his treatment of fencing, the writer of this breezy government document makes the observation that "the love of exclusive possession is a mainstay of society."

[28] "Statement to the Farmers of the Northwest from Washburn & Moen Company, On Some Aspects of the Barb Fence Question, and Results of the Patent System in the Northwest," June 30, 1881, AS&W Records, *loc. cit.*

[29] New Hampshire Secretary of State, Board of Agriculture, *Report of 1871,* 49.

[30] *American Agriculturist* (January, 1880).

[31] *The Great Plains,* 282.

It was in this setting, in the year 1874, that Charles F. Washburn, at the Washburn & Moen plant in Worcester, took note of unusual activity centering around the town of De Kalb in Illinois. As a result of his investigation, he decided to reopen the case for wire over wood and other standard fencing materials, hoping that this time it might be won, on the grounds—published but not publicized in years past—that wire for fencing "takes up no appreciable room, exhausts no soil, needs no annual shearing, shades no vegetation, permits close work for the plow and scythes . . . is proof against high winds, makes no snow drifts, and is both durable and cheap."[32]

[32] "Statement to the New Hampshire Legislature" (citing New York State Agricultural Society records of 1849), AS&W Records, *loc. cit.*

CHAPTER 3

INCIDENT AT DE KALB

At the De Kalb County Fair of 1873, on the outskirts of De Kalb township, there was shown a curious sample of fencing, hand made by one Henry M. Rose. The sample was a wooden rail, as was most fencing of the day. But the rail in this case was equipped with short wire points extending out in "sharp projections," and the apparatus as a whole was designed to be fastened to existing fences of smooth wire, board, or ordinary rail.

Rose was a farmer from the near-by community of Waterman Station. In attempting to control a "breachy" cow, he had evolved the "Wooden Strip with Metallic Points" upon which he had been granted patent No. 138763 on May 13, 1873. His design was not as good as a few other "armoured fencing" patterns which had appeared in the lists of United States patents issued five or six years earlier. Actually Rose's invention was not a fence but a fence attachment. It was not wire but wood with points of wire. It was a plain, rough-hewn exhibit and might well have gone unnoted and unknown, as had most other efforts by other men. But because Henry Rose's work showed up at the right time and place —the prairie farm belt of Illinois in the early 1870's—it became famous as the device which triggered action by three men who went ahead to become inventors of practical barbed-wire fencing.

These three—lumberman, merchant, and farmer—like other men, women, and whole families from surrounding towns and settlements, apparently came to the fair for pleasure, companionship, and the usual interest in seeing goods on display. The men

[29]

came with no thought of making a discovery. Yet, when by chance they met and stood together examining the crudely spiked strip of wood, each considering how it might fit his personal needs, there was borne in upon the consciousness of each the realization that what he saw gave promise of things to come. They studied the exhibit together for some time before they left the fairgrounds and parted at the gate. Whether they made mention of future plans, whether they spoke of adapting this "improvement in fencing" to the needs of other men of their era, is not known. But the files of the United States Patent Office record that within six months each of the three men had applied for patent on separate types of fencing, and each type was equipped— as Henry Rose's had been—with "sharp projections" made of wire.

One of the three was the German lumberman Jacob Haish, who had dealt in the buying and selling of *bois d'arc* seeds and had considered using *bois d'arc* branches twisted into strand-wire fencing. Since through this venture he already had noted the advantages of nature's thorny fences, he readily recognized the advantages of man-made thorns to be used in their stead. Since the men with whom he did business were concerned with the constant search for suitable fencing material, he was concerned with it too. Since he was of agile mind and appropriate interests, it was understandable that Jacob Haish should have taken special interest in Rose's exhibit at the fair.

The second man, Isaac Leonard Ellwood, had customers in need of fencing also, for Ellwood was a hardware merchant servicing a wide area around De Kalb. He was largely dependent on farmers for customers, and he evidently catered to them in a number of ways. They were welcome to stand around his store and talk together, and when they did not come for a long period of time, Ellwood sometimes drove his buggy to the country to see them, to deliver small goods, to act as auctioneer for the farmers, to talk up his business, and to inquire into theirs. He sold them, among other things, nails, staples, and small amounts of smooth wire for fencing off small lots. Because he was in touch with the rural population of the area, he was in a position to appreciate the fact that a real improvement in fencing could be important. It was reasonable that he too should have given special attention to a recently patented fence device.

But it was the third man, Joseph Farwell Glidden, who had the biggest stake in the matter. Glidden was a farmer beset with the worries of raising his crops without adequate protection. The need for providing some sort of barricade to keep out stray animals was one of the gnawing problems of his everyday existence, and he could see that an "armoured fence attachment" might help in remedying the situation. He considered it at least worth trying.

In the weeks following the fair, Joseph Glidden was busy with preparations for winter on his farm one mile west of De Kalb, but the lengthening evening hours of autumn he spent experimenting with ways to make prickers or spikes like the ones in Rose's invention. Having the benefit of Rose's example, Glidden did not pursue a like course of action but, in fact, reversed it. Whereas Rose's initial move had been to put armor on the offending animal, Glidden's first move was to arm the fence in the animal's path. In the beginning Henry Rose had put the prickered board onto the head of his "breachy" cow. He had thought that a cow thus armed would be kept from going through fences because of being pricked when the board was pressed against a fence. Not until he had required the unfortunate creature to carry the contraption with her everywhere she went did it occur to Rose to hang the board on the fence instead.[1] Joseph Glidden, on the other hand, seems to have realized from the start that barbs could be put to better use if attached to fences or—better still—to the material which would be used for building fences. He turned his efforts toward learning how to barb the ordinary smooth fence wire with which he was familiar, and it was not long before he was making barbs to put directly onto the wire itself.

[1] According to a story told by his son, Rose might have thought of applying barbs to the fence proper, but did not pursue the idea because he lacked machinery needed for such an operation, and because he felt that strips of wood could be made by farmers without machinery, "at home during the winter or rainy season." Arthur G. Warren, "History of the Manufacture of Barbed Wire Fencing," 25, AS&W Records, *loc. cit.*

Glidden experimented in his farm kitchen, with his wife—his second wife, Lucinda Warne Glidden—to help him. It has been suggested that it may have been Mrs. Glidden who encouraged him to become involved with fencing in the first place, and that her wish to protect her garden prompted him to work out the armed fence on a small scale. At any rate, Joseph Glidden saw that wherever he used the barbed strands, on garden or cow lot, the twisted wire pieces gradually slid along the straightened fence strand, and he realized that he must find a way to crimp the barbs so that they would stay in place. He took a coffee mill from the kitchen wall and fitted two pins into the end of the shaft, one pin precisely centered and one off center just enough to leave space for slipping the smooth wire in between. When the crank, at the other end of the shaft, was turned full circle, the wire wound around the center pin, making an eye; when the wire was snipped, two points or barbs were left extending in opposite directions from the eye.[2] By this method a fairly uniform barb was produced with each operation of the coffee mill.

When the barbs were strung on a strand wire, Glidden found that they still turned and slipped along the fence, however, and he decided that he might remedy the trouble by adding a second wire to the strand. He used parts from an old grindstone to improvise a twisting mechanism, and he called on Lucinda to turn the grindstone while he handled the wire. With this equipment in his farmyard, Glidden succeeded in twisting the auxiliary or second wire with the strand which already had barbs on it, and the result was a double strand or cable having wire barbs secured along its entire length.[3] He took down a four-

---

[2] *Ibid.*, 40 ff. (statement of Andrew Johnson).

[3] AS&W Interior Views, *loc. cit.*, II, Plate #289. "Mr. Glidden told me . . . he would have a boy climb a tree and take up the tree with him the end of a No. 9 wire (as he used No. 9 wire for the main strands) and a lot of formed barbs. . . . He would then put on the No. 9 wire a lot of the barbs which would run down the wire to the ground—when he had enough barbs on the wire he would come down the tree and they would stretch out the wire for quite a distance and fasten one end to a tree—then take another wire without barbs on it and fasten it to the tree—would then place the barbs on the wire in even spaces and then fasten the other end of the No. 9 wire to the grindstone and one would turn the grindstone and the other party would keep the barbs

The Gate and Beyond
From an oil painting by Peter Hurd

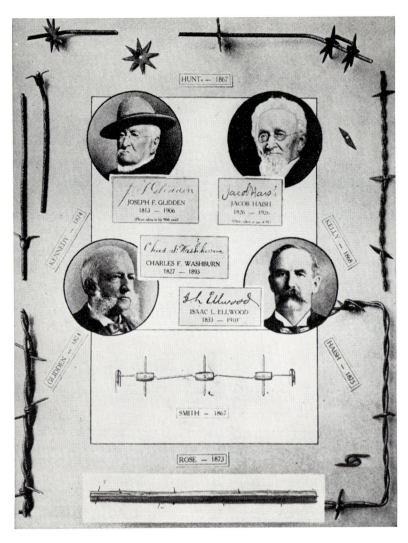

The "Big Four" of barbed wire—Glidden, Haish, Washburn, and Ellwood—surrounded by samples of early barbed wire.

rod section (sixty-six feet) of old board fencing across his barn-yard, and—little knowing that he was choosing the testing ground for barbed fencing—he replaced the board with his armored wire.

When Glidden noted the effectiveness of his new fence, he invited some of his neighbors to look at it. He took small orders from these and other farmers in the vicinity, and soon he was making barbed wire in such amounts that he was obliged to hire a man to work with him. Mrs. Glidden had served her turn as original helper, however. Although conflicting accounts were told of the part she played in the venture, it is generally agreed that Glidden's wife worked with him when he was first develop-ing his invention.

It was Isaac Ellwood, the merchantman, who later gave credit to the Rose invention for inspiring the three who had seen it on exhibit. In later years he described the incident:

> In 1873 we had a little county fair down here about where the Normal School now stands. . . . Mr. Glidden, Mr. Haish and myself were at the fair, and all three of us stood looking at this invention of Mr. Rose's and I think that each one of us at that hour conceived the idea that barbs could be placed on the wire in some way instead of being driven into the strip of wood.[4]

Following the fair, Ellwood too had busied himself with working out ways of using barbs, and when he heard that Glid-den had put up a new fence, he was curious to see what it was. He evidently inquired of the farmers who came to his hardware store, and then on a Sunday in early spring—probably when he could contain his curiosity no longer—he took his wife for an afternoon ride past the Glidden farm. The prickered wire was strung close to the roadside. When they came to it, Ellwood stopped the buggy and got out. Before he left, both he and Mrs. Ellwood inspected the fence, and Mrs. Ellwood made a quick ap-praisal of it. The Glidden fence, she said, was better than the one her husband had made.

in place and in this way they would twist the two wires together and have the barbs in proper places." Letter of H. O. Cary. See also page 227n. below.
    [4] *A History of De Kalb County, Illinois.*

Isaac Ellwood was furious at her statement. He was red-faced and short of conversation on the ride back home, but by the end of the day he admitted that his wife might be right. Next day, he saw Glidden in person, and, as a result of the judgment passed on an afternoon pleasure ride, the two men began negotiations whereby they would go into business together.[5]

The third man, Jacob Haish, took a buggy ride to the country also.[6] When he found that Glidden—about to be allied with Ellwood—was making a new type of barbed fence more practical than his own model, he sprang into action. Until this time, Haish had discounted the significance of reports he had heard concerning Glidden's fence. Some time earlier a friend had told him that Glidden's barb was much like one which he, Haish, was designing, and Haish thereafter centered his attention on a second design; but even then he had not attached much importance to what old "Uncle Joe" Glidden was doing. The few pieces Haish had made, he had sold to a farmer for fifty cents and thereupon had forgotten about them (according to testimony given at a much later date).[7] He kept working up new ideas for use on fence wire, but evidently was not satisfied with any of them. He seemed not to have determined exactly what course to follow. Then, when he went in person to see Glidden's fence and found that Glidden and Ellwood were combining forces, he must have realized that they posed a serious threat to any move he might make. Particularly would this be true if ever a patent should be issued on the Glidden invention.

It was known that Glidden had made application for patent on October 27, 1873, soon after he had worked out his method of putting the barbs on wire; but the patent had not been granted. Haish, although filing application later, had been awarded two patents on wire and one on a wire-stretcher, between January 20 and June 23, 1874, and he was then prepared to apply for an-

[5] Warren, "History of the Manufacture of Barbed Wire Fencing," 44, AS&W Records, *loc. cit.*

[6] Gedge and Boley, "History," *loc. cit.*, I, 55.

[7] See Chapter 7 of this volume.

other.[8] When he saw that by doing so there was a way further to delay issuance of Glidden's patent, he jumped at the chance. He applied for patent on his third and most important wire design, the "S" barb—so named because of the twist—on July 17, 1874, and also within the next ten days he filed interference papers on Joseph F. Glidden—thereby setting in motion the wheels of legal procedure which kept turning for years to come.

Had he known how long-drawn-out and complicated would be the legal controversy he was starting, he might not have begun the battle; but probably he would have, for Jacob Haish was a fighter. Born in Colsul, Baden, Germany, in March, 1827, he had come to America as a child. He had fought his way up from the status of an immigrant boy carpenter to ownership of a thriving lumber business and a position of prominence in the town. He was to go on fighting until he had completed a full century of energetic living. And when he would face death, only a few days before his hundredth birthday, he would still be fighting for his claim to fame, having long since put over the doorway of his "ornate residence" in De Kalb a placard reading, "Jacob Haish, Inventor of Barbed Wire."

Joseph F. Glidden was a onetime New Hampshire schoolteacher, born in Charleston, New Hampshire, in January, 1813. He had started out at about the age of twenty-nine to work his way to the West with two crude threshing machines and his own service for hire. Two years later he had reached Illinois, in 1844, and had purchased land one mile west of the village of De Kalb and settled there. He had been elected county sheriff in 1852, and later served on the County Board of Supervisors. By the time his association with the wire industry began, Glidden was a well-established citizen, a veteran farmer. Like most farmers, he had had some experience with smooth wire; he knew something of its advantages and its shortcomings; and when he hit upon his "improvement," he was able to understand the potentialities of what he was attempting. His experience with smooth-wire fenc-

[8] Although this was Haish's fourth application, it was held up and, when issued, became his fifth patent. See the chart at the end of this chapter.

[35]

ing conditioned him to realize that he had hit upon something important. And Isaac Ellwood was conditioned to realize it, too.

This seventh son of Abraham and Sara DeLong Ellwood had come to Illinois as a young man. He had left his birthplace in Salt Springville, New York, and spent his early youth "roughing it" as a teamster on the Erie Canal and as a prospector in the California Gold Rush. The savings from these exploits he had brought with him to De Kalb, where he set up a small hardware store. Thereafter he had been in close touch with farmers, and when he saw the Glidden fence, he knew how to weigh its possibilities against the price of lumber, nails, wire, etc. Whether to continue with his own invention in the face of Glidden's superior one was the question he had to decide. If—as his own story goes—he made the decision overnight, it was a night's rest well sacrificed and a night's work long to be remembered.

There is some uncertainty about the exact time when Ellwood first saw Glidden's handiwork. There are confusing accounts of the parts played by Mrs. Glidden and Mrs. Ellwood—one newspaper story goes so far as to suggest that it was the latter rather than the former who originated the idea of a coffee mill, in this case, from the hardware store.[9] But all reference sources agree that Glidden and Ellwood were friends, that Ellwood was among the first to learn of Glidden's invention, and that when he did see it, Isaac Ellwood reacted immediately.

Another newspaper story, published after 1910—too much later to be considered documentary—tells in good journalistic jargon how Ellwood approached Glidden:

"Joe," he is quoted as saying, "if I get this patented, will you give me half of all we can make out of it?" And Glidden is said to have replied that he hadn't allowed to make anything out of it, just to keep those dad-ratted pigs out of the garden."[10]

[9] Mary Isobel Brush, "Romance of Barbed Wire," *Chicago Tribune* (September 18, 1910). This opinion is thought to be the result of an inaccurate quote from a newspaper interview with John W. Gates on his way to Isaac L. Ellwood's funeral.

[10] John Spy, "John Spy Writes Inner Story about Barb Wire," *De Kalb Daily Chronicle*, n.d. (citing "a Chicago newspaper in 1910").

[36]

This version as it stands is a little too pat, and the implied lack of foresight on the part of Mr. Glidden is out of character. Fuller knowledge of the matter reveals that Glidden was by no means so apathetic as this dialogue would indicate. A letter from H. O. Cary, who knew Glidden personally, tells how Glidden used the old grindstone.[11] Other records show that he went steadily ahead with work on his idea, even though he had once offered to sell half-interest in it to a farmer. During the time when he made wire for some of his neighbors, evidently he also sold small amounts of separate barbs to be clamped onto existing fences by the individual fence-builder.[12] O. H. Nelson of Kansas claimed that he ordered wire from Glidden as early as 1868 (though the date cannot be corroborated and is considered a miscalculation), and with the wire, he said, "came pincers and a bundle of wire barbs" which he attached to about half a mile of smooth-wire fencing already in use, "to try it."[13] Within a short time after filing his first application for patent, Glidden invented a wire-stretcher (allowing for expansion and contraction), a second type of barbed wire, and (with P. W. Vaughan) a machine for making barbed fencing.[14] Moreover, it is believed that the beginning of arrangements between Glidden and Ellwood occurred during the long wait after Glidden had made application for patent on the original design.

Undoubtedly Ellwood did much to stimulate Mr. Glidden. It is known that Ellwood supplied the business acumen which later helped to make the Glidden product a great financial success, but in the meantime, Glidden seems to have been energetic

[11] See note 3 above.

[12] In this connection another Illinoisan, R. H. Pooler of Serena, claimed that in 1874 he made and sold separate barbs (3 to 10 per pound) for fifteen to twenty-five cents per pound, and pincers for one dollar each to farmers who wished to clamp barbs onto plain (No. 8 or No. 9) wire fences. On August 29, 1876, he was awarded patent No. 181537 for the barbs, and this along with rights to the pincers he sold to Washburn & Moen Manufacturing Company after being sued by them for infringement on the Glidden patent. Letter of R. H. Pooler to Charles Pritchard (De Kalb, Illinois), September 24, 1914 (Hayter Collection, University of Wyoming, Laramie). See also Chapter 19 of this volume.

[13] Hamner, *Short Grass and Longhorns,* 208.

[14] See the chart at the end of this chapter.

[37]

enough. Patent on his wire-stretcher was procured before he and Ellwood went into partnership, and the question of whether re-vision of the application on the original barbed wire was made at Ellwood's insistence or through Glidden's own ingenuity is immaterial. Ellwood was interested. He was in close touch with Glidden and his affairs. He encouraged Glidden when the first patent was turned down. Recorded facts show that Glidden first filed for patent in October, 1873; formal sale was completed for interest in the original invention to go to Ellwood in July, 1874; this was four months before patent finally was granted on said invention, November 24, 1874.

When Glidden had offered to sell half-interest to a neigh-boring farmer, A. Y. Baldwin, the price had been $100. The farmer "who through hard work and thrifty living had acquired ample means to invest much more" gave as his reason for refus-ing the offer a "lack of faith" in patents of any kind.[15] The price to Ellwood for the same half-interest was $130 plus $135 ex-penses—total $265. Ellwood's confidence, in contrast to Mr. Bald-win's lack of same, made him quick to meet the offer and enter the pact with Glidden. Together the two set up business as The Barb Fence Company, marketing their product through Ell-wood's store.

Jacob Haish was in the barbed-wire business too—and there was no mistaking the fact. Haish was a man of many words, espe-cially in reference to barbed wire. He had a penchant for writing. He liked to pile words one on the other and gather them together in great quantities. He was as extravagant with words as he was with ornamentations. In the same way that he decorated his resi-dence with carvings and furbelows, he elaborated with written words on the subject of his barbed-wire activities, embellishing each account with unnecessary superlatives and sometimes un-believable descriptions. Thanks to this inclination for writing, there were records left which disclosed the feeling of animosity which grew up between Haish and the Glidden-Ellwood com-

[15] Arthur G. Warren, "Barbed Wire—Who Invented It?" *The Iron Age* (June 24, 1926), 6 n.

[38]

bine. But it is necessary today to weigh these disclosures against the background of other evidence. In his enthusiasm for words Haish may have lost touch with accuracy; especially is this the case in reviewing his account of the first barbed-wire developments in De Kalb and his subsequent action in filing interference papers to delay issuance of patent rights to Joseph Glidden.

Haish was evidently as intent as anybody on working out a new kind of fencing device. He was experimenting with ways of arming fences during the same period of time when Glidden and Ellwood were trying to improve on Rose's "improvement." He was doing the same sort of things they were doing at the same time. Yet in all his voluminous writings he made no reference to the county fair incident and never suggested that Rose's invention had influenced him as Glidden and Ellwood had intimated. His words, though always superabundant, made no mention of the afternoon when he, like Ellwood, drove to the country for a look at Glidden's fence. In short, Haish gave credit to no one for inspiring or encouraging him, and he brooked no evidence which seemed to point to the work of other inventors as taking precedence over his. Said Haish:

> The subject of barbed wire is very interesting to me, as you may readily suppose, because I was probably the chief factor in its development. . . . As a lumber merchant and building contractor from the year 1857 to 1872, I was in constant contact with the lumber interests of the west, and had often noted the immense cut of fencing material, increasing yearly, and its bearing upon agricultural interests of the country, with its burdensome cost, which led me to think out and provide a substitute therefor. You may well imagine my efforts were very crude when I state it was in my mind to plant Osage Orange seed and when of suitable growth, cut and weave it into plain wire and board fence, using the thorns as a safeguard against encroachments of stock. . . . Of course I soon discovered the futility of the Osage Orange idea and commenced a somewhat random thinking along other lines . . . . I saw the coming of a new era in fence building. First was the Osage Orange, next attachments of metal to wood. At this time, I saw, as in a glass, darkly; later I saw wire married to wire

[39]

and no divorce. It was then I saw face to face, clearly, that this was the line along which to work. It looked simple, I might say, foolish, just a short piece of wire coiled between its ends around a straight parallel (horizontal) wire. I showed the device to a friend and he exclaimed, "Oh, H——, Joe Glidden is working on the same thing!" Without stopping to investigate what "Uncle Joe" had—you see "the King's business required haste" just now —I immediately switched to another form and manner of applying a wire barb to a plain wire, which proved so much easier to make by hand and fasten on to two plain wires, instead of one, that I adopted it, concluding to let "Uncle Joe" and what he was working at alone.[16]

Said Glidden, in a deposition:

That in April, 1874, deponent [Glidden] put up some 30 rods of said fence along the public roads, on his farm, and a few days after it was put up, Mr. Haish drove along in a carriage in company with a lady, and stopped, left his carriage and examined the fence, deponent being at the time a few rods distant therefrom. . . . That Mr. Haish came to deponent's place some time in May, 1874, and brought with him a mechanic and took dimensions and measurements of a machine that deponent had previously devised and had constructed and was using for twisting the strand of his wire together after the barbs had been put on to one of the wires.[17]

From these accounts it is surmised that a sense of rivalry between Haish and Glidden began at an early stage, and that after each was aware of the other's intentions to secure patent, the two men stayed clear of each other. Although Haish claimed that their separate concerns operated "amicably and at a profit" until February, 1876, it would seem that from the time when interference charges were filed against Glidden in June, 1874, there was not much chance for improvement of relations. Profits increased for Haish and for the partnership of The Barb Fence Company, but "amicable dealings between them diminished to the vanishing point.

16 Haish, "A Reminiscent History," 2 f.
17 Gedge and Boley, "History," loc. cit., I, 54.

On June 25, 1874, Jacob Haish filed papers at the Patent Office in Washington, charging interference against Joseph F. Glidden, hoping by this means to delay issuance of patent on Glidden's original application which was still pending. Haish had in the meantime found reason so to do, for he himself already had received patents on two types of barbed wire and a wire-stretcher, and had made application (nine days before) for patent on a third type of wire. He had not been the first of the three "friends" to file application for patent on the first of their respective inventions—Glidden's application was dated October 27, 1873; Haish's, December 22, 1873; Ellwood's, January 7, 1874—but Haish's invention was the first to be granted patent. His application was approved in twenty-eight days, while Glidden's was held up—part of the time because of the interference suit—for thirteen months. It was November 24, 1874, when patent No. 157124 finally was issued to Joseph F. Glidden for his barbed wire, trade named "The Winner."

Filing of interference did indeed hold up approval for his rival, but evidently it held up approval for Haish too, as his latest application, dated June 17, 1874, was not granted patent until fourteen and one-half months later, August 31, 1875. This was the patent for the famous "S" barb, which was Haish's third type of wire and fifth patent. This was the pattern which he had evolved after putting aside the type of barb which resembled Glidden's twist, and after "concluding to let 'Uncle Joe' and what he was working at alone." This was what he saw when "the King's business required haste" and he "looked with the vision of a prophet... down the vista of time and saw revealed the midday glory and triumph of the fair and shapely form of the 'S' barb, which was all this time taking shape and comeliness in the evolutions of the mind."[18] This was the design which came to be one of the most widely acclaimed of all types of barbed wire, the patent on which Haish was willing to sacrifice time in the hope that he might stall advances made by Glidden's and Ellwood's Barb Fence Company.

[18] *The Biographical Record of De Kalb County, Illinois*, 26.

Haish produced his own wire on the second floor of his carpenter-lumber shop. Industrious by nature, he seemed to thrive on the challenge confronting him. He advertised widely—and loudly. He continued making improvements in his "factory." When a machine which he wished to perfect could not be completed within the time allotted by the Patent Office, rather than give up, he had a mechanic make the machine and apply for patent, and then he had the mechanic assign patent rights back to the original inventor, J. Haish, Esquire. He built up his business and his personal reputation at the same time, relenting not once on the issues which he undertook to handle. He was, as a consequence, perhaps the busiest man in busy De Kalb during the three-year period from 1873 to 1876.

HAISH

Patent Number	Type of Wire	Date of Application	Date Granted	Days Interval
1. 146671	Short chain lengths	12–22–73	1–20–74	29
2. 147634	Ribbon Star	12–27–73	2–17–74	52
3. 152368	Wire-Stretcher	4–18–74	6–23–74	66
4. 164552	"Stick-tite"	5–27–75	6–15–75	19
5. 167240	"S-Barb"	6–17–74	8–31–75	440

GLIDDEN

Patent Number	Type of Wire	Date of Application	Date Granted	Days Interval
1. 150683*	Wire-Stretcher	3–14–74	5–12–74	29
2. 157124	"The Winner"	10–27–73	11–24–74	389
3. 181433	Oval Twist	1–26–76	8–22–76	198
4. 157508	Machine (with Vaughan)		12– 8–74	
5. 187126	Machine for twisting and spooling		2– 6–77	

* Reissues 6913 and 6914[19]

[19] Two reissues granted on this patent on February 8, 1876, apply toward making other types of barbed-wire fences. Reissue No. 6913 reserves patent rights on all two-point wire barbs wrapped any number of times around one or more fence wires united together. Reissue No. 6914 reserves patent rights on all round or other shaped four-point wire barbs placed on single-strand wire of any size or shape.

CHAPTER 4

PRE-GLIDDEN FENCES

I F, INDEED, JOSEPH GLIDDEN had thought only to provide protection for his crops when he made his first "armoured fence wire," if he had meant it to be no more than a back-yard experiment, he had reason to be well pleased over his partnership with Ellwood. The Barb Fence Company prospered steadily. Beginning with a rented building in the De Kalb township, the company was in a position less than a year later to acquire its own brick structure "70 feet wide by 180 feet long and two stories high." The rented building was across the street from a windmill tower which was utilized by sending a boy up the tower with a bucket of barbs and having him slide the barbs down a greased wire; the twisting was then done inside the building. Later the Glidden-Vaughan machine for barbing was added, and in the company-owned brick shop, "a small steam engine was installed to furnish power for the twisting."[1] The company soon engaged a salesman to take its product into surrounding areas.

Within two years the partners made a decisive move in the direction of solidifying their position as an increasingly serious and promising young company. They bought interest in three patents which had been issued earlier on separate forms of "armoured fencing," and attempted unsuccessfully to buy rights to a fourth. The wisdom of this joint action Glidden and Ellwood later regarded as next in importance to the formation of their partnership, for in years to come it paid dividends in both

[1] Gedge and Boley, "History," *loc. cit.*, I, 50–61.

dollars and prestige to the members of the monopoly which grew from the nucleus of The Barb Fence Company. In the meantime, the partners' decision to purchase prior fence patents was considered a show of confidence in the future of barbed wire.

The company was doing well and meant to do better. There was little overhead expense since barbed-wire-makers had only to order smooth wire and make it into barbed wire with the simple equipment they themselves devised. Haish was engaged in a similar procedure, and soon other small businesses in the area began to follow suit. As the practice spread, orders for plain wire to be sent to the little-known town in northern Illinois poured into the offices of wire manufacturers, especially the Washburn & Moen Manufacturing Company in Massachusetts. The sudden increase in demand for wire attracted attention of officials at the Worcester plant. They sent a representative to investigate, and as a result of this man's findings, Vice-President Charles Francis Washburn decided to go west to see for himself the developments at De Kalb.

In February, 1876, Mr. Washburn in all his dignity appeared on the streets of the unperturbed town, asking at first to see not Glidden and Ellwood but Jacob Haish. He contacted Haish, visited in his home, inspected his factory, and proposed to buy an interest in the business. Haish indicated that if he should consider the proposition to sell, the price would be high. He was interested, confident, but inexperienced. He evidently expected Washburn to bargain with him. "Had he been a typical Yankee," Haish later said, "and offered me $25,000, I believe I should have accepted it." But no such offer was made. "It was up to me [to state a price]," Haish explained, "[and] the price was $200,000. It would have been cheap at that, as I have been told that the lawsuits [incurred] cost his [Washburn's] company $1,325,000."[2] Washburn left without accepting the offer, writing to Haish, "Were I in possession of Aladdin's Lamp I might consider it." Thus Haish lost his buyer, and Mr. Washburn, having bid Jacob Haish adieu,

[2] Haish, "A Reminiscent History," 8.

went immediately to The Barb Fence Company. There he found Glidden and Ellwood easier to deal with.

Glidden was not averse to selling. He was at heart a farmer. The six hundred acres he had bought with savings from part-time schoolteaching and part-time threshing in the wheat fields was his chief concern. He was over sixty years of age. He had lost a wife and three children. He had cared for his parents in their old age. There was left to him at this period a second wife (Lucinda), one married daughter (Mrs. W. H. Bush of Chicago), and his farm. These were his interests in life. He was ready for the proposition which Mr. Washburn put to him. He was willing to retire— for a consideration. The value he placed on his holdings at this time, was, however, far in excess of the $265.00 for which he had sold his first half-interest in the patent to Ellwood two years earlier. He was now in a position to ask a good price and to get it.

Some arbitration was required and as a consequence no agreement was made at once, but in May, Washburn returned to De Kalb and the contract was signed. Glidden sold his interest for $60,000.00 cash plus royalty of $.25 per one hundred pounds of barbed wire manufactured by I. L. Ellwood and Washburn & Moen Company.[3] He soon retired a well-to-do man.

Isaac L. Ellwood was willing to talk business also—but not to retire. He was a younger man than either Glidden or Haish, twenty years younger than Glidden. Ellwood was energetic and able. He could work with Charles Washburn as well as with Glidden, and this was what the immediate contract called for. The Barb Fence Company was superseded by I. L. Ellwood & Company of De Kalb, "sole agents in the West and Southwest," and Washburn & Moen Manufacturing Company of Worcester was designated as agent in the East. Charles F. Washburn was "the silent but by no means inactive partner" of the combined operations.

One of the first steps taken by Washburn & Moen Company

---

[3] "This royalty was a little later reduced to 12½¢ per one hundred pounds." Gedge and Boley, "History," *loc. cit.*, I, 63.

after the settlement of terms was to inaugurate actions aimed at gaining control of other barbed-wire patents. Patent rights were a prime concern for the experienced officials of this great manufactory. Possession of patent papers had been the principal reason for Washburn's contacting Haish in the first place, for his company at that time already had control of patent rights on a machine for making Haish's type of barbed wire. Officials had taken the samples of barbs brought from De Kalb by the representative sent there in the summer of 1875, and had assigned an expert machinist to develop a way to produce armored wire automatically.[4] When the machinist had come up with a model machine for making one of the types being produced in Illinois at that time by hand-operated equipment, the machine was for Haish's type of barb. Rights to the patented machine were controlled by the company, and when the same inventor perfected machinery for making the Glidden barb, this too was controlled by the company. Thereafter the compelling force behind Washburn & Moen's actions and the main theme of their advertising was concentrated on their rights to patents.

Ellwood and Glidden already had made an important move in this direction by acquiring interest in three earlier fence patents, and now Ellwood and Washburn pursued the course further, looking into every reasonable claim to prior inventions—and a number of unreasonable ones as well.

All known "armoured fencing" devices—barbed or prickered, spiked or jagged—which before 1873 made use of some form of metal for "armour," were of two groups: those granted patent in the United States or in Europe as variations of defensive barriers; and those recorded in some form of written document—official or otherwise—but, for one reason or another, never patented. Few if any were known by Glidden, Ellwood, or Haish in 1873, and many were brought to light only as a result of the ensuing

---

[4] H. W. Putnam, head of the Double Pointed Tack Company, Bennington, Vermont, was granted patent No. 173667 on February 15, 1876, for a machine designed, at the Washburn & Moen Company's direction, primarily to make Haish wire. He was granted patent No. 187776 on February 27, 1877, for a machine designed primarily to make Glidden wire.

dispute. Others undoubtedly never were known beyond the premises where they were conceived, and some were recalled only in legend. It was thanks to the furor growing out of the litigation begun at De Kalb in 1874 that most "prior-use" fence experiments were revealed, for most of them had been developed independently one of the other, unknown one to the other, and unheard of by the public in general. Among the earlier forms, most were never patented or manufactured, but merely made "on the spot" by individuals protecting their own properties.

In the year 1857, in Austin, Texas, a man named Grenniger was strongly driven by this compulsion for defense. John Grenniger was a Swiss iron-worker living on a small plot of ground near the river bank.[5] He had a few fruit trees and, around this modest orchard, a mediocre board fence. To protect his trees from stray cattle which continually broke through and destroyed his fruit, he attached to the top of the fence a row of jagged metal strips. Some say he added also bits of broken glass. The structure was, in any case, a wicked contrivance, plainly not indicative of a friendly feeling toward man or beast. It might have been better if Grenniger had taken more thought of the men who owned the animals, for the Switzer was not well known in the community and apparently not very well liked, while his fence came to be very well known indeed—and not well liked at all. The citizenry became incensed over the cruel nature of this barricade, and because of it they tried by various means to run Grenniger out of town. Just what measures were taken and what pressures were exerted to accomplish his expulsion is not certain, but despite it all, Grenniger refused to leave. He stayed on in Austin, and it is said that he was murdered there in 1862.

Whether or not the reason for his violent death was in any way connected with the fence is not now known; but it is known that this man tried an early bit of improvising, from which he reaped no enviable reward. He filed no patent application, made

---

[5] In some accounts he was called "a market gardener" guarding the produce by which he made his living, but in most records John Grenniger is referred to as an iron worker.

no claim, and only a photograph to demonstrate what he had built remained.[6] His construction was not barbed wire. It was not even wire. It was more reminiscent of medieval customs than prophetic of modern ones. But it was one of the earliest known examples of protective fencing armed with spikes, and Grenniger was one of the earliest known experimenters in this field.

Far away from Grenniger's unhappy location in Texas, one Adrian C. Latta of Friendship, New York, wrote to the editors of *Scientific American* describing his experiences "in the year 1861, while [he was] a boy of ten summers." Mr. Latta told in his published letter of a means by which he managed to keep hogs from getting through the lower part of a board-and-wire fence, and he described his experiment as a forerunner of barbed fencing. Since he was dealing specifically with hogs instead of cattle, Latta reversed Grenniger's order of arming the top of a structure, using instead attachments to the bottom of his fence, where the hogs went through. He described the fence in his letter, written many years later:

> I proceeded with my wire pliers and pieces of wire, inserted the pieces between the twisted wire and wound the pieces around one of the long wires, putting the pieces or barbs in about an inch apart and cutting the ends off leaving them as sharp as I could with the pliers. The hogs got through a few times after the barbs were put in. However, the barbs had the desired effect as the owner saw his hogs were getting terribly marked and kept them at home.[7]

Luckily there seem to have been no dire consequences arising from Mr. Latta's boyhood exploit, but it may be assumed from the above that neither was there a furtherance of good feelings between the owner of the ventursome hogs and his young neigh-

[6] As indicated by a letter from Walter Prescott Webb to Roy D. Holt, January 7, 1930, it was Webb's father-in-law who was engaged as photographer to take the picture of a replica of the Grenniger fence. The model was constructed in an attempt to prove the existence of Grenniger's fence before 1873 in a trial to determine priority of inventions. Roy D. Holt, "Introducing Barbed Wire to Texas Stockmen," *The Cattleman* (July, 1930), 26.

[7] "Evolution of the Barbed Wire Fence," *Scientific American* (November 2, 1907), 307.

bor. Latta said that the fence stood and did service for fifteen years; but no patent for invention resulted and evidently nothing more came of the experiment.

In Iowa, a blacksmith improvising with the materials of his trade made what is considered to be "one of the first attempts at barbing," sometime near 1860 or possibly earlier. He bent a common horseshoe nail all the way around a strong wire strand, repeating the operation at intervals and binding the nails in place by twisting a small wire over the doubled-up nail and along the length of the strand wire. It made a decidedly barbed strip of wire fencing, heavy and awkward, but effective against any manner of livestock. Small amounts for private use could have been hammered out in the blacksmith's shop without much difficulty, but it is doubtful if more than a few strips ever were made. It is thought that the man may have been Christian E. Schone who "shoed horses for a stage company" in Brooklyn, Iowa, but there is little more than hearsay to determine if this was actually his name.[8] No conclusive evidence is now to be found concerning the blacksmith or his exact whereabouts, and only an engraved likeness of his product in the *American Agriculturist* of January, 1880 remains.[9] It is to be presumed, however, that he ran into prejudices such as confronted Grenniger and Latta. At any rate, again an experiment had been made, and the results again, if not rejected, were at least neglected.

Four more residents of Iowa—Hutchinson, Long, Morley, and Stone, by name—and a number from the neighborhood of De Kalb, Illinois—including Anderson, Ankeny, Beers, Cook, and Hibbard claimed in later years that during this same period of experimentation, dating roughly from 1850 to 1870, they too had put up structures which resembled the later inventions. But it was difficult to determine the validity of their claims. These fences, like the handiwork of Grenniger, Latta, and the blacksmith, were reported only after a lapse of many years and, like

---

[8] Kent Pellett, "When Iowans Battled for Barbed Wire," *Des Moines Register* (January 21, 1940), in Peterson Scrapbook, *loc. cit.*

[9] Vol. XXXIX, 11.

Grenniger, *et al.,* they then were brought into court and found to be without satisfactory foundation, without bona fide claim, or completely falsified.[10]

Some claims, of course, were based on genuine experiences, but it appears that most were the spurious fruit of a later age when barbed wire had become both popular and profitable. In the late seventies and eighties men who had not actually done so could be induced for a price to say that they once had barbed a wire fence of their own. But in the meanwhile, the real originators of the principle of man-made "armoured fencing," the unnamed farmers who improvised on their own farms, were hesitant or unwilling to own up to the discovery they had made, mainly because it was not in keeping with the sentiment of their time. To present sharp projections to livestock—or, at least, to any livestock except one's own—was intolerable. So strong were the feelings aroused prior to the last quarter of the century—before the time when Glidden and Ellwood and Haish became involved—that whenever one of the "unnatural" barriers appeared, evidence of its effectiveness was repressed over and over again. The beginnings of barbed wire were almost lost in the confusion of an era which was not sufficiently conditioned to its new environs to recognize the solution of its own problem. Recognition could not be forced; it had to come in its own time, when conditions most propitious for the reception of barbed wire were fully developed.

In the meantime, from one of the most unexpected places possible came the next related development. In France there was patented in July, 1860, a "fence and tree protector." In this invention Leonce Eugene Grassin-Baledans proposed the use of twisted strands of sheet metal as fencing. He, like the Swiss iron-worker, seems to have been most concerned with providing protection for trees, but in the illustrations accompanying his original letters which were granted patent, Grassin-Baledans sketched a variety of ways for arranging the metal strips, and one figure—Figure 9—showed a strand of twisted sheet metal with projecting points or prongs.[11] Although bearing little relation to the main

[10] See Chapter 6 of this volume.

[50]

body of the patent and the main purpose for which the invention seems to have been designed, that section of the patent which describes Figure 9 makes use of the principle of armored fencing, with a kind of barb. The section, old and handwritten, seems to say, in fact:

> Fig. 9: showing the shape of branches or threads of twisted iron accompanied by little ends of prickly iron which make spiney tips.
> This sort of guard is used to enclose the top row to make it less penetrable [less capable of being crossed or passed over].

Thus it appears that the first patented fence armed with pieces of pointed or prickly iron (*"fil de fer herissie"*) originated in France; and it appears also that other fence patents of particular significance were issued in France within the next few crucial years. Louis François Jannin's design—by coincidence remarkably similar to a later United States patent of considerable importance—was granted in 1865.[12] Two years later, in August, 1867, a third French patent was issued to Gilbert Gavillard, this one employing a T-shaped spine held between three strands of wire. In April, June, and July of the same year, the United States Patent Office granted to three American inventors the first United States patents ever issued on barbed fence wire—six years before Rose's invention. The months of the year are significant; by the end of 1867, the United States and France had registered an equal number of barbed-wire patents, but William D. Hunt's patent No. 67117 (July 23) preceded Gavillard's patent No. 77570 (August 27) by one month and four days.

The issuance of these French patents is thought to have had little effect on developments in America. Certainly no conscious effort was being made to outstrip other countries in the discovery, and probably few if any of the American inventors ever knew that Frenchmen were in any manner concerned with frontier

[11] This feature is found only in the original, not the reissue, of French patent No. 45827. Also in the original, Figure 10, though showing no barbs, is described as *"une colture de prairie,"* "prairie fencing."

[12] Both Jannin (No. 67067, France) and Michael Kelly (No. 74379, United States) used elongate diamond-shaped barbs on twisted double-wire strands.

[51]

fencing problems. There is nothing to indicate that the Americans who took out patents on barbed wire in the same decade as the French had copied the French work or had been influenced by it. Furthermore, the Americans do not seem to have built on each other's discoveries or benefited from each other's mistakes until much later, after the time when Glidden, Ellwood, and Haish saw the possibilities of improving on Rose's invention, and after patents were being published. The first makers of barbed wire were purely experimenters. But it was from this group of people who day by day were faced with situations which demanded new fencing that the inventors of barbed wire finally arose. Frenchmen patented it first, but Americans experimenting independently understood it best and ultimately perfected the product.

The three United States patents of 1867, marking official appearance of barbed wire on the American continent, were one in April to Alphonso Dabb for a "picketed wrought iron strip" to be used as an attachment on standard fences; one in June to Lucien B. Smith for what is sometimes known as the first United States patent on actual "wire fencing armed with projecting points"; and one in July to William D. Hunt for a spur-wheel design which, after having been brought into legal interference, was accorded priority rights over the Smith invention. All three were homemade experiments, but dignified with the appendage of recorded patents, they became historically important. For the most part, they were unknown in farming circles, however, and although in later years they were among the names best known to wire manufacturers, not one met with commercial success.

Dabb's invention was not practicable. Apparently it was not even intended as protection against cattle, but rather as a means to prevent human intruders from scaling stone walls or wooden fences. Its importance rests solely on the fact that the patent wording embodied the principle of arming fences defensively with "sharp projections."

Smith's difficulties were mainly legal. He could not test his ideas commercially after Hunt won priority rights over him. Although Smith's patent was granted first, twenty-eight days before Hunt's, it was decreed that Hunt held precedence for the reason that his application for patent was filed earlier than Smith's.[13] Actually the date of Smith's application has been questioned, and the circumstances under which the decision was made in favor of Hunt are hard to understand; but since there are no records to the contrary, and since fortunes were chanced and reputations risked on the rightness of the court decision in this case, it must be assumed that Washburn & Moen Company's legal advisers were sure of their ground when they stated in court proceedings:

> ... it is always to be remembered that the name of Hunt stands first and foremost as the real originator of wire armed for defensive purposes with sharp points or spurs. It is true that the patents of Dabb and Smith antedate the patent of Hunt; but Dabb's patent does not refer to wire and although Smith's patent antedates that of Hunt, the latter's application for patent was filed in the patent office prior to that of Smith.[14]

It is probable that Smith's invention would not have been satisfactory in any event, but he missed by a narrow margin the distinction of being the first applicant to receive a United States patent on actual barbed-wire fencing, this honor going to William D. Hunt.

Hunt seems to have deserved such prominence as finally was accorded him. He had made an important advance in arming fences. He worked long and deliberately despite the fact that he was handicapped at all times by financial difficulties. He began in 1865 trying several methods of attaching barbs to wire,

[13] According to information gleaned from records of the Washburn & Moen Manufacturing Company, the circumstances might be reconstructed as follows: Hunt filed on June 3, and was granted patent on July 23. Smith's patent was granted on June 25. Date of his application cannot now be ascertained exactly; but if it was after Hunt's filing date, it would have been within the short period from June 3 to June 25, and Smith's patent would have had to be processed with unprecedented speed and dispatch. It is possible that this Hunt application date was on a second or third application and that the filing date on Hunt's original application was several months (some say almost three months) earlier.

[14] Warren, "History of the Manufacture of Barbed Wire Fencing," AS&W Records, *loc. cit.*

and he put up a length of experimental fencing across a corner of his pasture as early as 1866. The next year, "perhaps in the spring of 1867," he had a model made to send to the Patent Office, showing the sheet-metal type of barb which he had settled on as being his choice of the best style. He borrowed $35 to meet patent costs, but even after the patent was granted, he still had not the means to promote manufacture. He seems to have felt that if he could get to the new farm and cattle-raising areas of the West, he could make a go of his idea; but one thing after another kept him from leaving his home in New York state until 1873 when, with high hopes, he set out for Illinois. Nevertheless, since he was still short of funds, he soon became discouraged, and when sickness overtook him, he counted himself lucky to sell full rights in his patent to Charles Kennedy of Hinckley, Illinois, for $1,725 cash.[15] Hunt gave up the venture at that point and returned home.

In the years to come, however, Hunt's patent was upheld as a "bottom patent," and he was acclaimed by the industry. Had he been possessed of financial resources to match the strength of his convictions concerning his invention, he might have made something of it.[16] Or perhaps not. Perhaps the time was not ripe in 1867, for even after Kennedy bought the rights in 1874, the Hunt wire was not a success. It was 1879 when Thomas H. Dodge, as counsel for Washburn & Moen and Ellwood, declared in his Argument for Complainants in fourteen suits brought simultaneously before the United States Circuit Court:

> The Hunt patent, as before stated, was generic in character, and hence all subsequent inventions of improvements were necessary branches or improvements, emanating from this first and original invention. Subsequent improvements may have varied in construction, but the Hunt invention underlies them all. . . . the original and first conception of Hunt, is capable of being embodied in barbed fence wire in various modes and forms, but they all embody the ideas of Hunt.[17]

[15] This was in October, 1874. Charles Kennedy's own patent, No. 153965, was granted in August, 1874.
[16] See Chapter 8 of this volume.

This was quite a statement, quite a victory for Hunt—but belatedly and in principle only, for Washburn & Moen and Ellwood had long since become sole owners of the Hunt patent (via Kennedy and The Barb Fence Company), and it was said of the Hunt wire that "probably not more than half a mile in length was ever produced—and that, laboriously, by hand."[18]

HUNT—Patent No. 67117

Hunt assigned his patent to Charles Kennedy	Oct. 15, 1874
Kennedy assigned ½ interest to Glidden & Ellwood	Jan. 12, 1876
Reissue	Mar. 7, 1876
Kennedy assigned remaining ½ interest to O. T. Earle and Earle transferred to Washburn & Moen Company	May 23, 1876

SMITH—Patent No. 66182

Smith assigned all his interest to Joseph F. Glidden (except part relating to the post—and except the states of Missouri and Kansas)	Sept. 12, 1874
Smith assigned to Charles Kennedy ½ interest for Missouri and Kansas	Sept. 12, 1874
Smith assigned to Joseph F. Glidden ½ interest for Missouri and Kansas	Apr. 7, 1875
Glidden assigned ½ his interest to Kennedy	Jan. 12, 1876
Glidden assigned ¼ his interest to I. L. Ellwood	May 8, 1876
Kennedy assigned his interest to O. T. Earle	May 22, 1876
Earle assigned to Washburn & Moen Company	May 23, 1876
Reissue	May 23, 1876

KELLY—Patent No. 74379

Kelly assigned to William Lalor & James Slammon	Mar. 13, 1869
Lalor & Slammon assigned to William Calkins	Mar. 11, 1875
Reissue—Haish bought part interest	Feb. 8, 1876
Calkins assigned to Thorn Wire Hedge Company	Mar. 10, 1876
Thorn Wire Hedge Company assigned to Washburn & Moen Company	July 3, 1876[19]

[17] Page 3, AS&W Records, *loc. cit.*

[18] Arthur G. Warren, *Barbed Wire—Whose Invention,* 4.

[19] Warren, "History of the Manufacture of Barbed Wire Fencing," 38, AS&W Records, *loc. cit.*

These first three American patents, marketable or not, served
the purpose of bringing the experimenters out from under cover
to be recognized as inventors, and served also as an impetus to
others. Dabb of New Jersey, Smith of Ohio, and Hunt of New
York—all areas at that time devoted to agriculture—were soon
followed by two more New York staters: Michael Kelly in 1868,
and Lyman P. Judson in 1871, each of whom secured patents on
variations which indicated improvements. The sequence of patents in the decade of the seventies, which opened with a backlog
of patented inventions, follows:

Patent	Inventor	Locality	Date
No. 45827*	Grassin-Baledans	France	July, 1860
No. 67067*	Jannin	France	1865
No. 63482	Dabb	New Jersey	April, 1867
No. 66182	Smith	Ohio	June, 1867
No. 67117	Hunt	New York	July, 1867
No. 77570*	Gavillard	France	August, 1867
No. 74379	Kelly	New York	November, 1868
No. 118135	Judson	New York	August, 1871
No. 138763	Rose, H. M.	De Kalb	May 13, 1873
No. 146671	Haish, J.	De Kalb	January 20, 1874
No. 147634	Haish, J.	De Kalb	February 17, 1874
No. 147756	Ellwood, I. L.	De Kalb	February 24, 1874
No. 152368	Haish, J.	De Kalb	June 23, 1874
No. 153965	Kennedy, C.	De Kalb	August 11, 1874
No. 157124	Glidden, J. F.	De Kalb	November 24, 1874

* French patent numbers

Judson's design was for a flat hoop-wire strip, scarcely notable; but Kelly's invention was important for several reasons.
Whereas Smith and Hunt had worked with a single-strand wire,
Kelly twisted two wires together to form a cable for barbs—
the first of its kind in America. Whereas other designs had not
been produced in quantity, Kelly's was. Whereas others were
not brought into legal contest, the "Thorny Fence," as Kelly and
his assigns aptly called it, became a strong contender for rights
as a basic patent of the barbed-wire business.

[56]

Kelly's wire was first brought into prominence by a "land poor" gentleman farmer, General Aaron Stiles, who was in search of a cheap but effective fencing material for his own use. J. M. Millington, whom Stiles had directed to examine patents on fencing, pointed out that Kelly's "Thorny Fence" met Stiles's specifications, and Stiles took an immediate interest in the patent. His interest seems to have been purely personal, however. It is possible that at this time, in 1873, he might have recognized also the commercial possibilities of the Kelly invention, but it does not seem probable. Apparently it was two years after Millington began his patent study before Stiles actually purchased rights in the Kelly patent, and in this interim many events had transpired.[20] It seems much more likely that his business interest developed only after he was made aware of the significance of the Glidden patent and the ensuing fight for patent rights.

At one time it was Kelly's patent No. 74379, granted in 1868 (more than five years before Glidden filed application for patent), that loomed as the greatest obstacle in the way of Joseph Glidden's efforts to secure patent on his "improved fence wire." Kelly's patent as originally issued was based partially on a provision for "twisting of a second wire to strengthen the first wire." Later Glidden's attorney found that, although Glidden's was a new form of barb and an improvement over Kelly's, still Kelly's wire would "dominate as to twisted wire." But the Kelly claim had missed the point, had "failed to specify what he [Kelly] had really invented," i.e., a means of locking the barb in place. According to William Boone Douglass, L.L.M., who described in layman's language the court proceedings in this connection, if indeed it was Kelly's original intention to lock the barbs rather

---

[20] Charles G. Washburn in "Barbed Fencing" (AS&W Records, *loc. cit.*) says, "The Kelley patents were purchased by Aaron K. Stiles, J. W. Calkins and W. T. Calkins, in 1873, for less than $3,000." However, he gives no specific dates, as do other sources, and makes no mention of two men who already had bought from Kelly and from whom Stiles and the Calkinses made their purchase. It would seem, therefore, that Washburn was writing in generalities on this point, and that the date he gave was in error. According to United States Patent Office records, the transfer to Wm. T. Calkins (and Stiles) was made on March 11, 1875.

than to strengthen the fence, an error had been made.[21] Kelly tried to make correction in a reissue of 1876, but, in the meantime, Glidden and his attorney had seen their chance and had seized upon it.

Glidden's specifications clearly stated that the twisted wire was intended to hold the barbs in place, and there is no reason to suppose that it was not so intended from the beginning. He had, of course, experimented with an old grindstone to twist one wire around another in order to secure the barbs in proper position. Why should he not so state his claim as to stress this feature of his invention? There was, after all, every reason why he should so state it, and if, at this stage, Ellwood had joined forces with him, Ellwood most likely would have seen to it that legal advice was secured. The Glidden papers read as follows:

> This invention has relation to means for preventing cattle from breaking through wire fences; and it consists in combining with the twisted fence-wires, a short transverse wire, coiled or bent at its central portion about one of the strands of the twist, with the free ends projecting in opposite directions, the other wire strand serving to bind the spur wire firmly in place and in position, with the spur ends perpendicular to the direction of the fence-wire, lateral movement, as well as vibration, being prevented.

As far as any contest from Kelly was concerned, these words resolved the issue. As Douglass expressed it: "Though his [Kelly's] invention solved the problem and anticipated that of Glidden, it was not claimed." Case closed.

Nevertheless, in 1876, Stiles and two men, J. W. and W. T. Calkins, organized the Thorn Wire Hedge Company for manufacturing barbed wire as designed by Michael Kelly in his first and only successful patent. In the same year the Thorn Wire Hedge Company assigned rights to the Washburn & Moen Manufacturing Company of Worcester, Massachusetts, with the proviso that the Thorn Wire Hedge Company should retain free

21 "How Inventor Kelly Lost His Millions," *Professional Engineer* (October, 1928), 15.

license to manufacture the wire, and the Washburn & Moen Company should pay royalty of "⅜ of a cent per pound upon all barbed wire [of Kelly pattern] manufactured by it or licensed by it."[22] This was, of course, two years after Glidden, Ellwood, and Haish had received patents on their respective inventions, and eight years after Kelly's first patent was issued; and it would appear that the success of the Glidden-Ellwood manufacturing project and the excitement fomented by Haish served to accelerate the reception of Kelly wire. Certain it is that the Thorn Wire Hedge Company, manufacturing Kelly wire exclusively, profited greatly from association with the owners and licensors of Glidden rights, and although the Thorn Wire Hedge Company continued substantial operations for a long time, it was largely subsidized by royalty payments from Washburn & Moen Company. The continued operation of the former was contingent upon actions of the latter, in the same proportions that the commercial success of the earlier patent was dependent on the businesslike management of the later Glidden patent. It was, in the final analysis, the De Kalb incident of 1873 which led indirectly to the revival of interest in the Kelly patent of 1868. Without Glidden and the sequence of events which his work set in motion, Kelly's wire was not likely to have prospered so soon; but without Kelly's wire, Glidden's fate was not likely to have been any different.

Kelly, Hunt, Smith, Judson, Dabb—these early inventors of barbed wire had little to show for their efforts. Yet it was they who had taken steps in the right direction. And it was these first halting steps which brought the essential principles of barbed fencing back from overseas and into the heart of agricultural America. These men brought to light in the East progress which already had been made in farm sections across the country. They served a good purpose. But it remained for a group of Midwest-

[22] The fee was reduced on December 2, 1878, to one-fourth of a cent per pound; on August 7, 1879, to fifteen cents per hundred pounds; and on June 12, 1883, to five cents per hundred pounds. Charles G. Washburn, "Barbed Fencing," 14, AS&W Records, *loc. cit.*

erners, on the threshold of the prairie-plains where barbed wire was destined to be tried and proved, to lift the lid unceremoniously from an explosive issue which helped spark the continuance of westward migration in nineteenth-century America.

The scene was De Kalb, Illinois.

CHAPTER 5

PROMOTING BARBED WIRE

O NE AMERICAN JURIST, during litigation concerning
barbed-wire patents, said:

> . . . many times . . . men have exhausted their intellects and their
> lives in fashioning, conditioning, and maturing the most abstruse
> processes and machinery without having contributed one dollar
> to the world's wealth or one throb of enjoyment to its happiness
> . . . and yet some of the most important and valuable discoveries,
> which have marked the progress of the arts and sciences, have
> been the effect of accident or the suggestion of some stray but
> happy thought, which came, as it were, unbidden.[1]

With regard to the "discovery" of barbed-wire fencing, this
observation was both right and wrong. It was by accident, in fact,
that Glidden, Ellwood, and Haish came upon the Rose exhibit at
the De Kalb fair; it was by chance that they met there. But it
was not as the result of any "stray" thought that each conceived
the idea of attaching sharpened points to wire instead of to wood.
It was because they were concerned with farming. It was because
they knew about wire fencing. It was because wire fencing was
advocated for use where there was a scarcity of rock and timber,
as on the plains and prairies of Illinois. It was not a "stray"
but a deliberate thought on the part of men who understood
agricultural problems. It was because they lived where they did,
and because they were concerned with the problems that confronted them, that these three men were able to contribute to
the industrialization of agriculture in America.

[1] Barbed Wire Fence Cases of 1882–84, Briefs, AS&W Records, *loc. cit.*

They were in the beginning three plain citizens. There was nothing which set them apart or marked them as different. They had good strong faces, and good Biblical names—Joseph, Isaac, and Jacob. Yet Joseph Glidden, Isaac Ellwood, and Jacob Haish were three early Americans caught in a flow of events which made it necessary that their private affairs should be known to history. They became public figures, with the consequent loss of personal privacy.

Of the three, Haish apparently was the least reluctant to accept notoriety. His unique method of courting publicity seemed sometimes to have been designed to attract attention to himself as well as to his wire products—or, at any rate, he seemed to make no attempt to avoid the limelight. Certainly he did not go so far as to change his ways. He continued doggedly on with a great outpouring of claims and counterclaims publicized on billboards, in periodicals, and in hand circulars. He was the most aggressive advertiser of the barbed-wire inventors. In fact, the popularity of his "S" barb probably was due as much to the quantity of his promotional advertising as to the excellence of the barb's design and construction.

Before Washburn & Moen Company had entered the business, Glidden and Ellwood had published circulars entitled *Farmers Take Notice,* and had included in these all manner of details concerning the construction of fences. Later, the pros and cons of legal actions were put before the public through publications. Ellwood, then in partnership with Washburn, printed a periodical known as *The Glidden Barb Fence Journal,* apparently as an attempt to counteract Haish's scathing accusations in a similar publication called *The Regulator.* In comparison with Haish's writings, Ellwood's were tame indeed, as he adhered to a more or less conventional pattern, yet into the pages of the *Journal* were tucked occasional notations of a nature more personal than professional. One interesting sidelight, for example, was called "What's in a Name," and it listed some of the Ellwood agents whose names happened to represent various occupations—Miller, Baker, Fowler, Shepard, Carpenter, Miner, Sawyer, Porter, Taylor, Farmer, Shearer, Hayer, Barber, Potter, etc. But the *Journal* was made up mostly of fencing news, items of farm interest such as weather notes, and a few wisecracks. It was good advertising, but no match for Haish's sensationalism.

Haish advertised in the same grand manner that he did everything. His posters showed, along with assorted pictures of strange-looking animals, drawings of the "S" barb as wire coiled, stretched, wrapped around trees, and loaded in boxcars marked "Transcontinental Through Line." One poster, which has been preserved, includes, in addition to illustrations, the extra feature of a jingle-verse in German dialect:

Mit der vires rount und rount, Haish fence ish sure to vin!
Stick posts 18 feet in grount, for der prices bplease walk mit in.[2]

It was typical Haish extravaganza, comparable in its way to the turreted and gargoyle-encrusted palatial residence which he later built with the wealth acquired from barbed wire.

Ellwood and Washburn used colored poster ads also, after the style of the times, and theirs too were heavily ornamented; but verses were omitted and sentiment greatly reduced. Washburn & Moen Company, typically New England, could not have been expected to do more. The company had displayed good Yankee sagacity by entering the barbed-wire business, and company officials, having had the wisdom and foresight to get into this Western venture, were determined to support it with enthusiasm; but they were unused to the ways of the West. They were agreeable enough about the necessary amount of sales appeal, and they were willing to let Ellwood do what he thought was needed; but they would not go beyond the point of decorum. Haish could publish his periodical, and Ellwood could publish one too; but the wire manufactory of Worcester, Massachusetts, did not follow suit.[3]

[2] The idea of sticking posts eighteen feet in the ground is of course preposterous. It can only be assumed that the directions were intended to mean that posts be spaced eighteen feet apart; especially does this seem to be a plausible explanation when it is realized that the practice of the times was to space posts far apart in regions where they were scarce and/or expensive.

[3] Washburn & Moen Manufacturing Company issued pamphlets as "notifi-

Washburn & Moen Company lent to the attitude of their con-
federate in the West a note of sobriety. What is more, the align-
ment added a store of skill, experience, cash, and industrial
know-how which was unsurpassed in the whole of the American
steel and wire industry of the times. No sooner had the two
joined forces than they took up the action initiated earlier by
Glidden and Ellwood when they purchased half-interest in the
Hunt and Smith patents. The new partners bought the remaining
half-interest in Hunt and Smith (May 23, 1876), gained control
of the Kelly "Thorny Fence" (July 3, 1876) and several other out-
standing patents, and tried—unsuccessfully—to buy out Haish.
Thereafter they stressed, in advertising to the public as well as
arguing before the courts, their rights and privileges as owners
of these important papers and as "sole manufacturers of Glidden
wire." On the rights to the Glidden, Hunt, Smith, Kelly, and Kennedy patents, Mr. Washburn estimated that he spent $120,000;
on the real estate and fixtures at De Kalb, plus "other inventions
and equipment," $30,000. The aggregate expense, he noted in
July, 1877, as "1.42 per 100 lb. of barbed wire fence made and
sold."[4] It was no longer a small operation with which Mr. Ellwood was concerned and from which Mr. Glidden drew tangible
profits. From the moment of alliance with the great Eastern wire-
drawing company, it was big business for Glidden and Ellwood—
and for the barbed-wire industry in general. And to think that
Mr. Washburn had come unsolicited to De Kalb!

Ellwood had made important moves before—buying in with
Glidden, securing rights to prior patents, forming partnership
with Washburn; and now by retaining "the west and the territories"—new, raw, and raucous as the region was—by holding on
to this half of America, Isaac L. Ellwood displayed good judg-

---

cation and warning" against infringement on patents owned by the company,
and during litigation with the Iowa Farmer's Protective Association some newspaper space was purchased; but all such advertising was conducted at a later
date and in a decorous manner. See Chapter 6 of this volume.

[4] Proceedings of Circuit Court of United States, Northern District of
Illinois, July, 1879; Washburn & Moen Manufacturing Company and I. L. Ellwood Company vs. Andrew Dillman, A. N. Klinefelter, W. S. Dillman (testimony from Charles F. Washburn affidavit), 21, AS&W Records, loc. cit.

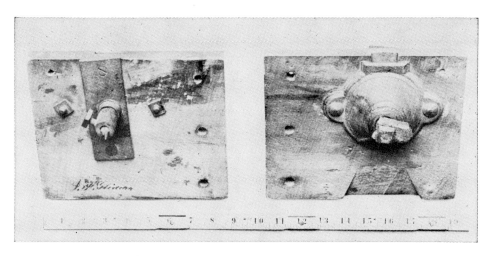

Two views of the famous coffee mill used by Joseph F. Glidden in the year 1874 at his home in De Kalb, Illinois, to form barbs for the first Glidden barbed-wire fencing.

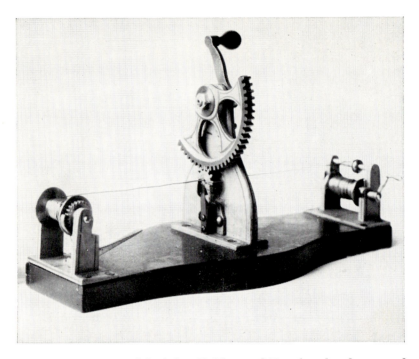

The 1874 patent model of the Glidden and Vaughan hand-operated
machine for making barbed wire.

ment again. The West was his kind of country, not Washburn's kind. It was, moreover, the clue to the future of barbed wire, and this Ellwood seems to have sensed from a very early date. Ellwood and Glidden and the two salesmen they had taken into their company already had evidenced special interest in areas bordering cattle ranges. The Barb Fence Company already had representatives in Texas, which was considered the key to the region as a whole.

On that day in 1874—November 24—when Glidden's application finally was granted patent No. 157124—"The Winner"— Joseph Glidden had written to a salesman, a friend and a relation by marriage, saying: "I cannot say definitely what we would like to do. We should very much like to have you interested in this fence business. . . . It promises to be a big thing and needs deliberation."[5] The salesman, Henry Bradley Sanborn, probably had seen the wire which Glidden wrote about. Apparently he too thought "this fence business" held promise of being "a big thing," for he began to travel for Glidden and Ellwood in areas surrounding De Kalb, and in 1875 he went to Texas as agent for The Barb Fence Company—and as the first barbed-wire salesman in the Southwest. There his partner J. P. Warner joined him, and with Warner's help Sanborn began the introduction of new fencing along the fringes of open range-lands.

Sanborn had found Texas a seething hotbed of controversy between farmers and stockmen. As the influence of the growing cattle industry increased, it had begun more and more to divide the men of Texas into the opposing factions of "free grassmen" and "nesters," the one faction holding nothing more important than preservation of the open range, and the other seeking closed ranges and protected fields as the requirement for settlement in new land. Between the two, the barbed-wire salesman was caught in a difficult situation, and rejected by both sides. Sanborn had settled near the railroad terminus, ordered wire shipped to him there, and had sent for Warner to help him cover the state by

[5] Warren, "History of the Manufacture of Barbed Wire Fencing," 48, AS&W Records, *loc. cit.*

one means or another, mainly by long buggy rides. Between them they had sold "the first ten reels" to a Gainesville merchant in north Texas, the "first carload" to an Austin hardware store in central Texas, and "the first carload sold directly to a Texas consumer" on the Gulf coastal plains. But they had not convinced either settlers or cowmen of the merits of their wares. They had been confronted with a combination of disbelief and sentiment which was not to be quickly overcome. Cowmen had scoffed at the thought that skimpy strands of wire would hold off Texas Longhorn cattle, while farmers had contented themselves with a wait-and-see attitude. Hardly anyone seems to have recognized the significance of the invention of such a product and some did not recognize the product itself. When shown a strip with two barbs on it as a sample of the new fencing, some men had guessed the barbs were posts for a model fence; one man had thought the piece was a bit for a horse.[6]

A number of factors contributed to the lack of enthusiasm over barbed wire. For one thing, Texans were dubious about any innovation from the North. Although the War between the States had been over for ten years, they still suspected that this might be another Yankee scheme to benefit the industrial North at the expense of the agricultural South. Lumbermen objected because they saw a threat to the sales they expected when railroads would be extended further to the west, and railroad men, anticipating the lumbermen's business, lent their voices to the protest. Added to this was the feeling that barbed wire was cruel, though on this subject there were widely varying opinions among agriculturists throughout the country. Some farmers who raised a few head of cattle of their own reported that the new fencing was "so great an improvement over simple wire that they prefer[ed] to use it and run the risk of injury [to cattle]."[7] Others contended that there should be a law prohibiting the use of the "unnatural fencing" because of the wounds inflicted on all man-

[6] Roy D. Holt, "Barbed Wire," *The Texas Monthly* (September, 1929), 175–76.

[7] *American Agriculturist* (November 1879), 157 f.

[66]

ner of livestock.[8] Opposition on humanitarian grounds was particularly strong among Texas cowmen, even though injudicious handling of cattle accounted for many of the injury cases, and tensions inherent between stockmen and farmers as well as between Northerners and Southerners gave rise to reports of many others. Ofttimes disturbances blamed on barbed wire were basically the result of personal animosities which would have occurred with or without fencing. As settlers came more and more to the grasslands, cattlemen became more and more antagonistic, and their adherence to the tradition of the Open Range, understandable though it was, presented the greatest obstacle in the way of Sanborn, Warner, and those who followed them in striving for acceptance of barbed wire in the West.

Sanborn had been the first to bring barbed wire to Texas. Sanborn and Warner had been pronounced "general agents for the United States for the introduction and sale of fence, being the first wholesale barb wire fencemen to take the road."[9] The first printed advertisements for Glidden wire—in the form of a thorough description of operations at De Kalb—had been circulated by them.[10] They had been representatives for Glidden and Ellwood, for Ellwood and Washburn, and later Sanborn was to be partner with Glidden in a ranching enterprise to demonstrate fencing. Sanborn and Warner were among the most important figures in the promotion of barbed wire. But their first trip to Texas had been disappointing, and probably no one had been more disappointed in it than Isaac Ellwood.

By the time Sanborn and Warner had come back in 1876 to check on territory they serviced in Illinois, Ellwood was ex-

---

[8] Bills prohibiting use of barbed-wire fences were brought before the Texas legislature in 1879, as in Connecticut in 1879, and Vermont and Maine in 1880. The bills did not pass in Texas, but one law requiring a board between top strands of barbed wire was in effect for a short period.

[9] Marsh, *The De Kalb County Manufacturer*, 8.

[10] The advertisement read, in part: "Mr. Glidden commenced making this fence but a few months since in a room 108 square, and twisted it by hand. We now twist by steam power and our brick factory is 708 by 1208 and two stories high, and employs 70 hands. Our capacity for manufacturing is over 5 tons per day. We have already manufactured and sold over 100,000 lbs. on trial and not one pound has been returned." Gedge and Boley, "History," I, 58.

panding production at De Kalb, combining interests with Washburn at Worcester, and anticipating greatly increased sales for the industry. Undoubtedly he had considered the venture into Texas a strategic move, for the opening up of a new market was of utmost importance to him at this time. The securing of the vast potential of the West was a primary goal. He had good reason for pressing the point. In the light of these conditions, Ellwood hired an enterprising Illinois farm youth named Gates, as a salesman "to push sales in Texas"—and by so doing, he threw Texas and the surrounding territory abruptly into prominence, and into confusion.

—•—•—•—•—•—•—

John Warne Gates was born on May 18, 1855, at Gary's Mill in northeastern Illinois. He came to Ellwood with a letter of introduction from Glidden, whose wife, Lucinda Warne, was related to Gates's mother. How much of a recommendation Glidden gave is not known. Gates had not the reputation at this time for staying long with a hard job, and presumably Glidden's letter was a help to him. But in all probability the young man's confidence in himself—to be displayed in later life with such vigor—contributed toward Ellwood's decision to take him on. At any rate, by this decision there was added to the list of characters taking part in the drama of the barbed-wire business the name of John W.—later known as "Bet-a-Million"—Gates, whose appearance on any scene was the signal for fireworks. The scene in this case was San Antonio, Texas, in the heart of the cattle kingdom. The time, "before the year's end" in 1876.

Gates was quoted as saying, when he attended Ellwood's funeral in 1910, that he went to work for "Colonel Ike" Ellwood at the age of nineteen and left for Texas soon afterward, yet it is generally stated that Gates was twenty-one when he arrived in San Antonio.[11] He was, in any case, a young man. It can hardly be said that his personality was set, but there were strong evi-

[11] *Chicago Tribune* (September 18, 1910). In this same newspaper article Gates is quoted as saying that it was Mrs. Ellwood, not Mrs. Glidden, who used a coffee mill to crimp the wire for barbs. (See Chapter 3 of this volume.)

dences even at this time of the confident, take-a-chance attitude which characterized him throughout his later years. He was ready to take a chance on barbed wire. He made his start with it in a big way, and he stayed with it in one capacity or another for the rest of his days. Although he engaged in the widest—and wildest—possible range of business activities during his lifetime and speculated in almost every conceivable venture, it was as a youngster selling barbed wire in Texas that Gates laid the foundation for his great financial success. His fate was sealed, along with Ellwood's, at old San Antonio, and thereafter the two—bound inextricably the one to the other—made history together.

San Antonio was quite a place for Gates to set up shop. Romantic and beautiful as it was, San Antonio in the 1870's was a frontier town replete with all the accouterments that the term implies. Since the days of the conquistadors it had been a trading center, a seat of government, a stronghold of the church, a scene of heroism, a meeting place for the high and the low, a jewel of Spanish grace set on a winding river. The atmosphere created by its early history could never be erased. But in the era following the Civil War, San Antonio boomed with business. In addition to everything it had been, it was now a mecca for cattlemen.[12]

When Gates got to San Antonio, his new store-bought clothes and the drummer's dull green satchel marked him as a beginner in his trade. But Gates was a good talker and already a hail-fellow-well-met. He talked his way into acceptance with other salesmen, and gradually won his way into friendly association with prospective customers. Apparently he stood around and visited with farmers on the plaza in the daytime and matched stakes with cattlemen in the casino at night. He made contact with both factions. But he did not sell much barbed wire, for the attitude which confronted him was little better than that which Sanborn and Warner had met with.

One story of the times recounts that "Ol' Jim," a neighbor's

[12] Although Fort Worth, Texas, has come to be known as "Cowtown" and serves as a center for the cattle business, it is still to "Ole Santone" that the Texas and Southwestern Cattle Raisers Association often repairs for its business meetings, and there that the Old Trail-Drivers often gather for reunions.

bull, "could go through anything," and the owner reckoned that "the bull would not stop for barbed wire."[13] But John W. Gates reckoned differently. He thought that what he had for sale would make an impression on Ol' Jim and on his owner too—if only it could be tried. He had to think up a way to prove it. Finally one night while he sat in a Mexican chili parlor, he had an idea. Gazing absent-mindedly through the narrow grilled window and watching a medicine-show performer peddling his wares in the plaza, Gates suddenly knew what he would do. He was jubilant. He grabbed the friend seated beside him and, according to one realistic description, shouted:

> I've worked something out. I think I've got it. We'll sell more barbed wire than you can shake a stick at. We'll do like Doc Lighthall. We'll give 'em a show, right out in front. Get the wildest damn cattle in Texas—corral 'em here with barbed wire and then let 'em try to get out. That'll show 'em. Ain't a cow-hand livin' won't go for that![14]

Next morning Gates went to the San Antonio city officials and got permission to build a corral on one of the city's plazas, and although he must have been required to make some explanation, Gates evidently persuaded the officials to keep his plans secret. The Military Plaza, between San Fernando Cathedral and the Spanish Governor's Palace, was the site settled on.[15] It was a good location in a conspicuous spot, and the building of a corral there was bound to attract attention. The work took a number of days and during this time Gates, refusing to say what he proposed to do with the construction, aroused the public's curiosity and general interest. He went to work setting posts, without a word of explanation, and only when he was well along with the job of

---

13 Holt, "Barbed Wire," *loc. cit.*, 176.
14 Herman Kogan and Lloyd Wendt, *Bet-A-Million: The Story of John W. Gates*, 45.
15 Some sources say it was the Main Plaza. The two plazas were very close —separated only by the Cathedral—and could have been confused, but it is believed that the Military Plaza was the exact location of Gates's demonstration. According to city records, James H. French was mayor of San Antonio from January 19, 1875, to January 31, 1885, but whether Gates went to Mayor French or to one Bryan Callaghan, is not certain.

stringing a new and peculiar-looking wire did Gates begin to talk
—with a sort of ballyhoo all his own:

> This is the finest fence in the world. Light as air. Stronger
> than whiskey. Cheaper than dirt. All steel, and miles long. The
> cattle ain't born that can get through it. Bring on your steers,
> gentlemen![16]

The time had come for a showdown on barbed wire.

There are many and varied accounts of the demonstration
which followed. Some say that 25 of the roughest and toughest
Longhorn steers were put into the arena; other estimates run as
high as 60, and one puts the figure at 135. Some claim that Gates
had previously arranged to have the fiercest-looking and yet most
docile steers that he could find and that his exhibition was a fake.
But at any rate a goodly number of people turned out to see the
show. They stood at a distance from the fence or perched on
stands for safety, since hardly a man in the audience believed
that the barbed wire was going to stop the Longhorns. The crowd
had gathered for the excitement—and for the laughs.

Gates played his part as a master of ceremonies to perfection.
He had the cattle driven in with flying hoofs and much fanfare. He took time to build up suspense for the spectators and
probably to lay bets of his own. But once inside the corral, the
cattle took over. Since they could see nothing in their way but
thin strands of strange-looking wire fastened to posts, the animals began to bolt into space; but when they came in contact with
the fence a few times, they retreated momentarily. Then, enraged
at being repulsed, they charged harder against the fence; but
the barbs were still there to stop the attack. Some stories tell that
at this point two men with flaming torches were sent into the
arena to stir up the animals. And then with tails raised, heads low-
ered, and hoofs pawing the ground, the Longhorns charged again
and again against the corral. The barbed wire held. The audience waited. The moment came for another onslaught. The steers
only milled around inside the corral, and their interest in going

[16] Chris Emmett, *Shanghai Pierce*, 136.

through the fence gradually subsided. They seemed resigned thereafter to haunch around and bellow their discontent. One report stated that "a post was pulled loose," but to the surprise of most of the spectators, little damage was done to the tight eight-strand barrier. It was clear that the fence had won the fight, had subdued its assailants—both man and beast. The experiment had worked, the barbed wire had held, and that—for the moment —was enough. John Warne Gates had proved his point.

It was said that "before nightfall Gates had sold hundreds of miles [of his product] at the prevailing price of 18 cents a pound."[17] It might be said, if it has not, that he slept well that night; or, he should have. His personal fortune was made, and he had succeeded in putting on what many varying and sometimes conflicting accounts all agreed was an epoch-making event. He had staged a climax in the history of barbed wire. Business boomed—almost literally overnight, and although there were difficulties yet to be encountered and objections to be overcome, it was evident at once that the purpose for which Gates had been sent to Texas—to speed up sales in the Southwest—had been accomplished. Barbed wire was soon to be sold by the ton, by the mile, and by the carload.

Isaac Ellwood, no doubt, thanked his lucky stars for the sequence of developments which had made his factory equal to filling the orders which now poured in, and Charles Washburn might well have congratulated himself also, for not even so great a manufacturing firm as Washburn & Moen Company could fail to be impressed with the rise in barbed-wire production during the weeks, months, and years following the San Antonio episode. Records show the increase for the industry, as follows:

1874—	10,000 lbs. made and sold
1875—	600,000 lbs. made and sold
1876—	2,840,000 lbs. made and sold
1877—	12,863,000 lbs. made and sold
1878—	26,655,000 lbs. made and sold

[17] "The Fence That Made Cattle History," *Steelways* (April 1, 1946). See also Washburn, "Barbed Fencing," 7, AS&W Records, *loc. cit.*

1879— 50,377,000 lbs. made and sold
1880— 80,500,000 lbs. made and sold
1950—482,000,000 lbs. made and sold[18]

It has been suggested that Sanborn and/or Warner had thought sometime earlier of staging a rodeo to publicize and dramatize the effectiveness of barbed wire, and that Gates's stunt was an outgrowth of the rodeo idea. It has been implied that Gates took more credit for the resultant upsurge in business than was his due. It has been intimated that some entirely different and unknown person conducted the demonstration and it was later attributed to Gates. By far the greatest number of records and most reliable of sources, however, concede that the idea was Gates's; and only the most skeptical reviewers question that it was Gates who actually put on the show. Who else would have had the temerity—unless it were Haish, and he has never been mentioned in this connection. No other character could have done it with the bravado of which John W. Gates was known to be master. All things considered, it seems safe to conclude that it was this brash young newcomer who gave the barbed-wire business the boost it needed, and set sales skyrocketing.

Gates was a salesman as well as a showman. He took barbed wire to many small Texas towns, and with his personal brand of persuasiveness he caused many a storekeeper to stock the new product and many a farmer to buy it from the stores. Hardware dealers as a rule were reluctant to handle the "new-fangled stuff," prickly with barbs and sometimes sticky with paint, yet Gates sold to them sometimes by the carload. An experience at the Richardson hardware store in Mexia, for example, was recalled by Mr. W. H. Richardson of Austin:

> [At first] no one would unload the wire . . . and no one knew how to handle it. But Gates and my father arranged demonstrations and showed them how. They built a chute up to the railroad car door and rolled it out. I remember that a spool tore a cowboy's boots half off, but Gates got the job done. He showed

18 Figures for 1874–80 are from *Great Plains*; 1950 estimate of "enough to string 502,000 miles of 3-strand fence," from Douglas A. Fisher, *Steel Serves the Nation*, 161.

them how to stretch it with a wagon wheel. He certainly was a good talker, because my father got only five cents a spool for handling the stuff. Pretty soon, though, he [Richardson] was selling it by the carload himself.[19]

There were other signs showing that Gates was "a good talker," for while selling barbed wire in Texas, he had also to sell himself in Illinois. He traveled back and forth between the two states, endeavoring to deal with problems in both places at once. He had not only left his boss and his business headquarters at De Kalb, but he had left his young wife and child at near-by Turner Junction. He made frequent trips to both places, attempting on the one hand to come to terms and make a new contract with Isaac Ellwood, and on the other hand to compose and reassure Dellora Gates. He thought he knew how to accomplish both tasks, but he was having trouble—especially with Ellwood.

The I. L. Ellwood Company at De Kalb, in partnership with Washburn & Moen Company, was unwilling to meet the terms which Gates sought. Gates insisted on a share of the profits greater than Ellwood would grant him, and when he demanded that either he be made a partner in the De Kalb company or be given exclusive rights to sales in Texas, Ellwood refused. Sanborn and Warner, as first representatives of the company, still held contracts for selling wire in Texas, and this Gates resented. He could do nothing about it, however, until these contracts expired on January 1, 1877. Then Ellwood renewed them.

Gates was caught short and he knew it. He resigned in a fury. He packed up Dellora and the child, and set out to start a new business in a new locale. He said he would move to St. Louis and start making barbed wire. He called on his Texas customers to rally to his cause and swing their business his way. He swore vengeance on the Ellwood-Washburn and Sanborn-Warner combine; he vowed he would beat "the big boys" at their own game.

[19] Kogan and Wendt, *Bet-A-Million*, 51.

[74]

CHAPTER 6

MOONSHINE AND MONOPOLY

THE COMBINATION of Washburn & Moen and I. L. Ellwood Company—hereinafter often referred to as "the Company"—was a formidable adversary against which to launch a career. To less determined opponents than Jacob Haish and John W. Gates, it would have looked to be an indomitable foe, for its position of superiority was founded on ownership of patents which dominated all others. But as long as there were points of law which could be brought to trial, counterclaims from many sources continued to pile up, and these the Company was required to meet, one by one.

There were twenty-eight lawsuits on "prior-use" fences. Some were based on "armour" which actually had been put up, in exasperation or desperation, to protect property; some were dreamed up at a date later than claimed; most were of the type which the courts called "crude experiments," not patented.[1] Valid or not, however, each required examination and trial, and each cost the defendants heavily. Glidden and Ellwood alone could never have financed such a battle; the Barb Fence Company could never have survived such an onslaught; but the strong organization grown out of the combined forces of Washburn & Moen Company and Ellwood spent on these twenty-eight claims an estimated $50,000.

The structures named in the suits were generally referred to as follows: Anderson fence; Ankeny fence; Beers fence; Brooklyn,

[1] Gedge and Boley, "History," I, 33.

[75]

New York; Crill fence; Combined wire, board, and nail; Cook fence; R. V. Douglas fence; Grenniger fence; Hair fence; Hibbard Gate; Hutchinson fence; Dr. Jayne fence; Long fence; McKinney fence; Manchester Fair fence; Morley fence; Jacob Outwater fence; Pendelton fence; Philadelphia fences; Plane fence; Rice fence; John A. Roebling's Sons fence; Stone's fence; Tolman fence; Twisted Wire (this may have been known also as the Freeman fence); Walker & Son fence; and Wilson fence. From among these, the most remarkable and most controversial—Beers, Morley, and Long—bear some explanation.

Edwin A. Beers, living near Mayfield, De Kalb County, Illinois, claimed that as a boy of thirteen he had armed a wire fence with wire barbs in 1857. A sample of the fence was presented as evidence in court in 1879, with the claim that the piece had been preserved for twenty years in an old tool chest in a barn. The court ruled against the Beers fence because analysis of the sample showed it to be Bessemer steel which was not made in America until the late 1860's and early 1870's.

Alvin Morley of Delhi, Iowa, claimed that he had exhibited barbed wire at a Delhi County Fair sometime between 1857 and 1862, and again a sample was presented as evidence, this piece reputed to have come from an old trunk in an attic. The Morley case was taken all the way to the United States Supreme Court before it was proved that the sample could not have been made with the crude tools available to Morley at the early date claimed.

The fence claimed by W. H. Long of Delaware County, Iowa, was a board fence topped with a prickered wire strand said to have been put up in 1873. It was discovered from railroad records that the boards for the fence were not shipped until 1875; and it was verified that pliers used to barb the sample were specially designed to make barbed wire of a kind used in the Delaware County area after 1873.

Settlement finally was made, so that when the long litigation was finished, it could be said that "there was not a single 'prior-use' fence which had not been utterly discredited; not a scrap of proof remained showing that anyone had in any way armed a wire with prickers or barbs prior to the invention of Hunt in 1867."[2] And rights to the Hunt patent, as well as to the Smith, Kennedy, Kelly, and their own Glidden patent No. 157124 were securely controlled by Washburn and Ellwood.

As the Company assumed responsibility for protecting the Glidden patent, it assumed also the right to approve or refuse approval of manufacture of Glidden wire or any patterns which infringed on the Glidden patent. On this second score Washburn and Ellwood came up against still other individuals, and more expenses, for there had sprung up in the wake of success not only many inventors but also many manufacturers of barbed-wire fencing.

The very simplicity of the product invited imitation. As long as plain wire could be ordered from wire-drawing factories, and as long as no legal precedent was set to discredit slight variations of barbs attached to wire, it was easy enough to become a competitor in the new business—at least on a temporary basis. Small factories operated throughout the area from Chicago to St. Louis, many of them without participating in the Washburn & Moen Company and Ellwood plan for licensing factories which manufactured under rights belonging to the Company. Some operators claimed immunity because they had filed application for a new patent; others set up plainly illegal operations. Their status was definitely *sub rosa*, their life expectancy as businesses was admittedly short, but while awaiting decisions from the United States Patent Office and opinions on the law of the land, they worked feverishly to share in the barbed-wire boom for at least a little while before being required to close down.

One such plant was operated by John W. Gates. Gates had gone to St. Louis, as he had said he would, when he left Ellwood in anger. He had begun making wire on a small scale. But nothing that Gates touched remained small-scale for very long a time. He was soon selling barbed wire fast and at a profit. He enlarged his operations, merged with others, and took a stand with any and

[2] Warren, "History of the Manufacture of Barbed Wire Fencing," 17 f., AS&W Records, *loc. cit.* Also Gedge and Boley, "History," I, 34.

all concerns that opposed the growing power of Washburn & Moen Company and I. L. Ellwood Company.

Gates did not want for buyers of his barbed wire, for he had kept personal contact with many customers in Texas and he was able to pick up others in St. Louis and its environs. His problem at the beginning of his operations in 1878 was not so much to make sales, as to make wire—to manufacture, legally or otherwise. He had no rights to the designs of barbs which he manufactured or to the machine he used to make the barbs. But because patent on the machine he used was not owned by the Company, he dared to use it without having claim on it himself and without caring if the patent infringed on Company rights.[3] He was thoroughly familiar with the system under which the Company granted license, but he had no intention of complying with it. He had no intention of paying tribute to Isaac Ellwood. He conducted an outlaw business, and since this business was within the province assigned by Company contract to Isaac Ellwood, it was up to Ellwood to stop it.

Ellwood got out an injunction and sent officers to St. Louis to subpoena Gates. But before he would submit to having papers served on him, Gates loaded his factory equipment on a barge and floated it by moonlight out on the river, moving from his location on the Missouri side of the city, across the river to the Illinois side, out of reach of the process servers. By the time Ellwood got legal proceedings started again on the far side of the river, Gates had floated back again—making barbed wire for sale in competition with the Company all the while!

This was, of course, pure trickery and could not be kept up indefinitely, but in the meantime Gates gained from it. For one thing, he had the satisfaction of making Ellwood look foolish, at least for the moment. But the chief result and long-term advantage to Gates was that he succeeded in attracting to himself other rebellious operators who were ready to oppose Washburn

[3] The machine which Gates used was invented by George C. Baker of Des Moines, Iowa, in 1875, and used by Baker when he began the manufacture of barbed wire in 1879. It was an important machine and figured in many important lawsuits, as did the Stevens machine which Haish controlled.

& Moen and Ellwood. Unlicensed manufacturers of the area saw in Gates the leader they needed, one who gave promise of being able to combat "the combine" which they feared. They were willing to go along with him and to take directions from him in the fight against licensing. They quickly organized into a group which assumed the nickname of "moonshiners" in honor of the moonlit night when Gates had floated out of the grasp of Isaac Ellwood. They became known generally as "moonshine" manufacturers; their unlicensed product, as "moonshine" wire. They fell in easily with Gates's plans, and it was not long before he had them ready to act at his command.

Meanwhile the Company was beset with many lawsuits pertaining to the patents under which licenses were issued. Even the long-time controversy with Jacob Haish was still on appeal. But Washburn and Ellwood conducted their business with confidence, feeling justified in their stand because they owned the patents basic to the industry, including patents on important machinery for making barbed wire. Legally and logically they had the right to require license fees from manufacturers usurping or infringing these patents, except that the question of priority on some patents was still subject to appeal in the courts. The Company employed men trained as expostulators to travel over the country and explain to dealers about the differences between Glidden wire and the infringers' product. Publicity of various kinds was tried. J. M. Millington, who had started out helping Stiles and the Thorn Wire Hedge Company, was employed as expostulator with the added assignment of locating infringers and attempting to settle with them out of court. But despite all such efforts to clarify their position and to establish order in the industry, the Company's stand was variously interpreted and greatly disliked.

Gates realized that while litigation was prolonged, the implications of the matter were so clouded in legal language as to be unintelligible to the average buyers and users of barbed wire. As for the manufacturers, Gates knew that they resented having the burden of paying license fees in addition to regular operating

[79]

costs. As long as he and his cohorts paid no license fee, they could manufacture cheaper than bona fide licensees of the Company. Also they could deal in a number of variations of standard wire, because by the slightest change in specifications, without materially altering the value and intent of the original, it was possible to apply for a new patent on an old and valuable design. While the application was pending, manufacture might proceed.

Since the wire was produced at a lower cost, it could be sold at a lower price, and by cutting the price, "moonshine" operators were in a position to undersell the Company and upset the market. The man who determined the rate of cut was John Gates, and he was in a position to enforce his decision. In the group he commanded, Gates required each man's check for $2,500—the amount to be forfeited by any member of the group not holding to the price set. As the number of his group increased and his influence spread, Gates was clearly on the way to establish a monopoly of his own in opposition to Washburn & Moen Company and I. L. Ellwood.

While he continued to compete for the growing market in the Southwest, Gates began to eye the great stretches of newly opened-up farm land in Kansas, Nebraska, Wisconsin, and territories beyond. Here at mid-continent appeared to be the business challenge of the day; here was open country on the very outskirts of manufacturing centers. Here were the small factories needed to add power to his organization, the area needed for widening his field of operations. Gates could see many advantages which would accrue from capturing this area for his group—and for himself. He was ready to expand into the Midwest, and he proposed to start with Iowa.

Iowa was one of the states leading in consumption of barbed wire, in the number of grange locals, and in the fight against the Company. It has been said that "If the prairie state of Illinois produced and manufactured the first practical barbed wire fencing, Iowa followed immediately in her steps. . . . During the seventies and eighties, Iowa had 15 different factories."[4] And most of these

4 Hayter, "An Iowa Farmers' Protective Association," *loc. cit.*, 335. This

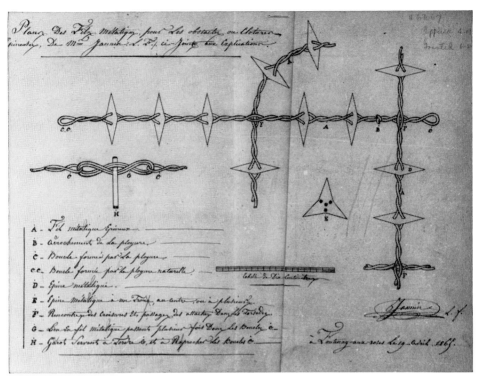

French patent No. 67067, granted on June 24, 1865, to Louis François Jannin. This patent is remarkably similar to one of the first United States patents on barbed wire, No. 74379, granted on February 11, 1868, to Michael Kelly. But Jannin's patent did not take hold in France as Kelly's did in the range cattle country of the United States.

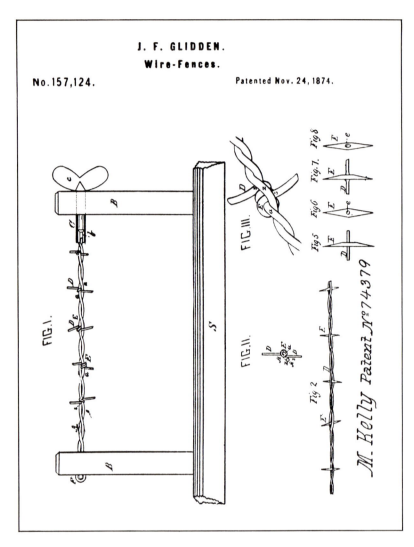

The original patent drawing of Glidden's barbed wire, "The Winner," patent No. 157124, issued on November 24, 1874.

interests were unitedly opposed to paying license fees to Washburn & Moen and Ellwood. "Free wire" enthusiasts organized in December, 1878, for the purpose of presenting a firm stand against the Company, and within a short while the group known as the Iowa Farmers' Protective Association openly defied "the combine" and encouraged all farmers to use "moonshine" or "free" wire fencing. This was insurrection, close to the home base in De Kalb, and again it fell Ellwood's lot to quell the trouble.

Ellwood threatened with lengthy letters. Charles F. Washburn in person journeyed west again, and failing to make peace, he authorized the unprecedented action of "getting out a series of pamphlets" to explain the situation to dealers and their customers. Meanwhile, Iowa newspapers, with the farm editor of the *Iowa State Register* taking a prominent part, proposed that the farmers buy not a pound of wire put out by "the trust." "The trust," so the papers stated, "[had] circularized every railroad and farmer in the midwest," and "with a whole galaxy of sleek well-fed eastern patent lawyers" had bought out one small factory after another.[5] Farmers, needless to say, were thoroughly puzzled, in some cases so much so that they did not buy wire from either faction for fear of reprisal from the other.

Mainly, however, the conflicting propaganda created more confusion than fright, and probably the Association project would have prospered for some time had it not been that their cause was betrayed from within their own ranks. When James A. Coon represented himself to Washburn and Moen Company as sole owner of the factory which the Association operated for the manufacture of "free" wire, he and the Association attorney C. C. Cole were caught by co-owners of the factory equipment, and their attempt at double cross was foiled. The Association went

seems to be a conservative estimate counting only full-fledged businesses without reference to others less well organized. St. Louis boasted of eleven factories in 1886, which, like Iowa's businesses, were subject to opening and closing and reopening without ceremony. The figures are considered dependable because they are given by Earl Hayter in his scholarly article. At the time of writing this article in 1939, Mr. Hayter had access to many records which are not now available.

5 Pellett, Peterson Scrapbook, *loc. cit.*

on with its factory, but in the fracas among its members, its fight against Washburn and Ellwood had lost ground which was not easily recovered.

Enormous sums of money were required for prosecution of affairs by both sides in the Iowa controversy. The Association thought at first to save the amount of $20,000 by going in with Jacob Haish on his already organized suit, but when this plan fell through, the farmers raised the needed funds and went resolutely forward with the fight. After separation from Haish, the Association retained its own lawyers; one of them, A. B. Cummins, conducted his business with such effectiveness that he was well noted by the defendants, Washburn & Moen Company and Ellwood, and was later hired by them.[6] Cummins *et al.* won for the Association two decisions in close succession, these being the only cases to break the Company monopoly for any appreciable time. Judge Treat in St. Louis and Judge McCrary in Keokuk, both in June, 1882, ruled that the Company patents in reissue had been "illegally broadened." It was necessary thereafter that the Company hold its ground on the basis of the original patents rather than reissues, and this they did accomplish, since the federal court at Des Moines in 1885 sustained the original Glidden papers and ruled that back damages for infringement be assessed against the Iowa Farmers' Protective Association.

Meanwhile 9 cases of alleged infringement were tried in Iowa and 53 in Iowa, Missouri, Kansas, Minnesota, and Nebraska combined. J. M. Millington, representing the Company as expostulator, closed 139 factories. Ellwood issued a number of "wordy letters" to which the "moonshiners" replied by brazenly courting the Company's customers with more publicity. "Our forefathers had spunk enough to cast tea into the sea," one local leader wrote in the *Iowa State Register* on March 2, 1881. "Have any of our farmers spirit enough not to use one pound of this wire which has the blood of liberty staining it?" Washburn & Moen Company and Ellwood went so far as to threaten suit against farmers using

---

[6] James A. Coon, ousted by the independents, was later employed by Washburn & Moen Manufacturing Company.

illegal wire, as well as against agents and dealers selling it. This was too much for Iowa! Farmers were bewildered, salesmen were angry, the state was in an uproar. It appeared to be a good place for John W. Gates to step in.

But at this point Gates suffered a serious setback. Before he could press ahead with his plans for expansion, he would have to overcome the effects of a court verdict. The Company had won judgment in a crucial suit against the troublesome and ever-present Jacob Haish. By a joint decision of Judges Thomas Drummond and Henry W. Blodgett handed down in Chicago on December 15, 1880, Jacob Haish's "famous 'S' barb" was decreed an infringement on patents judged to be foundation patents—i.e., Hunt, Kelley, and Glidden—in the possession of Washburn & Moen Company and I. L. Ellwood Company. Jacob Haish was thereby made liable for damages already accrued.

The effect of this legal decree was tremendous. In a manner of speaking, it brought independent manufacturers to their knees before the power of Washburn & Moen Company and Ellwood. Although it was quite possible to continue to operate at a profit under license, in the case of most fly-by-night establishments the owners were already liable for so much in back royalties or were so poorly financed from the start that they were unable to face settlement. Many small operators were obliged to sell out completely, a few faded into an unrecorded past, and those who were financially able made application for license to manufacture under the "foundation" patents. It seemed almost as if "the Company" had become "The Company."

Said the *Industrial World*, in its issue of December 23, 1880, from Chicago:

> It seems to be admitted on all sides that this is the most important mercantile decision that has ever been rendered in this country. It has created a most profound sensation and is the topic of conversation on the streets, in the cars, in the hotels, in business houses, and in fact wherever men congregate. Its importance arises from the fact that there has already been more than 100,000 tons used, and there seems to be practically no limit to the de-

[83]

mand hereafter; and to the additional fact that that portion of the vast amount sold during the past four years which has been manufactured by infringers of the patents now decided valid renders the parties engaged in such unlawful manufacture, sale and use liable for damages to the plaintiffs, the Washburn and Moen Mfg. Company and I. L. Ellwood.[7]

Charles Washburn was in Europe at the time of the ruling, but he hurried home to his offices and to consultations with Isaac Ellwood. The two went to Chicago and set up headquarters where, during January and February, 1881, they attempted to settle grievances brought before them. The terms of settlement were stern. It was said—by one of the "moonshiners" most bitterly and most busily opposed to regulation—that men were seen emerging from Mr. Washburn's room in the Grand Pacific Hotel "with tears running down their cheeks."[8]

Obviously the victor was not in a mood of reconciliation, nor could he have been expected to be. He was not vengeful, but neither was he moved to sympathy. He had spent up to this time (January, 1881), "in the payments of royalties, in the acquirement of patents and the litigation expenses ... $468,000 ... [and] had received $36,000 in royalties, making a net outgo ... from the point of ownership of patents ... of $432,000."[9] He was now assessing what he considered to be his just dues—and there is every reason to believe that "he" was a composite figure, for Washburn and Ellwood seemed agreed on how best to set up the transactions.

Twenty-nine infringing patents were turned over to the Company. Royalty to be paid the Company was fixed at seventy-five cents per hundred pounds, and the quantity to be manufactured by each licensee was set individually at between one thousand to five thousand tons annually (although one later contract, to be described in another chapter, was issued for ten thousand tons per annum). Although there were some slight vari-

[7] Gedge and Boley, "History," II, 41.
[8] "Briefs from Barb Wire Fence Cases of 1882–84," Arguments for the Licensor, AS&W Records, *loc. cit.*
[9] Washburn, "Barbed Fencing," 21, *ibid.*

ations, the contracts were generally uniform, all being based on a seven-point standard, summarized by Mr. Washburn's son as follows:

1. Licensor acknowledged novelty and validity of all the patents.
2. Agreed to manufacture and sell only the types attached to his license.
3. Monthly reports of sales, to whom made, price, etc.
4. Royalty to be paid of ¾ ct. per pound, independent of any question in dispute between the parties.
5. Should not sell barbed wire at less price than Washburn & Moen, the latter to furnish price list.
6. Right to cancel license upon breach of any of conditions.
7. Royalty paid under license not to be greater than that paid by any other party licensed after January 1881.[10]

Forty companies received licenses under the foregoing conditions, and of these, thirty-three were assessed back damages.[11] At the end of the proceedings, Washburn and Ellwood estimated their deficit at $110,493, the difference between the total outgo and income at the start of the meeting having been made up by the thirty-three illegal manufacturers, most of whom had operated at one time or another in collaboration with either Haish or

[10] *Ibid.*, 23.

[11] Licenses were granted in January and February, 1881, to the following, those marked with asterisks being the companies assessed back royalties: *Iowa Barb Wire Company; H. B. Scutt & Company; *Iowa Barb Steel Wire Company; Reuben Ellwood; *Ohio Steel Barb Fence Company; Pittsburgh Hinge Company, Ltd.; *Sherman & March; Thos. H. Dodge; *Lock Stitch Fence Company; *The Crandal Manufacturing Company; *Baker Manufacturing Company; *Northwestern Barb Wire Company; *St. Louis Wire Fence Company; *Lambert, Bishop & Company; *Watkins & Ashley; *Chicago Galvanized Wire Fence Company; *Cincinnati Barbed Wire Fence Company; *Noble G. Ross; *Edwin A. Beers; *Frentress Barbed Wire Fence Company; Robinson & Halledie; H. B. Scutt & Company, Buffalo; *Stone City Fence Company; *Cleveland Barb Fence Company; *Railway Barb Fencing Company; *Hawkeye Steel Barb Fence Company; J. H. Lawrence & Company; *Oscar F. Moore; *William J. Adam; *Fish & Connell; Norton & DeWitt; *Novelty Manufacturing Company; *Thomas Gibson; *Albert Henley; *Marinus W. Warne; *Herman E. Schnabel; *Farmers' Steel Barb Company; *Sandwich Enterprise Company; *Arthur H. Dale; and *Home Manufacturing Company. Compiled from lists in Gedge and Boley, "History," II, 59–60.

Gates. The task of delegating responsibility to the right man on the right point of law was finally accomplished—without consulting either of the Company's archenemies. The figures of the grayed and goateed German and of the brash young "moonshiner" were conspicuous by their absence from the peace table.

CHAPTER 7

PATENT LITIGATION

EVEN THOUGH JOHN GATES CAUSED NO END OF TROUBLE for Washburn & Moen Company and Ellwood, it was Jacob Haish who was at the bottom of most of the Company's legal difficulties. Barbed-wire litigation lasted for eighteen years, and for a good part of that period, Haish saw to it that lawsuits of one kind or another plagued his rivals. He started litigation with his application for interference against Glidden in June, 1874. He made a case of the Grenniger structure of 1857, and became involved with other early experiments; in company with fellow members of the anti-license Barb Wire Manufacturers Union, he supported practices whereby unreliable evidence was taken.[1] He lent his name and his financial backing to various organizations entered in the fight. While patents expired on certain inventions, while fortunes were made and lost on certain other patent claims, while there was evolved as an outgrowth of legal action a monopoly of the industry, Haish continued to see that the suit of Beat 'Em All Barb Wire Company was pressed against Washburn & Moen Company until it was brought before the United States Supreme Court in 1892.

By the time Washburn and Ellwood had consolidated their

[1] Warren, "History of the Manufacture of Barbed Wire Fencing," 17, AS&W Records, *loc. cit.* "In carrying out their plans, a room over a livery stable in Austin was hired, models of a Grenniger fence structure made, a corps of men was sent about the neighborhood to talk with old residents, who, if found amenable to argument, were sent to the livery stable, where their recollections were properly stimulated, and their memories refreshed regarding the details of the old Grenniger fence."

interests as joint owners of Glidden wire in 1876, Haish had built up a good business of his own. His "S" barb was a highly successful product. It was one of the first types of barbed wire acclaimed in Texas and other parts of the Southwest, and it continued to be popular there. It was the type most extensively used in the Midwest, particularly in Iowa. Even Washburn referred to it—as did everyone, including Haish himself—as "the famous 'S' barb." Jacob Haish had had high hopes that it would not be ruled an infringement on earlier patents, and the decision against him was a heavy blow. Apparently it was also a surprise.

Haish said—loudly—that the court decision was unjust and unfair. He complained that he had not been notified in advance of the date when the decision was to be given. He claimed that members of the Company fraternized with the judges and thereby influenced the judgment. He pointed out that originally the suit was to have been tried by Thomas Drummond alone, but that "some of the opposing force" managed to have Henry Blodgett appointed also; he contended that it was Blodgett, the handpicked magistrate, who rendered the decision in favor of Washburn & Moen Company. "The irascible German," as Haish was called, never passed up an opportunity to discredit Blodgett and the court action of December 15, 1880. Even in later years he suggested that it was more than a coincidence that in 1890 the Company located a plant in Waukegan "where Judge Blodgett lived."[2] And in his "reminiscent" pamphlet, Haish sarcastically phrased the title of his writing to refer to "the Celebrated Decision of Judge Blodgett," without any reference at all to Judge Drummond's part in the proceedings.

Haish was said to have put out "hundreds of thousands" of copies of his *Regulator* protesting the ruling. By the same token, Ellwood was said to have purchased "twenty-two thousands of

[2] The Washburn version of the incident stated: ". . . steadily increasing demand in the west for various kinds of wire and wire products led the Washburn & Moen Company, in 1890, to the belief that a great commercial advantage would result from establishing a manufacturing plant in the middle west. . . . The erection of this magnificent plant [at Waukegan] . . . was amply justified by the subsequent business expansion." Charles G. Washburn, "Industrial Worcester," 163, AS&W Records, *loc. cit.*

copies" of the printings of the court decision for distribution, and to have written at length about the case in the Company's *Journal*. Haish raised every kind of commotion he could raise. And when it was clear that despite his protest, the verdict was to be held against him, he came up with a startling new development, decidedly Haish-like in character.

It seemed that years before, when Haish was first experimenting with the idea of an armored fence, when he began by weaving branches of thorny Osage orange into board and rail fences, when he worked with wire prickers on single strands of wire and found that the prickers slipped and "bunched," he finally thought of "putting two wires together, forming a twist, with the barb between them."[3] It seemed that he made a sixteen-foot section of the twisted cable, and kept it lying around in his store until a farmer bought it for fifty cents and took it away. He may have made a few more sections of the same length, believing as did others that this was the only way in which wire for fences could be handled. But evidently Haish thought nothing more about the experiment and did nothing about it. This was sometime in 1873–74. It was years later, 1880–81, when a farmer named F. W. Pierce was in the lumberyard and got to talking to Haish about fencing. The farmer mentioned that he must have been the first purchaser of barbed wire because of the twisted double strand he had bought from Jacob Haish.

In recounting the incident, Haish said that he had forgotten about the sale, until here before him was the man who had bought the wire, had used it for fencing, and claimed that it was still in service. Here was a witness to show that a piece of wire with barbs had been put to commercial use at a very early date. Here was one more chance for Haish to add fuel to the fire that he had set under Washburn & Moen Company and Ellwood.

This was not, however, the only thing bothering Washburn and Ellwood and their attorneys. By virtue of its ownership of foundation patents, the Company felt secure in its position of dominance on barbed-wire designs and was prepared to uphold

[3] *The Biographical Record of DeKalb County, Illinois,* 56.

its position, but other issues were sometimes more difficult to resolve. Jacob Haish held control of the Stevens patent, No. 222608,
on an important machine for making barbed wire. Various persons had tried to buy the patent. Stevens had made agreements
to sell part-interest once to a Mr. Andrew Dillman, and once to
the Joliet Wire Fence Company, but in each case the sale failed
to be consummated because the purchasers did not carry through
with payment. Later Haish bought the patent. It appeared that
he was the sole owner when in 1881 legal transactions concerning
the machine were in progress; and in the light of evidence indicating that Haish and Haish alone owned the Stevens patent, it
seemed imperative that the Company should purchase it from
him, if possible.

Machines for manufacturing barbed wire were vital to the
industry. Haish and, in his turn, John Gates were not the first to
realize this importance. From the start, Washburn & Moen Company had seen that for them the value of barbed wire in any form
rested largely on the plausibility of production by automatic machinery. Even before the influence of the Washburn company had
been brought to bear on the matter, some of the barbed-wire
inventors themselves were designing the machines needed to
produce their respective types of barbs. Glidden made his first
wire by hand, but it was not long before he had a hand-operated
machine—the Glidden-Vaughan machine, registered as patent
No. 157508 on December 8, 1874. Haish, it will be remembered,
failing to meet the appointed date for submitting plans for his
machine, wasted no time in securing other plans. In the period
when both Glidden and Haish were establishing businesses, a
machine designed to facilitate production of the long-neglected
Kelly wire was granted patent No. 173491 on February 17, 1876,
and two days earlier "the first patented power-driven barbing
machine" was awarded patent No. 173667 to H. W. Putnam of
Bennington, Vermont.

The Putnam machine was the design "conceived" in August,
1875, and "fully reduced to practice and public use" in October,
1875; patent was applied for on January 30, 1876, and granted

on February 15, 1876.[4] This was the patent which Charles F. Washburn awaited before he personally set out on his original visit to De Kalb. This was the machine deemed of such importance as to warrant Washburn's participation in the new fencing business. This was the machine for making Haish's type of barb.

The Putnam machine for manufacturing Glidden wire followed soon afterward. It "was conceived in March 1876, built during the month of March and part of the month of April, and operated by power April 19, 1876, producing wire at the rate of 70 to 75 barbs per minute."[5] This was the machine perfected in time for Mr. Washburn's return to De Kalb to purchase interest in the Glidden patent. With the machine in operation, and with Glidden's rights assigned to the Company in May, manufacture of the wire was commenced in June, 1876, without waiting for issuance of patent. Patent No. 187776 was granted in February, 1877, and by January, 1879, Washburn & Moen Company had utilized the machine in making approximately nine million pounds of Glidden wire.[6]

The Putnam inventions served as a basis for much of the early commercial manufacture of barbed wire, but there were other important machines used by the Company and by its competitors. Some of the most notable patents on machinery were: Glidden & Vaughan, No. 157508, granted on December 8, 1874—bought by Washburn & Moen Company; Mitchell, No. 173491, granted on February 17, 1876—controlled by Thorn Wire Hedge Company and eventually by Washburn & Moen Company; Putnam, No. 173667, granted on February 15, 1876, and Putnam, No. 187776, granted on February 27, 1877—both made for Washburn & Moen Company; Stover, No. 196313, granted on October 23, 1877—independent; Stevens, No. 222608, granted on December 16, 1879—controlled by Haish; Baker, No. 295513, granted on March 25, 1884—used for making "Baker Perfect" wire; and Bates, No. 365723, granted on June 28, 1887—controlled by Washburn & Moen Company.

---

[4] Gedge and Boley, "History," I, 63–64.
[5] *Ibid.*   [6] *Ibid.*

The Company had great respect for the Stevens machine, and for Haish's control of it. Company lawyers were instructed to negotiate with Haish for this patent and for patents on barbed-wire designs also. Despite the decision of Judges Drummond and Blodgett, it was still possible to patent some particular feature of the barbing process, and this was what Haish claimed to have done. He claimed that his was a system for constructing the barb so that it passed between double-strand wires and around each separately, a system which permitted the barb to extend onto each strand wire and at the same time bind the wires together. Attorneys and engineers hired by the Company regarded this feature as important. Counsel Thomas H. Dodge, who once had been an examiner of patents in the United States Patent Office, felt that the Drummond and Blodgett decision actually enhanced the value of this phase of Haish's claim; he warned that it "could not be preached down." It was thought to be a mode of construction which licensees of Washburn & Moen Company and Ellwood "had so far adopted as to make them liable to suit by Haish ... if the Supreme Court should reverse the decision of the lower court, as to that special device." With fifty thousand tons of annual production of wire incorporating the "device" already licensed, the Company looked upon Jacob Haish as "a constant menace to the very profitable license system that had just been built up at such great cost of time, and money and labor."[7]

Manufacturers holding Company license pressed for an agreement which would protect them. They grew increasingly nervous as trouble continued to erupt in Iowa, where the turmoil had centered around Haish from the start. Because he and the Barb Wire Manufacturers Union already had done battle with the Company, this most recalcitrant of their number served as a rallying point for rebellious operators throughout the Midwest. Because he already had gathered evidence for suits against the Company, Iowa farm groups had allied themselves with him in the hope of saving "the $20,000 it would cost them to form a new case."[8] Haish was, as Mr. Washburn said, "a man ... determined

[7] "Briefs," 75-77, AS&W Records, *loc. cit.*

to fight, to wriggle, to scold and pull wires and issue ridiculous circulars; if necessary . . . [even] encourage Farmers Associations."[9] And for the very reason that the description seemed to fit him down to the last particular, "free wire" forces in Iowa and adjoining areas had joined themselves with Jacob Haish at the beginning of their fight. Furthermore, they remained loyal to him as long as he held on to them. Even John W. Gates could not loose them, but found—much to his surprise—that he needed Haish's backing in order to win their support.

The underlying current of influence emanating from this original opponent of "the monopolists" was still strong. It lasted through court action in Chicago, St. Louis, Keokuk, Leavenworth, and Des Moines. And at the time when Gates, displeased but determined, went to De Kalb for council with Haish, lawsuits still being formulated throughout the region were mainly the outgrowth of agitation fostered by Jacob Haish.

One thing, however, the Iowa farmers did not know, and even Gates on his journey to De Kalb, did not guess it. The Company's negotiations with Haish neared a climax. It was hoped that settlement might be attained, and with constant urging from its licensees, the Company explored all possibilities. Operators licensed by the Company had a right to expect action by the Company; more and more they insisted that they should have protection from suit by Haish, protection on price, and protection on tonnage allowable. To secure these points, they were willing to make concessions, and "of the nearly forty [licensees] all but three signed a paper authorizing Washburn & Moen Company to surrender to Haish all claim to either past damages or future royalties in order to procure assignment of his patents under which they could be protected from trouble. All they asked was that he should be limited as to tonnage and price."[10] Future trouble with Haish was to be avoided, even at a price.

---

[8] Hayter, "An Iowa Farmers' Protective Association," *loc. cit.*, 346.

[9] Letter from C. F. Washburn to I. L. Ellwood, Worcester, June 11, 1881, cited in *Iowa Journal of History and Politics* (October, 1939), 344.

[10] "Briefs from Barb Wire Fence Cases of 1822–1884," 90, AS&W Records, *loc. cit.*

The price of peace was never cheap; difficulties in agreeing upon it, never easy. In a fight with such a man as Jacob Haish, the difficulties outweighed even the cost. There seemed to be no end to the objections, annoyances, demands, and threats which the old rebel could raise. Even his own lawyers found him extremely trying. At one time when it seemed that settlement was finally in sight, when it was thought that there could be no other obstacle in the way, Haish tried to insert a clause which would have made Washburn and Ellwood pay all the costs and attorneys' fees, even for Haish's attorneys. This, it was said, was "no bagatelle." The Company balked. Ellwood personally declared that he was through; he had made his last attempt to come to terms with Haish. Negotiations were resumed, however, and once again a settlement was about to be effected, with only the most minor matters—such as names of customers, etc.—unfinished, when one of Haish's lawyers wrote on June 29, 1881, to his client, saying:

> . . . what a trivial thing [the listing of customers' names] that is to lay in your path on your way out of the clutches of the court, and out from under a heavy burden of possible damages. Haish, for heaven's sake, do think of this once deliberately before you make up your mind finally. It would grieve me deeply to see this chance go by, for should they finally get the better of us in the court, then you would get the sympathy and we [the law firm] would get the blame, whereas you deserve the blame yourself."[11]

Thus there hung on the thin thread of Haish's whimsy the balance of agreement which would settle once and for all the battle between Washburn & Moen Company and I. L. Ellwood, and their bitter enemy, Jacob Haish.

Finally one of the Company lawyers hit upon a way to phrase the minor issues which stood between the two parties. Attorney Thurston was said to have cried out jubilantly, "Eureka! I have it!" And, sure enough, the documents were drawn, the signatures affixed, and on July 26, 1881, a license from Washburn & Moen

[11] Gedge and Boley, "History," II, 46.

Company and I. L. Ellwood was "granted" to Jacob Haish of De Kalb, Illinois.

Haish assigned to the Company the following patents: Haish patent of February 17, 1874—star barb on ribbon wire; Haish patent of June 23, 1874—wire-stretcher; Haish patent of June 15, 1875—Eli "stick-tite" barb; Haish patent of August 31, 1875—"S" barb (reissued on January 6, 1880); Stevens machine patent of December 16, 1879; and Stevens applications for patents filed on December 8, 1877, and July 25, 1879. Haish was to pay royalty to the Company, and he was to receive payment in like amounts for the patents transferred. No monies were to be paid to him, however, unless and until monies were received from him. Moreover, he was allowed not more than 10,000 tons annual production. The papers drawn read, in part, as follows:

> Up to 4,000 tons, Haish would pay the Washburn & Moen Manufacturing Company 75 cents per hundred pounds royalty, and the Washburn & Moen Manufacturing Company would pay Haish the same amount of royalty on the same tonnage, so that Haish would pay no royalty upon 4,000 tons. On the second 4,000 tons, Haish would pay the Washburn & Moen Manufacturing Company 75 cents per hundred pounds, and the Washburn & Moen Manufacturing Company would pay Haish 25 cents per hundred pounds, which would amount to a payment by Haish to the Washburn & Moen Manufacturing Company of 50 cents per hundred pounds on the second 4,000 tons. If Haish were to manufacture the remaining 2,000 tons of his 10,000 tons, he would pay the full royalty of 75 cents per hundred pounds."[12]

Some of Haish's colleagues complained that Haish had "come to an understanding" with the Company, that he had made a secret agreement with Ellwood, that he had managed to settle the whole thing in a manner greatly to his own financial advantage. Lawsuits were instigated to show that he had had special consideration and was not treated as other licensees. Three of the forty firms licensed—with reluctance—after the Drummond and Blodgett decision—with E. M. Crandal as president of all

[12] Washburn, "Barbed Fencing," 25–26.

[95]

three—brought suit on the grounds that Crandal's groups had not joined other licensees to request settlement with Haish. Court wrangles mounted, with one suit dependent on testimony from another. The complex settlement was interpreted and misinterpreted from every angle, but there remained in the records nothing that would prove that a "separate peace" had been arranged, other than that described above. A Company attorney resolved the matter as well as could be expected, and to the satisfaction of the Supreme Court of Illinois, by writing:

> ... the rule is that all statements of parties endeavoring to make an agreement which is afterwards reduced to writing cannot be used for the purpose of explaining, changing or constructing the written contract, subsequently executed. Whatever may have transpired in the negotiations are supposed to be merged in the written agreement. Whatever may have been the intention ... the writing is supposed to be the true expression of what the parties eventually agreed upon.[13]

History stands on the written contract between Haish and the Company. It is assumed that without further ado Haish did finally sell his famous "S" barb patent, the Stevens rights, and others to Washburn and Ellwood; that Haish did take license from the Company; that he was not assessed back damages; that the remuneration he received was of sufficient amount to satisfy Haish; and that the value of this arrangement to Washburn & Moen Company and Ellwood was considerable, to say the least.

There remained in the courts only one case of significance to the barbed-wire industry, a case which has been called "one of the interesting suits of American history."[14] It had been filed by

[13] *Ibid.*, 20–24.
[14] To Honorable W. C. Gandy (attorney for Washburn & Moen Company), Chicago, Illinois, from Thos. H. Dodge (counsel for Washburn & Moen Company), Leland Hotel, Chicago, February 13, 1884. Extracted from the above: "A legal and perfect title was conveyed by Stevens to Jacob Haish by his, Stevens', subsequent assignment of January 28, 1881, of the letter patent granted to Stevens December 16, 1879, and of the inventions described in said Stevens' then two pending applications for letters patent, one filed on the 8th day of December, 1877, and the other on the 25th day of July, 1879, both of which patents the honorable commissioner of patents was requested to issue, when granted, to Jacob Haish, his assigns or legal representatives, as the owner or

the Beat 'Em All Barb Wire Company against Glidden's patent No. 157124, trade-named "The Winner." The suit was on appeal to the United States Supreme Court. Not only was Jacob Haish safely out of the clutches of the courts, but the Company almost was also.

owners of the entire interest therein. . . . Now, as all of the applications for patents embraced in Stevens' assignment to Haish were made subsequent to December 4, 1877, the first one being filed December 8, 1877, the second being filed July 25, 1879, and the third being filed August 10, 1879, it would appear from the testimony of the complainant itself [Crandal] that neither of these inventions was included in the agreement with the Joliet Wire Fence Company, and, furthermore, that Stevens invented the 'improved machine' after he left Dillman. . . . The patent and inventions embraced in the [then] pending applications assigned by Stevens to Haish, January 28, 1881, were based upon applications, three in number, filed by Stevens subsequent to December 7, 1877."

The complainant asserted that "Washburn & Moen Company did own half interest in this Stevens invention, and that therefore it could grant licenses under the then existing Stevens patent, as well as under the two then pending applications to Stevens." Defendant denied this. The case shows also that as business declined, Washburn & Moen Company and Ellwood "did abate a portion of royalties" so that regular licensees paid less than Haish was required to pay before he could in turn receive payment on rights sold to Washburn & Moen. "Briefs from Barb Wire Fence Cases of 1882–1884," Arguments for the Licensor, AS&W Records, *loc. cit.*

CHAPTER 8

BARBED-WIRE BARONS

SINGULARLY UNEVENTFUL was the meeting between John W. Gates and Jacob Haish. Gates had come to De Kalb expecting to set up far-reaching arrangements with Haish, yet when he left, no great decisions had been reached, no wordy pronouncements had been made. Knowing nothing of the attempts at conciliation between Haish and the Company lawyers, Gates attributed the disappointing turn of affairs to the despair of an old man. He simply wrote off Haish as a poor risk and a has-been, evidently never imagining for a moment that he himself was being put off by a cunning ruse.

When public announcement was made of Haish's contract with the Company, and Gates learned of the manipulations that had been carried on behind his back, he was furious. When he realized further the advantages Haish had won, Gates angrily set himself a new course. He determined that since Washburn & Moen Company and Ellwood had managed to establish a monopoly on the foundation patents, and had brought the old warhorse Haish to agreement with them in the patent fight, he, Gates, would manage to take interest with them—and eventually over them—in the patents. He was still out to beat the "big boys" at their own game, but he planned this time to dominate the business legally—and, of course, at a profit, too.

It might be said that financially he succeeded. John W. Gates became one of the wealthiest men in America. He did not always surpass his old rivals, or his new competitors in steel, railroads, and related fields; but if it could be said that there was a single ruler of the barbed-wire industry, it would have been—for a time, at least—John W. "Bet-a-Million" Gates.

Whether Gates actually beat out Isaac Ellwood, or came to an understanding with him, is hard to know. Eventually Ellwood retired from active participation in the Company and joined Gates in making crucial investments on the New York Stock Exchange. They seemed to have an on-again-off-again arrangement whereby they quarreled and feuded for a time, and then suddenly when Gates called the plays, Ellwood backed him to the hilt. Ellwood was Gates's ally, or not—apparently, at will. And he may have been outwitting Gates all the while, for although he never assumed the powers which Gates exerted in the world of finance, Ellwood became a man of great wealth—without having to fight as Gates fought.

Ellwood was a prominent man in his own right. He was appointed colonel on the Illinois Governor's staff, and was recognized in national political circles. In the campaign of 1900 he secured Theodore Roosevelt for a public appearance in De Kalb. He was at ease when dealing with old friends in his familiar surroundings, when entertaining new friends at his hunting lodge in Texas, or when meeting with Gates at the Waldorf-Astoria in New York. His fellow townsmen described him as "careful and systematic . . . charitable and benevolent." He was one of the main forces responsible for the establishment of the Northern Illinois State Normal School at De Kalb, and was appointed trustee.[1] When the college was dedicated, Ellwood's daughter was crowned queen of the celebration, and the Governor was received at Ellwood's handsome home, Ilehamwood—so named because "Ile" stood for Isaac Leonard Ellwood, "ham" for his wife

---

[1] Location of the college was evidently an important issue and one close to the heart of I. L. Ellwood. His son wrote in 1895: "All the towns in this part of the state naturally are after the school and are putting their best foot forward. . . . Father . . . is now in Springfield trying to stand in with the Governor as to trustees for locating the same, and there is the devil's own fight on this."— Letter of W. L. Ellwood to Henry Frye, May 23, 1895, in Ellwood Family Papers, University of Wyoming, Laramie.

[99]

Harriet Augusta Miller, daughter of a wealthy family to whom the property was granted by the government in 1833.[2]

Colonel Ellwood commanded attention in the Southwest when he purchased extensive lands in Texas, and the fine Percheron horses he raised on the Texas ranch, as well as in Illinois, were registered at important showings all across America and abroad. "He built great barns not only on his home place but on his various farms. His son made trips to Europe to select horses, "importing some of the Percheron stock directly from Perche in France.[3] Paintings of some of the famous stallions are still preserved, and beautiful gold and silver medallions awarded to Ellwood's entries at the World Exposition in Paris are kept today among the Ellwood family memorabilia.

Though "Colonel Ike," as Ellwood was often called, concentrated on Percherons and spurned the idea of investing with Gates in ownership of race horses, he appeared many times with Gates at fashionable race-track events. He was, in fact, Gates' companion in many experiences, in addition to being his partner in many business ventures. He was reported to have been present on the occasion when Gates was nicknamed "Bet-a-Million." Gates never liked the name and tried to drop it, as he dropped "Wild Bill" and "Moonshine," but "Bet-a-Million" he could not silence. He wanted to lay bets—at race track, poker table, or wherever he was—and he insisted that the stakes be high, even if the issues involved were the merest trifle, as was the case in the famous raindrop episode.

As the story goes, Gates and Ellwood were on a train traveling from Chicago to Pittsburgh, and because they had not enough members in their party to make up a card game, Gates sat sullen and dissatisfied, watching a gathering rainstorm through the window of his luxurious Pullman car. Heavy drops of rain coursed down the windowpane. Gates tapped the glass and spoke to Ellwood. "I'll bet this raindrop gets to the bottom of the pane be-

[2] Letter of May Ellwood (Mrs. E. Perry) to Henry D. McCallum, September 30, 1959.
[3] Ibid.

fore whichever one you pick," he said, and the game was on. One bet after another was made with stakes as high as a thousand dollars on each raindrop, and before the train pulled into Pittsburgh, Gates had won a veritable fortune.[4]

Perhaps even more interesting, though not so famous, was the flip-of-a-coin chance which sent Gates on this train ride. He had planned a trip around the world with his wife. The tickets were already bought, and Gates was about to give in to his wife's plea that he retire. He was in Ellwood's office, saying good-by, when the telephone rang. A mutual friend was calling from Pittsburgh to tell of a dispute between the proprietors of a big steel mill. Someone would be able to purchase the mill at a bargain price—one million dollars. Ellwood relayed the message to Gates; Gates reached into his pocket for a coin and solemnly flipped it into the air. The coin came down heads. "Well, it's Pittsburgh," Gates said. "I guess the world will wait."[5] He forthwith canceled the elaborate plans for world travel with his wife and boarded the train for Pittsburgh with Ellwood.

These two incidents, typical of Gates, were typical also of the relationship between the two men. If Ellwood was the accessory to Gates's extravaganzas, he was not the instigator. If he profited on Gates's speculation, he was practicing again the shrewdness he had exemplified from the start of their association. As biographer Warshow saw it, Ellwood seemed instantly to recognize Gates as a natural-born salesman, and from the moment Ike said, " 'Travel for me, boy,' and John replied, 'You're talking' . . . , a lasting alliance, often bent but never severed, was formed."[6] By the very strength of their early rivalry and the pitting of wits against each other, they seemed to develop something akin to respect for each other. Loud and blustering, raw and raucous as was the one, mannerly and intelligent as was the other, they knew how to do business together. Gates's ultimate victory over Ellwood was as inconclusive as was Ellwood's over Haish.

[4] There were other versions of the origin of this nickname, but the most popular and by far the most widespread was the raindrop story.
[5] Robert I. Warshow, *Bet-A-Million Gates: The Story of a Plunger*, 42.
[6] *Ibid.*, 21.

At one point Ellwood sold out to Washburn & Moen Company, only to buy back his part of the De Kalb plant a few years later. In 1891 he took his busines with him into the newly formed Columbia Patent Company (later the Columbia Wire Company), named in honor of the forthcoming Columbian Exposition in Chicago. This company was another one of Gates's schemes to enlarge his holdings. In anticipation of the expiration date in 1891 and 1892 of the important patents of 1874 and 1875—Glidden's patent topping the list—Gates gathered his friends around him—Lambert, Clifford, and Ellwood, among others. So closely did they work together in this new alliance for power that in one instance the purchase of St. Louis Wire Mill Company was executed with a check (for $1,137,233.71) "made payable to Alfred Clifford as Treasurer of Consolidated Steel & Wire Company, and endorsed on the back by Alfred Clifford as Treasurer of the St. Louis Wire Mill Company."[7] With these friends and supporters as key officials in the new company, Gates's Columbia Patent Company attained control of 95 per cent of the entire barbed-wire production of the United States, according to reports.

Gates bought out one company after another, scrapping their machinery if it could not be put to use for the Columbia Patent Company. In March, 1891, the Columbia organization purchased all patents on wire and on machines owned by Washburn & Moen Company, the latter group retaining rights to make the wire and use the machinery under all assigned patents (except that for "Baker Perfect" which would not be allowed until after February 27, 1894).[8] In 1898 the American Steel & Wire Company of Illinois was organized and in a short time took over most of the remaining small factories, under Gates's chairmanship. In 1899 the firm of Washburn & Moen Company was consolidated into the American Steel & Wire Company of New Jersey, with Gates as chairman of the Board of Directors, and Ellwood as chairman of the Executive Committee.

[7] "This check is one of the prized exhibits in our Museum at Worcester." Goodrich, "Formation of the American Steel & Wire Company," 4, AS&W Records, *loc. cit.*
[8] Gedge and Boley, "History," II, 84.

Having scored with and/or against Ellwood and having managed to keep him in line by keeping company with him, Gates next directed his vengeance against another foe. Having out-"moonshined" the "moonshiners" by organizing them in consolidation, Gates undertook to out-finance the financiers. With much of the same zeal and some of the same tactics he had used in fighting Washburn and Ellwood in the early days, he now prepared to fight the masters of finance—J. Pierpont Morgan and Andrew Carnegie.

This time, however, Gates had little chance of winning the enemy over to his way, and no chance of being taken into theirs. Gates made the mistake of thinking that if he dealt with these men, he might also enter into their expensive and exclusive social life. He had the money, but the entree he had not. As an individual, Gates was not welcomed. He was acceptable as an investor but not as an intimate. He was considered a crude Westerner, "a typical Chicagoan," an outsider, and the treatment accorded him on this basis made bitter and unsavory the battle which Gates waged against the acknowledged heads of industry. Carnegie, to whom Gates liked to refer familiarly as "Andy," had the annoying habit of deliberately referring to Gates as "Mr. Yates." To his face or behind his back, it was always, "Mr. Yates." Morgan used more direct assault. He told Gates, after using him to advantage, that Gates never would be acceptable on a Morgan-run board of directors—and he meant it. In 1901, Gates's American Steel & Wire Company was incorporated into the newly formed giant organization of the United States Steel Corporation, and Gates was left out of the directorate, at Morgan's insistence.

Washburn & Moen Company, having passed from the hands of Columbia Patent Company to the American Steel & Wire Company, was taken into the new United States Steel and thereby continued to serve as a nucleus around which, since the time of Ichabod Washburn, the wire industry was built. Gates had brought the Company in, and he had expected a top post in the new corporation. It was an insufferable blow to his pride to be excluded. He probably did not lose money, but even if he had, that would not have mattered as much to him as the loss of prestige and power. With great wealth at his command and with Ellwood and other confederates to go along, Gates was able to move into other fields and to command greater enterprises and greater wealth than before; but he never got over the Morgan slight.

For solace Gates turned to Texas, scene of his early success in barbed wire, and with typical Gates intuition, he arrived in the Lone Star state again at a propitious moment—in time to play a part in another great spectacle which was destined to revolutionize life in the Southwest. Although he certainly was not responsible for and never was credited in any way with the initial discovery of oil in Texas, "Bet-a-Million" Gates was in the right spot, ready and able, when needed to build pipelines and port facilities for handling the flow of riches which gushed out of the ground at the famous Spindletop oil well in January, 1901. He was there to claim a share of profits also from the speculation and wild trading which ensued.

Gates built up the city of Port Arthur, Texas, close to the oil field, and made it a shipping center. He built up also The Texas Company, whose pipelines, oil, and gas became the basis of new fortunes. For these two works alone he might have been remembered. But in the minds of men who recalled the boisterous close of the nineteenth century, he was best remembered as "Bet-a-Million," a man whose talents fit the times in which he lived. Earlier or later, the American economy would not have supported so unrestricted a "plunger," but in his day he was a figure of success. At the time of his death in 1911, change was already being felt. The day of the showman was passing. But Gates was one of the fortunate few who "appeared at the perfect time for his talent, and went when his works and he were no longer needed."[9]

Although Gates was to be counted the wealthiest of the barbed-wire barons, and Ellwood as the one enjoying success the most, Jacob Haish was not to be discounted on either score. Haish was still very much a power in the business. He was wealthy and influential. In De Kalb, he held a position of prominence. In 1884

[9] Warshow, *Bet-A-Million Gates*, 179.

he organized The Barb City Bank and was its first president. He built an opera house; contributed "willingly and cheerfully" to the building of the Normal School; owned "the most palatial residence" in De Kalb, "a grand and imposing edifice [which] he conceived in his own fertile brain"; and his factory was considered "one of the noted institutions of his city and his state."[10]

Furthermore, Haish became affiliated with a school known as Colorado Seminary, located in the heart of present-day Denver, Colorado. By an agreement of 1886, Haish gave to this school "one-half of all the gross receipts derived from the sale of Haish barbed wire within the territory embodied within the State of Colorado, and the territories of Wyoming, Utah and New Mexico until such one-half of the gross receipts should amount to the sum of $50,000. . . . In consideration of this agreement on the part of Mr. Haish, the Colorado Seminary agreed that the department of the seminary devoted to . . . the mechanic arts should thereafter be known as and called the Haish Manual Training School."[11] In 1910 and again in 1920 the contract was modified, but in the end the Haish family was still counted among the benefactors of the University of Denver, successor to Colorado Seminary. Even in this Western state far from his home, Jacob Haish was looked to as a patron.

It is probable that, despite the more impressive aspects of other "monuments to his industriousness," his barbed-wire factory at De Kalb held special meaning for Jacob Haish; certainly the manufacture of barbed wire did. Wherever there is found a chronicle of the life and work of this man, wherever the irascible German-born immigrant is mentioned, there is sure to be found the most detailed account of his part in the business. Unexpected accomplishments such as "the first wooden spool upon which the wire was coiled . . . the first paint or varnish [on wire]," the first spool shipped by rail or water, and the first automatic machinery for barbing were credited to Haish in local publications, and these

[10] *Past and Present of De Kalb County, Illinois*, II; *The Biographical Record of De Kalb County, Illinois.*

[11] Letter of Harry W. McEwen, trustee of Jacob Haish Estate, to Earl H. Ellis, staff of University of Denver, December 3, 1949.

generally corresponded with Haish's claims in his "Reminiscent History."[12] Nothing, however, jerked at the heartstrings, or revealed the anguish which must have prompted much of Haish's action, as did his own description of Charles F. Washburn's first trip to De Kalb:

> He [Washburn] came into my office unannounced, introduced himself, became my guest, sat at my table, enjoying my hospitality to the limit. He was a fluent converser, with high ideals, with a fine appreciation of art and music. In short a cultured gentleman. The final outcome of this visit was a willingness to buy.[13]

The rest, of course, is history, and far different from what Haish must have expected. The aura of "dreams come true" was replaced by bitter disappointment. The thought of what he had missed must have been the ghost that haunted Jacob Haish for the rest of his life and drove him relentlessly through all his battles concerning the barbed-wire industry.

Nor could Joseph Glidden be overlooked in his later years. Living on at De Kalb, he enjoyed a more peaceable existence than the others. He was well-to-do, content. Furthermore, he had the satisfaction of having his patent No. 157124 for an "Improvement in Wire Fences" pronounced the winner in the long patent fight, when in 1892 the Beat 'Em All Barb Wire Company suit, begun in 1885, finally was heard before the United States Supreme Court. "This was the first time the question of the validity of the barbed wire patents reached the Supreme Court during all the litigation commencing with the suit against Jacob Haish in 1876."[14] By the time the final decree was rendered, the basic pat-

---

12 "The first spool of barbed wire ever shipped to California, I packed in a half barrel. It was considered dangerous to ship such a long distance in any other way. . . . To preserve the wires from rust was the next step to be considered. Paint placed in troughs in front of the twister was tried, but when the twister was revolving, the fresh paint flew in all directions. That was given up. After many trials I succeeded in securing a dip paint, or varnish as it was then called, which was very satisfactory." Haish, "A Reminiscent History," 3–5. See also *The Biographical Record of De Kalb County, Illinois.*

13 Haish, "A Reminiscent History," 8.

14 A decision by Judge O. P. Shiras in 1888 upheld the "novelty" of the Glidden patent, but declared it "invalid of prior use. . . . a petition for appeal was filed and allowed, and citation was made to the Supreme Court of the United

ents of Hunt and Kelly and Glidden had expired, but the verdict of 1892 was a history-making decision. Mr. Justice Stephen J. Field dissented upon the ground that there was "no novelty" in Glidden's invention, and indeed the certainty of the absolute origin appeared to be impossible to prove, but the decision of the court was explained, in part, as follows:

> We are not satisfied that he [Glidden] was not the originator of the combination claimed by him of the coiled barb, locked and held in place by the extra twisted wire. It is possible that we are mistaken in this; that someone of these experimenters may, in a crude way, have hit upon the exact device patented by Glidden, although we are not satisfied from this testimony whether or by whom it was done. It is quite evident, too, that all, or nearly all of these experiments were subsequently abandoned. But it was Glidden, beyond question, who first published this device; put it on record; made use of it to the public, by which it was eagerly seized upon, and spread until there was scarcely a cattle-raising district in the world in which it was not extensively employed. Under these circumstances, we think the doubt we entertain concerning the actual inventor should be resolved in favor of the patentee.[15]

By so saying, the United States Supreme Court sustained the rights of Joseph F. Glidden's patent for the product already trade-named "The Winner."

By virtue of this decision, Glidden was established as the most renowned of all the leading figures in barbed-wire history. He was, however, the most withdrawn, and although his name was known wherever barbed wire was of concern to an individual or a community, he was retired from the business and he meant

States. . . . The case was argued . . . December 16th and 17th, 1891, and decided February 29th, 1892. . . . The case was reversed and remanded with instructions to enter a decree for the plaintiff [Washburn & Moen Company] for an accounting, and for further proceedings in conformity with the . . . opinion. This decision was rendered after the expiration of basic patents, i.e. Hunt, Kelly, and Glidden patents. At the time it was rendered the patents in force were largely for special styles of barbed wire and for machines. The machine patents were perhaps the most valuable." Gedge and Boley, "History," II, 49–52.

[15] Douglass, "How Inventor Kelly Lost His Millions," *loc. cit.*, 32.

to remain so. Only once again did Glidden take an active part in barbed-wire affairs, and that was at the request of H. B. Sanborn.

Sanborn was the young man to whom Glidden had written on the day the original Glidden invention had been granted patent in 1874. Sanborn was the man whom Glidden had chosen as first representative for the Barb Fence Company. Sanborn was the long-time friend, family relation, and favored protégé of Joseph F. Glidden.

Born on September 10, 1845, in St. Lawrence County, New York, Henry Bradley Sanborn, "like many other forceful young men" of his era, left home in his youth to make his way in the West. Sanborn had an uncle in Minneapolis, in the heart of a mid-century boom area, and Sanborn went to work in 1864 traveling as a salesman of the wooden gutters which his uncle manufactured. While showing his wares at the farms around De Kalb, Sanborn met Joseph F. Glidden, and in time was invited to take a room at the Glidden home. For several years he made his residence there; there he met Ellen M. Wheeler, an orphaned niece also living with the Gliddens; and in 1868, Henry Sanborn and Ellen Wheeler were married.[16]

Sanborn had been partner with Judson P. Warner in Colorado, where Warner ran a horse farm and Sanborn handled the sale of horses, when Glidden had called him back to De Kalb to enter the barbed-wire business. He had begun selling in the farm region where he had formerly sold wooden gutters, and he had made his first sale of wire—"two or three reels"—at Rochelle, Illinois. Sanborn had gone to Texas in 1875, had sent for Warner to join him there, and by 1876 the two of them had developed a fair business, with headquarters at Houston, Texas.

Sanborn operated mainly in the northern part of the state, however, and by 1877 he had settled there and had built a large home ten miles west of the town of Sherman.[17] He had purchased

[16] Letter of John W. Crudgington to Frances T. McCallum, April, 1959. See also The Sanborn Scrapbook, Amarillo City Library, Amarillo, Texas.

[17] The farm home remained as a landmark until the early 1950's. The *Sherman Democrat* of August 29, 1954, published a picture of the house along with an article saying, in part: "To prove to the skeptical that horses and cattle

2,000 acres, which he later increased to 10,000 acres of Grayson County prairie farm land. With creek beds in the vicinity affording enough wood for fence posts, and with near-by rail termini affording transport of wire from the De Kalb factory, Sanborn had been able to set up what amounted to a model farm project for demonstrating the effectiveness of barbed wire. He later bought a large farm in Clay County where he devoted most of the acreage to grain, but the Grayson County property was more of a stock farm. It was, moreover, his home and the center of his activities during the 1870's.

Sanborn was interested in raising fine horses—some of the foreign-bred draft animals of the type Ellwood doted on, some of the race-track variety Gates preferred, but mostly quarter horses. His "large sale stables at Dallas, Texas" were well known and well advertised. It is said that he had on exhibition there "French draft and Coach horses, roadsters, saddle and standard bred trotters, Jacks and everything in the horse line . . . from his ranch 12 miles out of Sherman."[18] One old-timer still living in the area in 1957 told of selling oats for the horses raised by Mr. H. B. Sanborn:

> I could sell to him without the trouble of taking the oats into town, and at a better price to-boot. I got interested in his horses, this way, and one day when I had a little money in my pocket, I went to Dallas to the races so's I could bet on a Sanborn horse running there.
>
> I went up to the first fella I seen at the race track and asked him for a one dollar ticket on Mr. Sanborn's Prospect. Then I went to watchin' the races. Sure enough, Prospect come in ahead of the

would learn to stay away from the sharp pointed fence, Sanborn bought a Grayson County ranch west of Sherman and put it under barbed wire. That was the first [large tract] of Texas acreage to be enclosed in the fencing that the range riders hated, the 'nesters' loved, and the Indians came to call 'the devil's rope'. . . . Ranchers and farmers from over the Southwest came to Grayson County to see the Sanborn place and its fence. Carloads of the fencing rolled into the country over the rapidly expanding railroad system. . . . The devil's rope had become part of the Southwest. It was used to enclose even the graveyards where many of its bitterest foes lay buried."

18 Sanborn Scrapbook, *loc. cit.*

rest, and I was ready to collect some real money. But when I went back to that bookie fella, he wouldn't pay; said my bet was on another horse in the same race—named Prinmart, and he showed me that name on my ticket that, out of ignorance, I hadn't even looked at before.

I was madder'n anybody; told him he'd tricked me for sure, as I'd only come to the races to bet on Mr. Sanborn's horse that I knew. I talked as hard and fast as I could. But this fella wasn't alone in his business. There was a partner of his sittin' up high in a little box, up over our heads, and he was eyein' me mighty close. He never said anything, but he was there—listenin' and lookin' and ready, as anybody could see, to take sides and witness for his partner. So, I moved off a bit to think things over, and when I did, I looked back at the name over that man perched up in the box, and it was enough to make me lose interest in horse racin' for good and sure. It was a name I knew from hearsay only, but there was no mistakin' it. It was Frank James, brother of Jesse, who had got my money I'd meant to put on Mr. Sanborn's horse.[19]

Sanborn's experience in Grayson County convinced him that the best way to sell barbed wire was to put it to use on the scene. He was anxious to win over the big Texas cattlemen who still held out against him, and he thought a large-scale demonstration of ranch fencing in the midst of ranch country farther to the west would be the best way to reach them. By 1880 he was determined to try it. He was by this time a man of some means and was willing to invest heavily in a ranching project, yet he apparently realized that he could not launch so ambitious an undertaking as the one visualized, unless he had help. He approached Joseph Glidden on the subject.

Glidden knew little about Western ranching, and apparently he cared less. He did know and care about barbed wire, however, and he was—as always—the willing supporter of H. B. Sanborn. Even when he learned that the venture he was asked to back in this instance would involve the purchase of thousands of acres in the Texas Panhandle, Glidden agreed. In 1881, Sanborn and Glid-

[19] Paraphrase of story told by Mr. R. G. "Rip" Shelton, Whitesboro, Texas, to Henry D. McCallum, 1957.

den bought 125,000 acres, to which another 125,000 acres of Texas Public School land later were added, fenced it round-about with 150 miles of Glidden wire, and stocked it with 1,500 cattle branded with the panhandle ——O . Sanborn was in charge of the whole project; Glidden was merely a partner in the investment. The older man visited the ranch in 1884, but only for a short time. He wanted no part of ranching for himself, but preferred to remain at home in retirement at De Kalb. He was an old man, out of place in Texas, and he knew it.

Glidden—no less generous than Ellwood and Haish—donated a sixty-four-acre tract for location of the Normal School at De Kalb. It was "a part of the old homestead which had been entered by him from the government when Indians still crossed it with their trails."[20] And it was a part also of the site where practical barbed-wire fencing had originated—the Glidden farm one mile west of the village of De Kalb.

At the college installation ceremonies in 1899, Joseph F. Glidden broke ground on his own tract. It was said that, at the suggestion of Jacob Haish, Glidden used a lead pencil, "emblematic of literature and education."[21] Perhaps it could have been said also that the occasion itself was emblematic of something, since Glidden, Haish, and Ellwood, all were participants. For these three who had once stood together looking down on a sample of a new kind of fencing to stand together again looking up to a new kind of progress was a notable achievement. It brought about a co-operation which neither legal counsel nor judges of the court had been able to promote in eighteen years of litigation. It smoothed over the enmity which had existed since the county fair of 1873. It marked the close of a dispute which the highest tribunal had disposed of by its judgment of 1892. If it failed to reach beyond the scope of patent records to the root beginnings of armored fencing as devised by unnamed experimenters of other times and other lands, it nevertheless marked also an ending. For it rounded out, on a note of acceptance, a century of quest by the fence-makers of a new world.

[20] *The Biographical Record of De Kalb County, Illinois.*   [21] *Ibid.*

PART TWO
Barbed-Wire Fence-Builders

CHAPTER 9

"THIS COCKEYED WORLD OF CATTLE FOLK"[1]

NOT FAR FROM THE SAINTS' ROOST SETTLEMENT and closer still to Robber's Nest, in the Texas Panhandle, Sanborn and Glidden purchased their ranch property. The ranch itself was dubbed "Panhandle," and in early registers the name as well as the appropriately shaped brand were so recorded. Later, as the story goes, a cowhand, upon first seeing the brand burned into a steer's hide, called out surprisedly, "Panhandle, nothing! That's a d—— frying pan!" and Frying Pan Ranch it was ever after. But the name Panhandle had become permanently affixed to the region, and the Panhandle term remained in the lore of ranching because the land served not only as a passage to Texas grasslands but also as an adjunct to the whole of the Southwest's natural range land. Although the words were not wholly synonymous, "Panhandle" in the annals of the early West generally meant "cow country."

The Frying Pan was not a typical cow country ranch at the start. Sanborn was more of a barbed-wire salesman than a rancher, and his partner a barbed-wire inventor. They had come into the Texas Panhandle to promote their product. They hoped to show with one mammoth application that theirs was the long-sought material suitable for fencing the Western plains. Since Sanborn had succeeded in demonstrating with fences on his own land in the farming areas, he was anxious to demonstrate in the ranching area also, for Sanborn could see that the cattlemen entrenched on the unclaimed plains of the West and Southwest

[1] Hamner, *Short Grass and Longhorns,* 207.

[115]

would be fence-builders on a large scale—the best potential market of all. It was to prove his wares to "this cock-eyed world of cattle folk" that he and Glidden founded the Frying Pan.

The Panhandle plains, like adjoining areas, had few towns, not much acreage under cultivation, and little prospect of permanent development. The open, semiarid stretches between the Rocky Mountains settlement and the Mississippi and Missouri River valleys did not attract farmers until after other more desirable areas had become crowded. Even after government forts had been established and the Southern Plains tribes of Indians had been subdued, the character of the land itself still turned back the few homesteaders who came early to the region. The only evidence of vegetation on the great tablelands of the Oklahoma and Texas Panhandle was the variety of grasses, and, with the exception of the Palo Duro Canyon, the area was "high and dry and lacking in wood and water."[2] When the time had come that there was better equipment to cope with the conditions of nature, there was another deterrent in the form of the cowman whose very presence discouraged the advance of late-comers to the region. Agricultural settlement was not wanted—even if it were feasible. This was the land of the Open Range; this was the realm of the cowman.

It was 1890 before farming actually featured in Panhandle affairs, yet by the start of the 1880's, settlers were venturing onto the plains in increasing numbers. Cowmen in the Texas Panhandle noted that suddenly, with the beginning of a new decade, there were no extensive tracts which had not been broken by scattered plots belonging to small landowners. The last big ranch to be started on "free grass" had been established. Range land over which the state had assumed priority was being offered to homesteaders in 160-acre parcels, and cowmen began to realize that rights of ownership when protected with fencing gave settlers an advantage. Cowmen wanted no part of this advantage for themselves. They would not adopt the methods of the invader.

[2] Nordyke, *Cattle Empire*, 10.

They would fight with every other means at their command, but they would not buy land and fence it.

Sanborn came to the Panhandle not as a farmer, though. He came not to demonstrate fencing as a means of keeping cattle *out* of a plot which he wished to cultivate but as a means of keeping them *in* the feeding grounds allotted to them. When he began work on the Frying Pan, there was not another ranch like it in the whole of the Western plains country; there were great ranches— but not under fence. The enclosure of so large an area of grazing land was unprecedented.

Sanborn brought his superintendent from Grayson County to direct the building of the fence. Posts were hauled by bull team from the Palo Duro Canyon forty miles away. A special order of extra-heavy Glidden barbed wire was sent from the factory to railroad termini 250 miles from the ranch, then brought by wagon freight at $2.50 per hundred pounds. Posts were staggered, one on one side of the wire and one on the other, only one rod apart.[3] The cost of the fence alone was $39,000, but it stretched 150 miles of barbed wire as enclosure for 1,500 to 1,600 head of cattle. As Gates once had made Texas the testing ground for barbed-wire fencing, Sanborn now planned to make it the proving ground. He had chosen this "kind of twilight zone with the light of civilization behind it, and the darkness of savagery before"—the area where "the settler hadn't rattled in with his butcher-knife wagon," and the cowman ruled supreme.[4]

Glidden, meanwhile, had stayed on in De Kalb. Surprising as it may have seemed for an aging barbed-wire inventor in Illinois and his favorite representative in Texas to combine efforts in so bold an undertaking, it was understandable that the two should work well together. Glidden had always supported Sanborn. He had boosted Sanborn as salesman for the Barb Fence Company, had helped him retain his position with Washburn & Moen Company and Ellwood, and had gone on Sanborn's note to

[3] Hamner, *Short Grass and Longhorns*, 210.
[4] Dale, *The Range Cattle Industry*, xiv; Nordyke, *Cattle Empire*, 36.

the Company for a loan which was apparently used to buy out Warner's part of the sales business. And evidently Glidden never quibbled about the expense of the Frying Pan venture, though he made it clear that he wanted no part of ranch life for himself.

When Glidden made his first visit to the ranch, in 1884, he came wearing a high silk hat, and showing a very scant knowledge of the fundamentals of life in the Southwest. He looked little like an Illinois farmer, and acted less like a Texas rancher. He judged native short grass at the ranch to be "not enough to feed a goose"—and he said so, aloud. He persisted in wearing the high hat even in the face of constant winds and frequent sandstorms—and despite the embarrassment of having it rescued once with a lariat. He found it no easier to understand the people and their ways than had Sanborn; moreover, appreciation such as Sanborn had learned to feel for the land itself seemed to escape Glidden entirely. He went back to De Kalb, and in time turned over his interest in the ranch to his daughter and her husband W. H. Bush of Chicago.

Although Sanborn retained his home in Grayson County, he spent an increasing amount of time at the Frying Pan, and as a consequence he became increasingly interested in the Panhandle area as a whole. By the time the Fort Worth & Denver City Railroad had been extended into the region in 1887, Sanborn was deeply involved. From a portion of the ranch, he developed a city called Amarillo, the location of which came to be an issue of great importance to him. There was a bitter dispute over designation of the county seat, as well as over the point of connection with the railroad, and when the townsite which he had chosen was overruled and building was begun approximately a mile away, Sanborn purchased the flimsy buildings and moved them to his own property. He even bought "the well and the windmill which supplied water in barrels to the residents. . . . In about six months he had moved the town, all of it, to his site except the newly completed courthouse."[5] There was a Texas law which forbade the removal of the county courthouse for a

[5] Letter of John W. Crudgington to Henry D. McCallum, April, 1959.

period of five years after it was built, and so, despite the fact that Mr. Sanborn was successful in locating the town and in having Amarillo designated as county seat, the original courthouse remained one mile away until 1893.

Though the controversy was regrettable, the situation as it existed attracted widespread interest. "In early Texas history moving a courthouse was not unusual," writes Amarillo historian John W. Crudgington, "but moving the county seat away from the courthouse was enough of an unusual twist that the *St. Louis Democrat* sent their star reporter to Amarillo for a story."[6] Finally the old site was enveloped and much of the old bitterness thereby erased. The city flourished, as did the ranch, and by 1890, Amarillo was considered one of the largest cattle-shipping stations in the world. H. B. Sanborn's success was assured—though his popularity was not.

Sanborn took up permanent residence in Amarillo. He was a part of the life of the Texas Panhandle. But he was never accepted as one of the fraternity of Westerners. Newspapers of the day referred to him as "a New Yorker" since he had been born in New York state, as "a millionaire capitalist," and as "probably the wealthiest man in Texas"—but not as cowman, rancher, or typical Texan. Tall and handsome, Sanborn went about in a fine Prince Albert coat with proper gray pants, and peering from his considerable height over the heads of most men, he went his way, usually, alone. His standoffish manners and highhanded actions did not improve his relations with the people of Amarillo. Not even his continual devotion to civic needs relieved the tension between them. In time the condemnation of his conduct tempered, but probably because of the sorrow which came to him in the tragic loss of his only child—a son, Elwood Bradley Sanborn, very promising when he died at age twenty-one. Among the many Sanborn mementos at the Amarillo City Library is a newspaper clipping which describes the young Elwood in the company of his father's friends and associates "at a pleasant leap year party at the Glidden House" in De Kalb. Many

[6] *Ibid.*

[119]

bequests from the Sanborn family remain in Amarillo, notably a park donated to the city on the condition "that it be forever named Elwood."[7]

Throughout the state this "first representative of barbed wire" was well honored and long remembered. An early book of Texas biography said of H. B. Sanborn:

> . . . had it not been for his persistent work in the face of many obstacles and violent prejudices against the "new-fangle" contrivance, the present generation in this state would not be so familiar with that style of fence, which now networks the entire country from east to west.[8]

In the same year that Sanborn began operations in the Panhandle, there occurred an event which led to the making of more ranch history for the area. On November 9, 1881, the state capitol at Austin, Texas, burned. The building was so badly demolished that little could be saved—except a pile of water-soaked pages painstakingly salvaged by Hans Peter N. Gammel, a Dane, who later compiled from these papers the laws of Texas. It was necessary that the capitol be completely rebuilt. Resolutions were rushed through the legislature so that in February, 1882, provisions were passed whereby state-owned lands would be set aside as payment for the erection of a new statehouse. Texans wanted a capitol larger than any other state could boast, and they stipulated that it must be at least one foot higher than the United States Capitol in Washington. For this they would be willing to pay—giving in exchange for the building, three million acres of Texas Panhandle plains. The men who undertook the job, and were to receive the bounty, were Abner Taylor, Amos Babcock, and two brothers, Charles B. and John V. Farwell—all from Illinois. They were organizers of the Capitol Syndicate, a company receiving financial backing from England. The cornerstone was laid in 1882; construction was begun in 1883 and continued until

---

[7] The reason for spelling the Ellwood name with one "l" in virtually all connections with the Sanborn name is not explainable. The monument in the Amarillo park is marked "Elwood Bradley Sanborn."

[8] B. B. Paddock, *A Twentieth-Century Historical and Biographical Record of North and West Texas*, 311–13.

1888. An impressive structure took shape on the capitol grounds in Austin. The building was made of native Texas granite shipped over a short-line narrow-gauge railway, hauled by convict labor, and fitted by Scottish stonecutters. It was a work of considerable magnitude and a source of considerable pride.

Not even the grandeur of the new statehouse, however, outranked in importance—or in excitement—the molding of the three million sprawling acres of raw, undeveloped land into one of the great ranches of all time, the famous XIT. The ranch property spread through the length of the Texas Panhandle, covering the Staked Plain, or Llano Estacado, where early hunters, traders, and Spanish padres were said to have used stones to stake the path to water in the wilderness. The ranch was named XIT because as "almost any embryo cowboy" knows, says J. Evetts Haley, the ranch property extended across or into Ten (X) counties in Texas (IT). It was high plains, rolling northward to an altitude of four to five thousand feet, and stretching "downhill" in the south to approximately two thousand feet above sea level. In the eyes of most voters of Texas at the time, it was "worthless land," part of a veritable "desert." State officials had few misgivings about trading it to the Capitol Syndicate.

Reports on the nature of the land were sent from many sources to the Syndicate people in Chicago and thence to London. It was generally said that the area was a vast, almost limitless expanse of rich life-giving grasslands. Contrary to the impression held by most Texas lawmakers, it was thought to be fertile and capable of supporting crops of grain and vegetables as well as thousands of head of cattle. Every report contained one special proviso, however, and this was a warning which Texans would have known how to evaluate, but which absentee landowners were not in a position to gauge realistically—i.e., a notice that the success of any venture which might be undertaken in the area would be dependent first and foremost on the provision of water.

Rainfall varied from year to year, and in times of drought there was no place to turn for relief. Although it was expected that water might be secured from wells drilled to not-too-deep a horizon, there were not actually flowing wells to prove the theory. The area was, frankly, the last part of the entire high plains region to be opened up and inhabited for the very reason that it was "high and dry and lacking in wood and water." But it was not the desert which Texans who passed it off on the "greenhorn Yankees" had supposed it to be.

The majority of the reports were in the vein of the one made, at the request of Babcock, by a Dr. Hunt, who wrote:

I visited the [Quaker] Colony [of Estacado] in August and September 1880. The first crop ever planted on the plains was then growing and maturing. All planted on sod, broken the winter previous.

The season was favorable, having had plenty of rain; corn, oats, millet, broom corn, sorghum, all did well. I never saw a better sod crop in all my ten years' observation in Kansas; and larger and nicer melons, cushaws and pumpkins I never saw anywhere. Irish potatoes did moderately well, sweet potatoes were excellent. All garden vegetables did well to their chance, being planted in sod.

I arrived here [again] the 15th of June last [1881]. The season was not favorable; corn light; fall wheat, spring oats, millet, sorghum, rice corn, broom corn, melons, sweet potatoes all made fair crops where they had a fair chance. Irish potatoes and garden vegetables were generally nearly a failure, on account of drought and bugs. . . . So I am prepared to make the following statements: First, the fertility of the soil and its capability to produce all kinds of grains and vegetables is established beyond doubt. Second, the rich grazing qualities of the grasses is also beyond question. . . . The climate is above the malarial line and is very healthy. . . . But. . . .[9]

The conclusion was inescapable: in "unfavorable" seasons a supply of water from wells must be available.

At a distance the warning sounded not too formidable. The Chicago syndicate went forward with plans for stocking the range with cattle, and one of the members, John V. Farwell, who later

[9] Nordyke, *Cattle Empire*, 49. See also L. F. Sheffy, "Old Mobeetie—The Capital of the Panhandle," *West Texas Historical Association Yearbook* (June, 1930), 93.

became head of the ranching project, ordered also the planting of an experimental garden patch.

John Farwell was a believer in agriculture. He welcomed the boom of the cattle business, but always incorporated into his plans was the goal of ultimately planting the Texas properties to seed—under irrigation, if necessary. From the beginning he authorized testing for water wells. He insisted on larger and larger vegetable plots, "and also some corn, millet and alfalfa." He sent cultivators, harrows, mowers, rakes, plows for the plains, and at one time he sent 5,000 one-year-old trees for planting a grove at the ranch headquarters. Despite the comments of many, like the cowboy who remarked, "Reckon the XIT intend to grow theirself a little wood," agricultural tests were continued.

John Farwell showed interest too with his brother and the other executors in preparations for receiving cattle at the XIT; and he gave particular attention to the fencing project which would serve not only for bounding and partitioning the enormously extensive properties but also for containing the cattle. This, he must have estimated, would protect the fields he planned to put to seed in this great development which one day—he was sure—would be an agricultural stronghold. He held out with determination on this point. He was persistent. And also he was powerful. He saw to it that there was no stinting on fences for the XIT.

On this score, John Farwell had no trouble. His brother, C. B., and Abner Taylor too, were in favor of fencing—with barbed wire. Unlike the owners of other large herds, these men were owners of land also—or at least the land would be theirs when the building of the state capitol was completed. They were not free-pasture men. They were not champions of the Open Range. They themselves, though controlling cattle, were not even cattlemen in the usual sense of the term. But neither were they squatters or nesters, come to break up the land into small farms and settlements. They were in a unique position; they were owners whose cattle would obviously benefit from fencing, and they were ranchers who believed in confinement of herds, although the

extent of their ranges belied the use of such a word as "confinement." Their outlook presaged an over-all change in philosophy
for the cattle industry. They were among the first to put into
practice the theory that cattle-proof fences were advantageous
for Western cattlemen as well as for agriculturists.

Barbed wire was brought to the XIT on freight wagons,
along with saddles and boots and food and salt and clothing, "and
lemons and cigars for the general manager." To the northern portion, posts of red cedar were hauled for fifty miles from government land along the Cimarron River in New Mexico, and wire
was brought from the railroad station of El Moro near Trinidad, Colorado. The Syndicate contract called for the unloading
of four eighty-rod spools of wire at quarter-mile intervals along
the fence line. When the southern portion of the ranch was fenced
sometime later, the clause stipulating the placement of spools
was omitted; but for the fencing of the northern sector in the
early stages of founding the ranch, the best possible arrangements were made.

Following the course set by Sanborn and Glidden on the
Frying Pan, this was to be a case where fencing came first, and
the ranch would not be stocked until it was fenced. It was made
clear to every man on the ranch that fencing was one of the jobs
that had to be done before the first herds could be delivered, and
every man responded accordingly. Some, working during the
day, surveyed by the stars at night. They fenced off first their
precious hand-built watering system so that with the arrival of
cattle brought from the south to this unwatered land, the "thirst-
crazed" creatures would not trample and destroy the troughs and
pits from which they must learn to drink. Cowpunchers turned
fence-builders, three hundred of them working feverishly to receive the 50,000 cattle involved in a $7,000,000 operation. By
1885 they fenced 476,000 acres into their first big pasture, "the
largest in the country under barbed wire."[10]

That was in July, 1885. In the winter a prairie fire destroyed
many miles of the structure. The reaction of XIT men, as de-

[10] Nordyke, *Cattle Empire*, 87.

scribed below in a passage from Nordyke's *Cattle Empire,* was characteristic: they worked "in winter weather" rebuilding the fences, and they began another big fencing project at once:

> Meanwhile, over on the long western line of the ranch, barbed wire was being unreeled by the hundreds of miles for the new fencing Taylor and C. B. Farwell had ordered. . . . The survey-ors moved ahead, determining the line and marking the post loca-tions. Behind them came the post-setters, pounding holes two to three feet deep and tamping dirt around the posts. The bracers followed, and behind them were the wire-stretchers and the staplers. . . . Slowly, the [new] fence crept across the prairie and by late December [1885], the fencers reached the center of XIT's north-south axis. There they were days away from the nearest settlement and had to haul water 35 miles for themselves and their work animals.
>
> One night they were menaced as headquarters had been men-aced. A prairie fire came blazing out of New Mexico and the men had to flee, with equipment, horses and mules, to the protection of the sandy bed of a dry creek. The fire brought down ten miles of new fence and left a sea of soot to puff up pants legs and sleeves and into the eyes of the workmen. Patiently [Surveyor] Mabry and his men backed up and rebuilt the destroyed part, and kept working ever southward.[11]

Wire used on the northern portion was not Glidden wire, but the wide, flat ribbon wire newly patented in 1881 by Jacob and Warren M. Brinkerhoff of Auburn, New York. And for the southern portion a rough, four-point type of wire was ordered. So far apart were the extremities of this three-million-acre spread that supplies were delivered by different agencies in different states, and wire for the southern range was hauled by mule teams from Colorado City, Texas, instead of by two-horse wagons from Trinidad, Colorado. Prairie fire and drought made the freighting more difficult, and this circumstance in turn brought on added troubles for Scotsman Shannan who had contracted to build fences on the southern range. He wrote to J. Evetts Haley on November 27, 1927, saying:

[11] *Ibid.,* 110.

. . . The freighters would not scatter them [the materials] along the fence line, but dumped them all in one place. Lots of them threw the material off at Singer's Store, thirty miles from where we wanted it. . . . This meant that we had to re-haul it before we could use it. I never worked so hard in my life as I did there for eighteen months. We put in sixteen hours a day and seven days a week. I erected eighty-five miles of fence at $110 a mile, and lost about thirty dollars a mile on the contract. But that fence was different from anything in the country—it was put there to stay always.[12]

By 1890, XIT cattle were trailed to Montana pastures to fatten for the Chicago market, and so great were the XIT herds that "they covered the cow country from the Yellow Houses to the Yellowstone (River)." In Texas, XIT ranges produced some of the early strains of Texas purebred cattle, and XIT farms when put under irrigation supported cotton, grains, and garden produce. Oil and gas, too, played a part in the latter-day prosperity of the ranch, although most of the income from this source came in the form of lease revenue rather than royalty, as proven production appeared most often on the fringes of the ranch property and beyond. But from the time of its beginnings in the early 1880's, the name of the Capitol Syndicate represented substantial prosperity. It was a name known and respected throughout Texas, hailed in financial circles of Chicago, and carefully appraised by speculators in foreign lands. The name was so often applied with reference to the barbed wire used on the southern part of the ranch that this brand of four-point wire is known in some parts of the Southwest as "Syndicate wire." The broad, flat, ribbon wire from the northern range, meanwhile, has many times been cut into six-inch strips for mounting on cards to be sold to the curio seekers who came to the famous XIT country.

As for the capitol building, some years after its completion, Big-Foot Wallace pronounced it an improvement over the original cabin put up "to keep Indians from scalping the lawmakers," but at the same time Big-Foot could not see that there was im-

[12] J. Evetts Haley, *The XIT Ranch of Texas*, 87.

provement in the laws being made. "There's no more brains and talent," he said, than in the old building.[13] Most Texans viewed their fine capitol with more satisfaction, however. On May 2, 1888, *Senate-House Bill No. 38* providing for acceptance of the building was approved in the Texas Legislature. On May 16 passage of *House Bill No. 91* authorized funds for furnishing the building and for grading and fencing the grounds. And at the present time the granite capitol still stands witness to the ability and integrity of Babcock, Taylor, and the Farwell brothers— though at dedication ceremonies on May 6, 1888, rain leaked in on the festivities, and the capitol roof had to be repaired before any land was finally deeded to the syndicate. The capitol land, the great XIT ranch, long since has been broken up and sold off in parts, some for grazing, some for planting. Though never supplied with ample rainfall, under irrigation the land blossomed, and those farm settlers who managed to hold on through years of hardship finally were repaid.

The XIT was "the largest ranch in the cow country of the Old West," says Haley, "and probably the largest fenced range in the world."[14] It was not, like the Frying Pan, founded by, for, and with barbed wire, but its fifteen hundred miles of fences comprised reportedly the greatest barbed-wire fencing project in history. And the ranch served, without doubt, as an important working example of the theory which the "cockeyed world of cattle folk" found hard to learn: that it could be advantageous for ranchers to fence animals *in,* as well as for farmers to fence them *out.*

[13] J. W. Wilbarger, *Indian Depredations in Texas,* 664.
[14] Haley, *The XIT Ranch of Texas,* 3.

CHAPTER 10

"THE BIG DIE-UP"[1]

I T HAS BEEN ARGUED that the opening of the West made possible the success of barbed wire, and it has been argued, contrariwise, that the success of barbed wire made possible the opening of the West.[2] In the decade of the 1880's, both points of view seemed valid. Fencing of some kind was bound to be found eventually—as was the solution to the problem of water supply and other essentials—yet there could hardly have been a period more propitious for solution to the fencing problem. The flow of migration was at flood stage, and the gates to the West were open. As the drive to settle the plains increased the need for fencing, the provision of suitable fencing accelerated the settling of farmer and cattleman side by side on the plains. In the interest of both fencing and expansion, the proving of barbed wire was a paramount issue.

There was hardly a time or a place which could have served both interests better than the locating of the Frying Pan Ranch and subsequent development of the XIT in the early 1880's. The Cherokee Outlet on the east was a part of the Indian Territory and not open, while ranges of Montana and the Dakotas in the northern plains were too remote to serve as showcase areas; parts of Colorado and Wyoming in the central plains, however,

[1] W. Turrentine Jackson, *et al.*, *When Grass Was King.*
[2] "The effect of barbed wire on the West was enormous and it was many-sided; the effect of the West on barbed wire was enormous also, but wholly uncomplicated:—the development of the West meant success for barbed wire." Dale, *The Range Cattle Industry.*

were within reach of the Texas Panhandle, as were the ranching sections of New Mexico, and from these centers influences spread to the north and west. Land laws applying to new states and territories were being altered to fit more nearly the needs of Western living, railroad supply lines were being extended, agricultural settlement was being encouraged, and immigration from European countries was being invited. Fencing was more than an accessory to migration onto plains and prairies; it was a prerequisite. Fencing of the Frying Pan affected more than the Texas Panhandle; it affected the whole of the Great Plains region. Moreover, the success of the program was achieved at an opportune moment in the fortunes of barbed-wire fencing.

The proving of barbed wire by Sanborn's and Glidden's ranching venture came just in time to counteract unexpected developments which threatened the whole barbed-wire industry when, from 1882 to 1885, misfortune stalked the cow country, and much of the blame for it was attributed to barbed-wire fences. Some of the fences were erected to form enclosures, but this type of structure was still scarce on the plains. The fences which brought strongest reaction and direst threats were parallel barriers erected by cattlemen of the Texas Panhandle and adjacent areas in an effort to keep cattle in the north from coming onto southern ranges. They were called "drift fences," because they blocked the way of unattended cattle "drifting" from one part of the ranges to another. They were used to protect the ranges in various sections of the plains, but chiefly atop the Texas Panhandle.

Soon after 1880 the plains were "inundated," as one historian put it, "with thousands of ranchers and millions of cattle without stamina or experience to survive there."[3] The Panhandle country in particular was crowded with newcomers, and its ranges were badly overstocked. Grasses were depleted and in danger of being ruined. A series of severe winters caused cattle unconfined on northern ranges to turn tail before the blizzards and "drift" south. There was no natural barrier to stop them,

[3] Ray Allen Billington, *Westward Expansion*, 683.

no man-made barrier to keep them from pushing on to what little remained of Panhandle grasses.

Finally Panhandle cattlemen, in a desperate effort to protect what was left to them, proposed the erection of an east-west barricade of barbed wire as the beginning of a program for restoration and preservation of their ranges. They had no mind to build an enclosure, or to confine their separate herds. They were not about to be committed to a policy of keeping cattle *in*. They planned only that the northern boundary of each man's accustomed range or each corporation's holdings be banded with drift fences to keep out intruding animals.

Beginning in 1881–82 the fences were built, taut and strong, with three or four strands to the pane, no cross wires and no cross corners. Some were put up by individual cowmen or individual ranching corporations to protect individual ranges; others were co-operative efforts by a number of cattlemen who controlled adjoining ranges. The average cost was estimated at $250.00 per mile, though in some sections it was said to have been "as high as $400.00 a mile . . . and some not half as much."[4]

Like present-day drift fences which are picket or board structures put up along highways to prevent snowdrifts, the early drift fences of barbed wire were built in disconnected sections. Individual fences sometimes were joined, but usually not. Where joined, however, they were parallel and, in effect, almost continuous. Cattle finding their way to the end of one long stretch were soon confronted with an overlapping offset, and not many animals could find the way further. Few were determined enough to pass through a series of such constructions. Though there was not a long unbroken fence line, though the slender strands whistling in the wind off the prairie looked frail and insubstantial—and very much out of place—they nevertheless formed a wall of wire which proved to be a sufficient barrier in the path of cattle moving from north to south. Sections built in 1881–82 were so effective that additional sections were put up the following year, and

[4] J. Evetts Haley, "And Then Came Barbed Wire to Change History's Course," *The Cattleman* (March, 1927).

by 1885 barbed-wire drift fences had been erected across the entire Texas Panhandle, from Indian Territory on the east to New Mexico on the west, and beyond.

Up to this time the only means for driving back stray cattle was the fence-rider or line-rider who set up regular winter camps along the northern line of a cattleman's range. As more cattlemen moved into an area, however, and as northerners allowed more animals to drift southward, line-riders were less able to cope with the situation. Cattle had less fear of the horse and rider than of the storm, and when great numbers of cattle came "tails to the wind" before a blizzard, the only thing a rider could do was to follow them and eventually corral them for return to their rightful owners. Under these circumstances, the visitors had to be tolerated until spring roundup.

Roundup, held twice a year, was an integral part of Open Range operations. It was the occasion for keeping cattle ownership straight, settling water-hole rights, formulating general policies for range cattlemen, and providing social gatherings. With its intricate but jealously guarded system of exchange, roundup almost was enough to defeat barbed wire. But line riders were expensive and roundup system was sometimes unwieldly. As the cost of fencing was reduced and its effectiveness increased, as pressure from farm sectors and from overstocked ranges grew, it seemed inevitable that barbed wire finally would be put to use. Cowmen still opposed enclosure, and since they usually did not own the land they used, they could not enclose it even if they wished; consequently, an unclosed drift fence to bar the northern line, and in some cases other boundaries as well, was sufficient to meet the cowman's immediate need. Drift fences for protecting overgrazed areas appeared to be a promising development as work on the fences continued. And promotion of barbed wire seemed to be touching a new high.

Barbed-wire manufacturers in distant cities watched for reports of the drift-fence experiment; dealers and salesmen in Texas and near-by areas looked on confidently; and cattlemen in all parts of the West watched as the project went forward. However, there was no one watching at the time of crisis when blizzards struck the plains in the winter of 1885–86 and again in 1886–87.

It was December 31, the last day of 1885, that the worst of the weather began. An eyewitness to the storm in Kansas reported it:

New Year's Eve about eleven o'clock a gentle snow was falling. Suddenly the north wind became a howling gale. . . . My father [had] completed a house on his claim in the Gate Valley that day, and as with other settlers, nearly starved before they could get out again and procure provisions. At Englewood [Kansas] I had brought a girl from 15 miles west, as my partner for a big New Year's Eve dance. I managed to get her back home six days thereafter. [Then] on January 7th [1886] another blizzard occurred much worse. . . . Everyone ran out of fuel. First purchasing all fence posts from the lumber yard, the yard then sold all its heavy dimension lumber for fuel. In about ten days a third blizzard struck"[5]

In such weather cattle turned by instinct toward the south, and when intense cold was borne on driving winds, the animals would not turn back and face the wind. No one needed to be watching on the ranges to know that when the fury of hard-driven snow was swept uninhibited across the plains, cattle moving fast before the storm pushed straight for the south, where barbed wire measuring "from 10 to 40 miles at a stretch" awaited them.

They moved "like grey ghosts . . . [with] icicles hanging from their muzzles, eyes, and ears," toward the Texas Panhandle, and directly into the fences.[6] There they were stalled; they could not go forward, and they would not go back. They stood stacked together against the wire, without food, water, warmth, or shelter. They pressed close against each other in groups all along the fence line, and sometimes they gathered in bunches reaching as much as four hundred yards back from the fence.[7] Still there was

[5] Angie Debo, ed., *The Cowman's Southwest, Being The Reminiscences of Oliver Nelson*, 272.
[6] Nordyke, *Cattle Empire*, 69.
[7] Nordyke, *Great Roundup*, 157.

not enough warmth in their huddled forms to counteract the cold, and within a short time they either smothered or froze in their tracks. At the storm's end their bodies were found piled against the wire, some of them standing stiffly upright, others looking as if they had bedded down in a swath of snow. It was "the big die-up," where thousands perished along Panhandle drift fences alone, and hundreds more along lesser barriers on other ranges.

Early in the winter of 1886–87 extreme cold struck again, and again there was little opportunity for reaching stock on the plains, little chance to feed and shelter them, to rescue them from ravines and canyons, icy waters, and barbed-wire fences. In creek beds and draws they bogged down quickly, and on northern ranges they sometimes died "within two hours after the storm struck."[8] Those that got through to southern regions ran right into the fence, for by this time nearly the whole of the Texas Panhandle was banded with barbed wire, and in adjacent areas also there were some drift-fence constructions. Again the number of cattle trapped by the fences was staggering. News of the losses spread a pall across the ranges. Said the foreman of the Swan Land and Cattle Company: "I never saw such a sight. There are big mounds of cattle, nothing visible but horns, for the snow had drifted over them and you are spared meantime the horrible sight of seeing piles of carcasses."[9] It was a time of deepest gloom in the cow country, a time of "stiff heaps in the coulee, dead eyes in the camp."[10]

Cowmen estimated losses as high as 65 to 75 per cent for many herds, as the count was made along the north line of the Rocking Chair and the XIT ranches, at the co-operatively constructed fence which followed the course of Sweetwater Creek, and at the townsite of old Mobeetie. It was said that a man from the LX ranch skinned 250 head of cattle to the mile for 35 miles

[8] Fred Tracy, "Reminiscences of No-Man's Land," MS in the University of Oklahoma Library, 4.

[9] John Clay, *My Life on the Range*, 290.

[10] Roy D. Holt, "Barbed Wire Drift Fences," *The Cattleman* (March, 1935).

along one section of drift fence.[11] In the Panhandle, it was "the big die-up" again.

This had been, of course, an unusual storm, referred to as "the worst of the prairie era." The winter would have been recorded as a disastrous time for cowmen even if there had not yet been fences in the West, and when it was followed by worse than usual drought, it became memorable to all. This one blizzard had wrought misery across the entire Western range country and in the prairie settlements as well. "Like a cold rock out of the skies" it had hit, causing houses to shake, trees to "whistle" in the roaring wind. Snowdrifts were as high as 30 feet. One stockman, hoping to get hay to a few of his cows, lost his way in his own barnyard and "most certainly would have wandered off to the prairies, had he not struck a cottonwood tree which gave him his bearing." Another recalled that by the time he could harness his team and hitch up a wagon, he could not reach the cane piled in the field "20 rods away." Wrote another:

> Snow drifts were like hills. There was a straw stack in the field ten rods away, but the cattle would not leave the creek where they were out of the wind. They got water out of the creek. The ice was more than six inches thick, but later froze to the bottom, two feet deep. . . . [Also] a deep ravine ran through the pasture and the snow filled it. Cattle made paths across the ravine in the snow, and when the thaw came were lost when they broke through the caked snow and drowned.[12]

Obviously, all stockowners—with or without pasture fences or drift fences—were in desperate straits, and those whose animals had been turned onto the plains faced the greatest losses of all. Many of the animals that managed to avoid drift fences froze or died of thirst on the open range, where there was nothing but snow and ice to eat and to drink, no shelter, no protection from wolves and coyotes and cold. Because of these circumstances, losses on open range ordinarily exceeded losses caused by drift fences, but in the years 1885 to 1887, the opposite was true. Ani-

[11] Nordyke, *Great Roundup,* 158.
[12] Peterson Scrapbook, *loc. cit.*

mals left to roam far from the protection of barnyards and hay-
stacks, outside of the occasional pasture fences, across the open
plains where nothing but natural instinct could help them, met
with a worse experience than they ordinarily would have encountered, because they were blocked from their natural routes
of retreat.

There was no escaping the fact that drift fences had been the
cause of many otherwise unnecessary casualties. Cattlemen on
both sides of the fence were sick at heart. They tore down long
sections of wire and broke other sections into parts. They cursed
the day they had first begun the venture. But it was not because
the barricade was unsuccessful that the plan had failed. Cowmen
had built their barrier too well; the material which they had used
had held back range cattle too successfully. It was the calamitous
effect on cattle repulsed, rather than the failure of barbed wire
to repulse, which had brought on the trouble, and as a consequence, there was no longer any question of the effectiveness of
barbed wire for fencing. There was only resentment—growing,
mounting, raging resentment, which was sure to cause a serious
setback in plans for the future of barbed wire.

The drift-fence disaster added weight to arguments of the
opponents of barbed wire who already had called the product
"unnatural" and "inhuman," and already had denounced it "on
humanitarian grounds." As the count of range losses increased, as
news of the catastrophe spread, earlier accounts of "cruel injuries" long forgotten were recalled in many localities. One after
another livestock owner recollected and retold experiences from
the past when barbed wire was first used in crude fence structures. Sympathetic townspeople remembered how sharp-pronged
barbs had damaged animals exposed to barbed wire strung
around feed lots or cemeteries. Voices from every direction were
raised in accusation against the very nature of the product, as
antagonism was leveled at fence-makers and fence-builders alike.

Most of the trouble arose in the West, where cattle were not
only most numerous but also most vulnerable. Western cattle
never had known confinement. They were still half-wild, closely

related to native strains, unfamiliar with fencing of any kind. When maneuvered into a pen for the first time, they bolted against the wire in much the same way that the bewildered steers had performed for Gates in San Antonio. In the beginning, they probably did not see the fence at all, for the wire was small as well as unexpected, and when they did see a barrier before them, it was the nature of the animals to run the harder because there was an obstruction to be overcome. When the obstruction was armed with spurs and spikes, the sting of punctured flesh only drove the cattle to charge again, with necks bowed and heels flying. Sometimes they were badly gouged and torn before their first encounter with a fence was ended; sometimes they were only scratched. But in warm weather, and especially in wet summers, even a slight injury, if it drew blood, attracted screwworms, and screwworm infestation under conditions on the Open Range was serious, often fatal.

In open country where cattlemen dealt with large numbers of cattle scattered over large areas of land, it was impossible to keep close watch over all ranges at once. On farms or in pastures close to ranch headquarters, cures might be effected by prompt treatment of injured animals, but infection contracted or worms nurtured in cattle and horses grazing extensive areas often went undiscovered for a long time. Minor injuries, which ordinarily might not have been serious, sometimes proved fatal because of neglect. Cattle fenced *in* many times could be saved, though only to be cut again when they next tried going through barbed-wire fencing. It was the cattle fenced *out* and left to roam that died by the thousands.

Those few cowmen who had gone ahead with fencing of their own surveyed the outcome with shocked disbelief; those who had not fenced, but owned cattle cut on fences built by other men, were up in arms. There was evidence that some ranchers with small fenced lots may have clipped the sharp points off the barbs on fences known to be damaging stock, but in most cases fences either belonged to someone else or were too far distant to be cared for. On the well-established ranches, the ranch hands had all they could do "doctorin' the sick" or "skinnin' the dead" for the price of the hides. In some states, laws were enacted to prevent the use of barbed wire or to prescribe the manner in which it could be used. In territories and some other sections under federal jurisdiction troops were ordered to assist in removing unlawful fence structures. Homesteaders on the public domain fenced, but cattlemen, who neither owned nor leased property, could not. Enclosure was not permitted without land title.

Farm settlers were dismayed at the terrible turn of events. Though not bearing responsibility for ranchers' livestock, they were alarmed, nonetheless, at the waste and destruction. Armed to defend themselves for the first time since venturing onto the plains, they had piled reels of barbed wire onto their wagons and moved farther west to government lands. They had built fences not in retaliation but for self-protection, and the fencing had been accomplished before there was time to gauge the consequences. When cowmen found cattle cut and wounds infected, when animals began to die and cattlemen counted the losses, it was too late to retract the advance of farm settlement. No one had anticipated a form of "big die-up" affecting the entire plains country, yet farmers and cattlemen both were trapped, for when the range cattle business suffered, the whole region suffered. And in the heat of their dilemma, both were roused to anger, for the undercurrent of enmity between the two factions came seething to the surface again, and the old conflict was resumed.

When the drift-fence toll was added to increased casualties from screwworms and infection, the double dose of trouble was felt in manufacturing circles also. Cattlemen facing bankruptcy and defeat were ready to drag down with them the makers of "that infernal fencing" which had been the ruination of the range. Resentful of their predicament and staggered by their losses, they raised loud protests, and non-cowmen, viewing with horror "the inhuman injuries" inflicted by prickers made of metal, and foreseeing the pinch of economic crisis, joined in the plaint. The Western populace turned on Eastern manufacturers in a body;

[137]

the barbed-wire business seemed doomed. Except for the fact that the trouble was mechanical and could be remedied easily, the whole barbed-wire episode might have been ended before it was well begun.

Manufacturers were quick to react, and fortunately they were able to adapt their product readily. It was decided that if barbs were made small enough to prick but not penetrate, damage would be reduced. Furthermore, it was thought that if cattle could see the fence which stabbed and jabbed them, they would soon learn to avoid it, and if the wounds inflicted in the meantime were such as to warn without actually injuring the animals, losses could be reduced immediately. Strand wires large enough and prominent enough to be readily visible, with small barbs, appeared to be worth trying. Analyzing the matter in a new light, manufacturers sought easy visibility rather than infliction of pain. Although this was a reversal in principles of barbed-wire design, a new type of product was presented within a short time, and there were developed many patterns of wire less vicious and more obvious.

Inventors responded quickly also. In fact, inventors may have been ahead of schedule, for actually the idea of visibility had been incorporated—whether consciously or not—in designs conceived long before. Even Hunt's patent showed some such characteristics. But because most early attempts had been awkward, the principle of using wide strands with small barbs had not been accepted. By 1879, however, the trend toward "obvious" styling had begun, and reports of cattle dying on the ranges started the movement in earnest. By the middle 1880's, "obvious" wire design was developed to such a high pitch that it seemed at the time to be an altogether new and sudden innovation. Within three years after Sanborn and Warner and Gates had first brought the "devil's rope" to the cattlemen's part of the country, the change was noticeable, and within five years the types of barbed wire which were plainly "vicious" gave way to newer types of "obvious" wire.

Inventors had new designs by the hatful, new ideas up every

sleeve. There was again a rush for the patent office. With the same excitement that had brought applications for patent on fences meant for farmers and agricultural settlers in the earlier migrations, there now were streams of applications on patterns designed to win the cattlemen, to silence the noisy commotion reverberating from the Western plains. There appeared on the market all shapes and patterns of barbed wire, among them the most fanciful and most unusual types ever patented, as inventors and manufacturers equipped their product with whatever contraptions they could devise to attract an animal's attention to the fence, to advertise its danger.

It can be surmised that Sanborn's farm locations and the Sanborn-Glidden ranch must have demonstrated the success of Glidden's "Winner" wire with barbs formed to be less pointed and less sharp. Other designs manufactured by Washburn & Moen Company and Ellwood, and sold by Sanborn and Warner, were put into use on a wide scale, and brands produced by Haish and Gates and their confederates contributed also to the spread of fencing throughout the West. At the same time, migration spread also. It was said that "in the 8 years since the introduction of 'a cheap fencing for the prairies . . .' white settlements had advanced further westward than in the 50 years preceding."[13] Barbed wire was playing a big role in the advance.

In the hope of rescuing themselves and their customers from calamity, leaders of the barbed-wire industry moved rapidly into full-scale production of "obvious" wire, and as a result, business never let up entirely. Prospects for makers and marketers appeared good, even in the years which were marred by heavy losses from injuries and drift-fence casualties. Tensions eased, sales began to rise slowly, and then suddenly to soar to new highs as cattlemen, realizing that they could not go back, moved toward a new kind of range rule based on—of all things—barbed wire.

[13] Holt, "Barbed Wire," *loc. cit.*, 174–85.

CHAPTER 11

"KING OF THE COASTERS"[1] AND BROTHER JON

F IRST OF THE BIG COWMEN to cry out with characteristic big cowman vehemence against the evils of barbed-wire fencing was Abel H. "Shanghai" Pierce, a prominent south Texas rancher who was present when John W. Gates staged the important corral test at old San Antonio. Pierce did not foresee the possibilities of other types of barbed wire, such as "obvious" and "modified" patterns, but he saw at once the effects of "vicious" wire—and he said so, in his usual forceful manner. As a witness to Gates's demonstration, he announced that he would not have that kind of fencing put in the way of his Texas Longhorns:

> "It may keep 'em in, by God!" he commented. "But my cattle would cut themselves and die from screwworms, and I'll be damned if I treat my critters that way."[2]

Abel H. Pierce was, even at the early date of 1876, the acknowledged "king of the coasters." His cattle "kingdom" spread across the Texas counties of Wharton and Matagorda bordering the Gulf of Mexico, and the parts of this region which his and his brother's ranch hands did not ride were parts controlled by the Pierces' onetime employer and all-time enemy, W. B. Grimes. Between them, the opposing forces of Pierce and Grimes ruled an enormous area of lush, unfenced coastal grassland centered around the Tres Palacios Creek.

[1] C. L. Douglas, "Cattle Kings of Texas," *The Cattleman* (December, 1935; January, 1936).
[2] Emmett, *Shanghai Pierce*, 136.

The rivalry between Shanghai and his former boss was of long duration, and it was the stronger because each had won his rights to the land by hard work and vengeance. Abel Pierce, in particular, held his position as a cattleman of prominence—and of pre-eminence over Grimes—not only because of a strong will backed by a strong voice but also by virtue of hard-earned understanding and canny appreciation of the practical procedures of ranching. Shanghai knew about cattle from working with them. He knew to the mouthful the needs of his herds, and he knew from experience how they would react to most situations. Armed with both knowledge and intuition, he actually was able to foresee and sometimes to forestall serious threats to ranching interests. It was understandable that his opinion should carry weight with other cowmen—and it was customary that he should express his opinion freely.

It was said that "anyone who had seen [A. H.] Pierce could truthfully say that he had heard him."[3] The big voice was as much a trade-mark of the man as was the six-foot, four-inch frame. The sounds which Pierce emitted were likened variously to "the sound of a foghorn," "a hurricane's roar," and "the bellow of an angry bull." Sometimes he stood on the second-story gallery of the rambling Pierce ranch house and shouted orders to men working cattle in pens a mile away,, and he expected the orders to be heard and to be executed. The carrying quality of his voice was enhanced, moreover, by the vigor of the personality behind it, for what A. H. Pierce thought, he said—without lowering his voice.

Where Shanghai brought his cattle out of creek bottoms and up from salty marshes to range on native grasses of the wide and sunlit prairie, he was far removed from the outreaches of agricultural settlement. He operated in the tradition of "free grass men." He followed the cowman's code and there was nothing in that code to say that he must own the range land which his cattle grazed on or the watering places which they frequented. He controlled the land without owning it, and he felt little apprehension

[3] Ralph A. Records, "A Cowhand's Recollections," *The Cattleman* (June, 1943).

[141]

about anyone else's laying claim to it. This was Open Range, and Shanghai was convinced that it would remain so. "As long as water runs and grass grows here," he said, "this will be open prairie."[4] And on the strength of this conviction he had built his cattle kingdom.

Shanghai knew as well as anyone that fencing posed a threat to the practices of free grazing, and on this basis his opposition to any form of enclosure was strong and deep-seated. But at the start he opposed barbed wire not so much as a threat to his land but as a threat to his animals. His immediate concern was for his precious "critters." When in the course of time it was seen that barbed wire was indeed a means by which settlement might advance into the plains country and settlers might be enabled to compete with cowmen for domination of unoccupied areas, Shanghai was forced to reassess the whole problem of fencing. But his animosity began and ended with the effect of barbed wire on his cattle—and on the balance of power between himself and his brother, as opposed to W. B. Grimes.

Though he could see nothing, hear nothing, and speak nothing except that which was applicable to cattle and the cattle industry, Abel Pierce was nonetheless obliged throughout his life to contend with a man who operated on a very different philosophy. Shanghai had as his partner in the Rancho Grande ranching venture his brother Jonathan Edward Pierce; and Jonathan was—like Cain—a tiller of the soil, a planter.

Jonathan could not agree with Shanghai's opinion that nothing was worth raising except cattle, and that in all the vast expanse of coastal plains and prairies no section should be set aside for cultivation. He was not averse to cattle-raising. He invested in cattle with Shanghai and reaped the profits therefrom; but "Jon," as he was called, could not acquiesce to the theory that this land was meant only for range land and was not good for anything else. He believed that it was good for the sowing of seed. He was a farmer at heart, "never so happy as while plowing with a yoke of

---

[4] From Pierce family lore, as related by Grace Pierce Hefflefinger to Frances T. McCallum, 1958.

oxen," and he was determined to set his plow into the soil of south Texas where fate and his brother had brought him. He was, needless to say, a veritable "thorn in the side" of Abel.

Jonathan it was who originally envisioned a permanent headquarters, El Rancho Grande. Jonathan it was who "drove stakes in the ground . . . where the prairie [was] dotted with Indian pinks and primroses, buttercups and daisies, marigolds and verbena . . . [against] a glorious back-ground of noble oaks and lordly elms." Jonathan it was who loved the land. While to Abel Pierce land was but pasturage for his stock, Jon Pierce held it sacrosanct. Land in itself was important to him, and he wished to have some of it for himself, his brother Shanghai notwithstanding. Although Shanghai, like most users of the newly won West, gave little thought to the ultimate disposition of anything so abundant as the seemingly boundless stretches of plains and prairies, Jonathan kept always in his mind the thought of ownership. Let Shanghai count his wealth in head of cattle if he would, for he was a cowman; but Jonathan counted by acres owned. He believed that the time would come when herds would not range free wherever the water would run and the grass would grow. He believed that homesteaders' plots would break up the open expanses needed for free range rights. He believed in owning land and, for himself, in planting it.

Jonathan was a much different man from his brother. Younger, shorter, "less noisy" than Shanghai, yet he was a big man, in every sense of the word—and destined to be one of the big landowners of his time. He wanted to be a farmer, a stay-at-home, and from the day he stepped off a schooner onto the docks at old Indianola to follow his brother into the employ of W. B. Grimes, he began to be just that. Almost at once he planted seed to supply the Grimes table with the unheard-of delicacy of fresh garden-grown vegetables. He planted flowers, experimented with grains and with orchards. He worked cattle and invested in a herd of his own for the main purpose of making money to buy more land. He broke the prairie sod with oxen, having in all six prized pairs of them to be put to this use. And he developed the acres which he owned in partnership with Shanghai to the fullest potential of productivity. He built on their joint property not only a home but a whole settlement—office, store, carpentry shop, blacksmith shop, potato house, hog house, and goat house; barns, carriage house, smokehouse, crib, hide house, and a hide press; and later a church and Masonic temple. Like a feudal village and a central manor house, Jonathan's community was built around the main ranch house; but in other respects it was a cross between a Western cowman's ranch and a Southern gentleman's plantation. It was headquarters for some time for the cattle operations which supported the entire venture, and it was also a planter's paradise.

Jonathan's life seemed by comparison with his brother's to be mild and quiet, yet neither he nor Shanghai was spared the violence and vicissitudes which commonly plagued pioneer Americans. Jonathan had three wives, Abel two, both men being widowered due to medical shortcomings of the times. They married sisters first, Jonathan making much fun of Abel's surprise at finding that they were brothers-in-law! Shanghai's only son, Abel, died in infancy and the mother, Fannie, a few months later. Jonathan's Nannie was injured when a fine span of Arabian horses reared and fell on her, and she died nineteen days later of peritonitis. His second wife died in childbirth, and the infant daughter being cared for by relatives in Galveston sickened and died of a strange milk poisoning which struck the city. Both Abel and Jonathan had other children (Abel only one, a daughter), but these early tragedies left their mark.

Jonathan's beloved Rancho Grande was gutted by fire. As an old man he was obliged "to move from the oak grove, away from the sound of the mockingbird's song," to live in a hotel he had built in the near-by town of Blessing.[5] But in the course of seventy-six years, J. E. Pierce found happiness, and the deep satisfaction of carrying on many projects dear to his heart. While A. H. ruled as "king of the coasters," demonstrating ably and impressively the practices required to make a cow kingdom in the lowlands of the Texas Gulf Coast, J. E. provided proof of the fertility

[5] *Bay City Daily Tribune,* n.d.

[144]

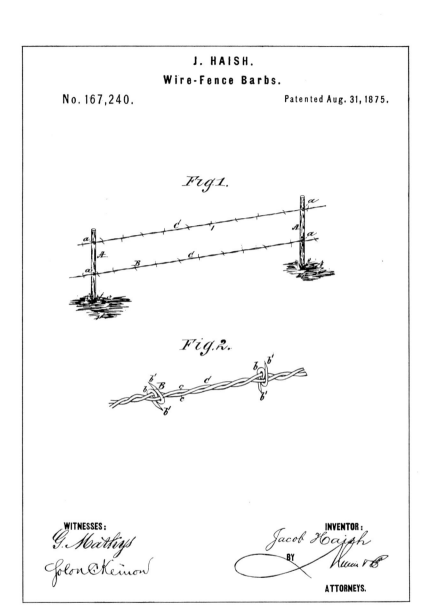

J. HAISH.

Wire-Fence Barbs.

No. 167,240.

Patented Aug. 31, 1875.

Fig.1.

Fig.2.

WITNESSES:
G. Mathys
John C. Kenson

INVENTOR:
Jacob Haish
BY
Kuun & Co
ATTORNEYS.

Jacob Haish's barbed wire, shown here in the original patent drawing, was issued United States patent No. 167240 on August 31, 1875.

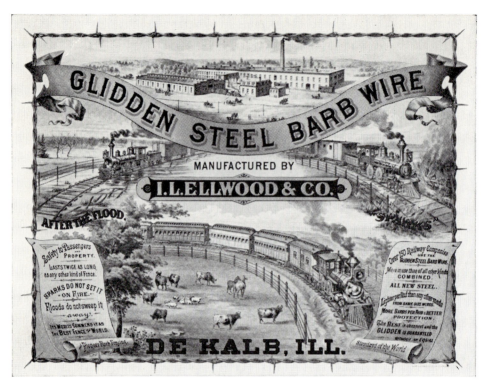

An 1877 advertisement of barbed wire by I. L. Ellwood & Company.

of the area. He demonstrated the fact that the land, even where slightly salted from the sea, was good for cultivation. He directed the development of enormously large tracts and sold off small plots to be settled by others. Men from Illinois, Wisconsin, and Colorado invested in his land ventures, and a colony of Swedish immigrants who settled on his acres referred to him, out of fondness, as "King Jon." While Shanghai was known as cattle king, Jonathan was lord of the land. It was thought that at one time the brothers owned between them more than a million acres. While Shanghai tended cattle as it was agreed he should, while he was busy buying and selling, "borrowing" and branding the herds of "mossback sea-lions"—which, he maintained, he had got out of the Gulf—while he spent most of his time away from the ranch, Jonathan stayed at home and tended the land, close by the banks of the Tres Palacios where it glided down to the sea.

Farmerlike, Jon Pierce turned his thoughts early to the problem of fencing for the rancho. Casting about in search of something to make up for the shortage of lumber in the area, he found the McCartney rose, a recently imported wild rose hedge which he planted as a barrier across a corner section "to keep out horse thieves and other depredators." The hedge grew quickly and soon presented a dense stand of dark-leafed bushes growing in great mounds of brambles and matted branches. Its thorns were thick and sharp and tough. According to Jonathan, any thief who tried to go through the Cherokee or McCartney rose hedge was "hardly fit for business after the trip."[6] Following severe cold snaps in winter, Jonathan found his cattle—and Shanghai's, too—huddled against the hedge for shelter, and he realized that it served as a defense against the elements as well as against "depredators." In spring when the early planting was done and the fields lay exposed to ranging livestock, the hedge which had been started ostensibly for the protection of livestock provided protection against them also; for, where thieves could not pass through to molest the animals, neither could the animals pass through to molest planted fields on the other side of the briar hedge. Since

6 Emmett, *Shanghai Pierce*, 46.

here at last was a means of providing protection for crops, more and more of the thorny bushes were planted until, in time, a hedge of Cherokee rose grew the whole way around the rancho —thirty-seven miles of it, a "blaze" of blossoms in springtime, and in all seasons a thicket of thorns.

To brother Abel, however, crops were not important. It was only because Jonathan's plans fell in with his own that he consented to go along with the ever-increasing planting schedule set up for Rancho Grande. No farm-minded brother ever could have persuaded a cowman to buy land, to farm and to fence it. Certainly no brother of Shanghai Pierce's ever could have persuaded *him*. Only two things counted with Shanghai: one, love for his precious "critters"; the other, rancor for his former employer, W. B. Grimes. And in the matter of purchasing land and enclosing it, the influence of both Grimes and the "critters" would be needed to force Shanghai into changing his views. He looked at fencing as at any other thing—in terms of its effect on cattle, on the cattle business, and on Grimes. If barbed wire would not help with the cows in his pasture and would not hinder Grimes' cattle, he was not interested; if it would, he was. For Shanghai it was as simple as that.

Grimes was a cowman too, of course—and a good one. He was at one stage the largest cattle owner in Wharton and Matagorda counties, and he often boasted that he was the wealthiest. His wealth was in cattle only, though; land he simply used without bothering to own it. He was a free-range man and, except for a short period of time when he bought land in order to protect himself from the Pierces, he held in his own right only eleven acres of Texas property. He once had said that he "would rather leave the land than to buy a chunk of it," and subsequent developments gave him the chance to prove that he meant it.

This, apparently, was the cue that Shanghai needed. Although he had been of the same mind as all free-range men in earlier years, Shanghai saw that by buying land himself, he would be able to control the land which Grimes used without owners' rights, and this gave Shanghai cause to change his stand. He began investing—sometimes with Jonathan's approval, sometimes without—in properties which Pierce cattle already grazed, and then he chose carefully—piece by piece—the adjoining portions which would do the most damage to Grimes. He bought, when he could, the very sod from under the hoofs of Grimes' herds; and when this was not available, he bought the next best—land which eventually would encircle the acreage used by Grimes. Therefore, when he fenced the ranges he had purchased, Shanghai enclosed also the ranges which Grimes always had considered as free and open to his use. In this way the prairie could be kept open for Pierce's "critters," "wherever water ran and grass would grow," while Grimes' stock would be blocked out, or closed in.

This was hitting where the blows hurt worst. This forced Grimes, in spite if not in fright, to buy land also. He purchased 3,074 acres right in the "big middle of Shanghai's circle," and retained possession just long enough to put up a plank fence—"at great labor and expense"—to block passage to the Pierce property.[7] As a result of this brief lapse from his stand against land ownership, Grimes turned the tables on the Pierces to the extent that Shanghai backed up his brother's land-buying plans and, before either of them realized it, the Pierce brothers were working together with plans for fencing.

His feelings about Grimes had gnawed deep at the vitals of Abel Pierce for a long, long time. But even under the pressure of such vengefulness as he felt toward his old enemy, it is doubtful if Shanghai would have attempted to do anything which was not advantageous for the raising of cattle; at least he would not have tried anything which would be injurious to them. Evidently he had found that with the change from "vicious" to "obvious" types of barbed-wire fencing, the dangers which he had anticipated from this source were largely eliminated; evidently he had decided that cowmen could benefit after all from some of the practices concerned with owning and enclosing land. The chance to defeat Grimes was the spark which gave impetus to his new way of doings things, but the final factor which changed "Old

[7] *Ibid.*, 89.

Shang" Pierce from a "free grass man" to a landowner and builder of fences was the proven suitability of barbed wire as fencing for the prairie-plains. It was not easy for him to make the adjustment. Negative influences were stronger than positive ones in formulating his decision, but even drastic action was worth the effort so long as he was rid of Grimes.

The choice of fencing for the Pierce brothers was not, however, a matter to be taken lightly. It was costly and it was precedent-setting. The region of Pierce's domain was a land where both animal life and the elements tended toward extremes. Mainly stoneless and sparsely timbered except along the creek bottoms meandering from the horizon down to the sea, this land was rich and rolling, bathed in sunlight and sometimes swept by hurricanes. It would support nothing flimsy or fragile. Although hedges well rooted in the ground were stable and could be counted on for protection, there were not other kinds of native-fencing materials which would serve. Although hedge fences could be bought cheaply and planted quickly, they could not be grown fast enough to meet the needs where thousands of newly acquired acres were involved. Even hedges already grown were not equal to the demands of ranching on a large scale, yet Jonathan Pierce went right on planting them. He was planting rose hedges three days' journey from home when his son Abel B. was born in 1874—because they were the best windbreaks and boundaries he could provide. But it was essential that something more suitable should be found. He tried having timber hauled by oxen so that certain of his fields could be fenced off with logs, but since native timber was scarce and not suitable for splitting into rails, Jonathan was still on the search for some new material which would be adaptable to his needs.

Barbed wire meanwhile had come more and more into favor with Westerners generally, and even the Pierce brothers were watching it with interest. They noted the changes and improvements. They noticed too that livestock became accustomed to it in a shorter period of time than had been expected. Cattle avoided barbed-wire fences after very few experiences, and each successive generation of bovines became increasingly apt at discovering the hazards of direct contact. While man had made adaptations to the ways of animals and had altered manufacture accordingly, animals had made adaptations too. It was a happy combination of circumstances for manufacturers, a joy to A. H. Pierce to find that "critters" could learn so fast, and a boon to J. E. Pierce's over-all plans and ambitions for use of the land.

Shanghai called on an old friend, found him fencing, watched the results, and ended by ordering barbed wire. Any pretenses which he had practiced before were forgotten, any stalling for time was ended, any hope for returning to free range and open prairie relinquished. There had been advantages to waiting, but now the time had come when fencing would be more advantageous. Shanghai ordered wire of the same kind his friend was using: a flat, ribbon strip with flat barbs clamped on at five-inch intervals. The wide-strand wire was more easily visible than ordinary round wire, and the barbs stamped from metal plate were more obvious than barbs made of narrow twisted wire. It was, apparently, a Brinkerhoff design, patented in 1881—a good example of the type of wire manufactured and featured as a means of counteracting the objections which had been raised on "humanitarian" grounds. This wire was advertised as a type "more readily seen" and less likely "to hook into and tear the flesh." A short time later, south Texas hardware stores stocked Brinkerhoff wire, along with "Waukegan" and other of the famed Washburn & Moen Company products. But Shanghai sent his order, which he wrote out in his own hand, directly to Lambert and Bishop, Gates's "moonshine" confederates who operated in the "Barb Town" of the 1880's, Joliet, Illinois.

Jonathan had oak logs from the river bottoms hewn for corner posts, and he bought cedar boughs for the remainder of the fence lines. The six yoke of oxen used for plowing were put to work hauling—and, for the sake of sentiment, were later kept to haul wood to the Pierce houses until the day their driver, old "Uncle" Jimmy, died. Rancho Grande buzzed with activity as the Pierces put up fences fast and furiously—as fast as they could purchase the pieces of land which were calculated to do the greatest damage to W. B. Grimes. Land which Grimes by right of many years' occupancy had considered to be his own the Pierces encircled along with their own properties, and then they bought outright the pastures which Grimes was using. They fenced him around about; they fenced him out; and with rolls of prickered steel which made the feat possible, they drove him far to the north of their domain and out of the state of Texas.

Eventually A. H. "Shanghai" Pierce, as bitter an enemy as a man could have, was given the opportunity to purchase "all the property of Mr. W. B. Grimes—on Tres Palacios including every-thing—Except about ten acres—on which is the Family burial ground [the aforementioned eleven acres] for $10 000.00 Cash—Land, fences—Houses, barns—Machinery tools—of course cattle are not included."[8] Shanghai felt that at last the score was settled in his favor, and he was able to escape a little from the clutches of the great anger which had gripped him for so long. But he had only a brief respite, for Grimes was not yet moved so far away that the two could stay clear of each other forever.

In the course of a few years, Grimes settled with Major An-drew Drumm on the narrow Cherokee Outlet in Indian Terri-tory beyond the Texas Panhandle. His land was so situated as to lay athwart the trail which cattle from south Texas were bound to travel on the way to Kansas markets. Cold and bleak in winter as it was, in other seasons it was valuable pasture land for cattle that needed fattening after the long drive from the Texas Gulf Coast. It was open country, far removed from the green grasses of the coastal plains where Shanghai—thanks to barbed-wire fencing—had "run him off"; but it was real cow country. In spring and fall it offered the indispensable feed and water which trail animals at this point desperately required. But Matagorda Coun-ty cattle took the route through the Cherokee Outlet only once. Thereafter the Pierce brothers sent their herds by other trails to other markets, or—for reasons best described as "personal"—kept

8 *Ibid.*, 93.

the "critters" safe at home until such time as the railroad extending into Matagorda and Wharton counties during the 1890's came to the Tres Palacios for them.

CHAPTER 12

"STARTIN' IN TO PLAY H—— WITH TEXAS"[1]

Suddenly, in the 1880's, ownership of land seemed desirable to many important cattlemen of the Southwest, and in the wake of ownership came the need for protective fencing. Shanghai Pierce's shift from the policy of free range rights to the practice of land enclosure became typical of the era, as drift fences came down and line fences went up on all sides of controlled ranges. Suddenly it was acknowledged that barbed wire was the cowman's tool as well as the farmer's, a weapon to be used by and for stockmen instead of against them. A rash of new fences appeared in various sections of cow country, and this time it was the cattlemen who erected them.

Such a shift was little short of revolutionary, since it meant that certain far-seeing cowmen had forsaken the tradition of the Open Range. With the decline of injuries caused by the new fencing, acceptance of barbed wire by its biggest and bitterest adversaries—the buyers whom Ellwood and Sanborn and Gates had wanted most to reach—was in the offing at last.

The change was so sudden, however, that few people realized its far-reaching effects. Cattlemen simply enclosed the land which they intended to purchase, along with the parts already owned. Many Western interests were caught unprepared in the rift between influential cowmen buying and fencing huge sections of pasture land, and other cowmen still maintaining their hold on the ranges which they were accustomed to using. Small cattle-

[1] *Austin American Statesman* (June 13, 1937).

[152]

men who could not afford purchase of the acreage that they
needed; ranchers with a few head of cattle and a few acres of
their own, but no rights to near-by creeks and waterholes; sheepmen whose herds could not be held on limited ranges; and the
"landless gentry" of cowmen who owned very large herds but no
land—all were placed in jeopardy when barbed-wire fences were
erected as a sign of priority over very large tracts which cattle
"kings" controlled. And the situation was made more difficult because of the fact that land enclosed sometimes was not yet the
legal property of the fence-builder.

Cowmen justified their action in several ways. In the first
place, those intending to establish large ranches in most cases
expected to buy the land or to lease whatever portions they did
not buy. As a group they were in earnest in their plans to make
honorable settlement in one way or another—especially where the
state was concerned. When individuals in their group obstructed
action on leasing regulations or when lawmakers stalled passage
of leasing legislation, many leading cattlemen made sincere efforts to arrange for orderly payment of rental fees. Charles Goodnight, venerable "discoverer" of and virtual ruler of the Texas
Panhandle, for example, was involved in a long dispute over lease
terms. Although he did not accept leasing and fencing peaceably,
to prove that he was ready to pay rental to the state for use of
public lands, he once marched up the broad main street of Austin to the state capitol, with a husky man beside him pushing a
wheelbarrow full of lease money—over $100,000 in cash for his
own and the T-Anchors Ranch.[2] Colonel Goodnight, like others
of integrity, faced up to the consequences of mistaken judgment
on fencing, and where he or other men of strong character gave
direction to the cattlemen's groups, discord was reduced to a
minimum.

Trouble enough remained, however. Cattlemen enclosing
land adjacent to that which they owned—or proposed to own—
sometimes fenced in a homesteader's claim, a nester's planted
field, or a water hole prized by the rancher who leased or owned

[2] J. Evetts Haley, *Charles Goodnight*, 393.

[153]

rights to the water. Many times small operators were driven off of land which they had purchased outright. Cowmen behaved as if the range land was inherently theirs; they insisted that farm settlers had no business there anyhow because land west of the one-hundredth meridian never could be used advantageously for anything but ranges. Also they felt that they were not the only group responsible for injustices and continued unrest. They contended that farmers often moved into range areas purposely, and deliberately broke into the pattern of range life.

The biggest reason, though, for the cowmen's fierce fight to keep the range for themselves was the absolute necessity for extensive grazing grounds and for water. In order to protect investments already made and to plan feasible investments for the future, they were obliged to have range land; and suddenly they found that barbed-wire fencing offered the best means for securing it.

Once the owners of big herds, users of big ranges, began the land grab, small operators soon followed suit. But it was too late for some who found themselves fenced in, and too late for others who found themselves fenced out. The march of posts with wire encompassed everything—small flourishing ranches, newly staked settlers' claims, public roads, trails, watering places, and cultivated farm lands. Virtually every kind of Western inhabitant was affected at least indirectly. Few people realized, however, that a climax was at hand. Few understood that in the unraveling of so muddled a situation the patience of all parties would be tried to the breaking point. Few grasped the appropriateness of Big-Foot Wallace's commentary when he said that "bob wire" was "startin' in to play H—— with Texas."[3]

Big-Foot Wallace was a man with a lifetime of experience behind him when he spoke these words. No one doubted that he knew about exciting events and daring deeds of the past, but few people noticed what he had to say about barbed wire because no one thought of him as a commentator on developments of the future. His exploits as Indian scout and Texas Ranger had won wide

[3] *Austin American Statesman* (June 13, 1937).

[154]

acclaim, but in his late years he was generally thought of as something of an eccentric. The public paid him little heed, forgetting that his admonitions were predicated on a thorough knowledge of Texas and a rare understanding of Texans.

Though born in Virginia, William Alexander Anderson Wallace had come to Texas early in its history, arriving soon after the Battle of San Jacinto, where in 1836 Texas had won its independence from Mexico. He had gone as a member of the ill-fated Mier Expedition into Mexico, and had come back alive only because he was lucky enough to draw a white bean instead of a black one. He had ridden "probably the most dangerous mail route in all Texas . . . the road . . . lined on either side from San Antonio to El Paso with graves of those who had fallen . . . at the hands of Indians or . . . Mexicans."[4] He had covered Texas in one capacity or another from the Red River to the Río Grande, and had left his stamp on Texas legends all along the way. He was so big and broad that his arm-spread measured six feet, six inches; so bold that he wrestled in the dark with Indians greased in bear fat; and it was told in more than one folk fable that he ate "bob wire" for breakfast!

In the years of his retirement, when "in necessitous circumstances," he was granted 1,280 acres of land by act of the Twenty-first Texas Legislature.[5] It was said that he "was able to defend his little ranch out on the Medina River . . . from the ravages of Indians, Mexicans, cutthroats and thieves," but when civilization spread out in that section of Texas, Big-Foot was emphatically unable to withstand the advance of settlement and "the manipulations of the shrewd land sharks."[6] He who had recognized "trouble abrewin'" was himself caught in the fight as barbed wire caused dissension to burst into violence all around him.

Big-Foot Wallace's prediction was borne out by nature when, to the consternation of Westerners in general and the discomfiture of cowmen in particular, the weather continued to in-

[4] Wilbarger, *Indian Depredations in Texas,* 113.
[5] H. P. N. Gammel, *Laws of the State of Texas,* IX, 1396.
[6] Wilbarger, *Indian Depredations in Texas,* 114.

trude itself upon events affecting the fortunes of barbed wire. The same drought which in 1883 began the sequence of bad-weather cycles culminating in the disasters of 1884 and 1886, the same long, dry, hot summer which played a part in making acceptance of barbed-wire drift fences impossible, precipitated trouble for barbed-wire boundary fences also.

Any unusual dry spell in the semiarid plains regions meant that cattlemen required more extensive grazing lands than usual. When the scant grasses of one range were gone, cattle needed to be moved to another range, and when one watering place was dry, it was necessary to provide another very soon. In time of drought cattle ranged over great distances—or else they perished. By 1883 boundary fences recently constructed in the rush for land made impossible the normal movement of herds from one locality to another. Ranges already depleted by overstocking were quickly overgrazed, and cattle without access through privately owned property to the ranges beyond were stranded without nourishment. As the drought lengthened, grasses grew shorter and were sooner browned. As prairie fires attacked what little grass was left, even the prickly chaparrel was devoured. Creeks dried up, rivers crept along at their lowest and slowest. Cowmen saw their worst fears realized as heat and thirst drove weakened animals to their death, and in instances where the way to relief ranges was blocked by barbed-wire fences, "free grass men's" indignation drove them to new heights of anger, new threats of revenge.

All livestock owners who were dependent on free grazing agreed that in order to meet such an emergency they must combine forces. They saw that in spite of past differences, they must work together to open a way to whatever grass and water remained beyond the barbed-wire barriers. Small stockmen for the first time teamed with men who owned large herds and with ranchers who, in the spirit of the times, "took advantage of opportunities to brand stray cattle." In desperation the new alliance turned to cutting fences that retarded their passage to open country. Many an honest man who saw his defenseless cattle stopped by a fence, simply "snapped the wires like threads [to] let his cattle pass," and many a wrangler clipped the tight strands in his path. Honest or otherwise, all stockmen who had need to move their animals moved them. The builders of fences—big landowners and cattle "kings," some farmers, all who had erected boundary fences—were attacked from every angle, as well-meaning ranchers joined cattle thieves and disgruntled cowboys—strange bedfellows though they were—to wage war against barbed wire. The provocations of the day brought all opponents of fencing together, and drove them to the practice of fence-cutting, in protest against that unwanted commodity which was encircling the public domain and barricading the ranges, and which evidently had come to "play H——" not only with Texas but with the entire West also.

Texas was, however, as good a place as any to begin. It was different from other regions because of the fact that Texas was the only state which administered its own public land. In other states, unoccupied lands came under the jurisdiction of federal authorities, but since Texas alone had been an independent republic at the time of admission to the union, Texas alone retained control of the unoccupied lands within her boundaries. Moreover, Texas, California, and New Mexico, most of all among the Western states, had been opened up by Spanish governors who had offered large land grants, not only in appreciation of services rendered to the Spanish crown but also as inducement to settlers for the West; and Texas as a state continued to operate under the influence of the liberal Spanish land system designed to encourage large holdings. The Mexican government had granted one labor ($177\frac{1}{7}$ acres) to farming families, one league (4,428 acres) to cattle-raising families, and five leagues to each *empresario* who brought one hundred families to settle in Texas. The Republic had given land to veterans of the Texas War of Independence and the State of the Confederacy, and had made ample provisions for homesteaders. In 1850 a Texas farm averaged 951 acres, and on the unclaimed land there were many large sections held unofficially by so-called range rights.[7] With native cattle already in

[7] Dale, *The Range Cattle Industry*, 22–23.

the area and extensive stretches of range land still available at the close of the Civil War, Texas more than most areas offered a stable basis for cattle ranching; as a consequence, this vast region of "free" land, the public domain of Texas, soon came to be the main target of the range cattle industry.

It was in this capacity, as center of interest for cattle raisers, that Texas came to be also the center of friction over fencing and the site of armed encounters. Dissatisfaction with barbed wire was both ahead of and close behind acceptance of the product, so that wherever fences were put up there was protest as well as praise. Opposition to barbed wire always was strong in Texas. From the beginning, cattlemen contended that it was an injurious device which caused losses in range cattle; enemies of cattlemen later declared it to be the instrument of cattle kings who sought to usurp the public lands. Unfortunately, both accusations were partially true. There were many instances of cattle dying from infection of barbed-wire injuries, and many cases of unlawful enclosure of public property. Whereas the one was caused by a mechanical deficiency, the other was the reflection of a sociological prejudice; but whereas the one was quickly remedied, the other was not. Injury to animals had been but the first and outward sign of a deep and constant threat to every cattleman whose stock grazed free on unfenced range land. Long after the cry of "humanitarian" opponents was quieted, the cry of opponents to "monopoly" still held forth.

Under the system of fencing first and leasing or buying later, state-owned lands were particularly vulnerable to illegal occupancy, and by the time fence-cutting was undertaken, there were thousands of acres of unlawfully enclosed public land under fences in Texas. It was in protest against these unlawful procedures that fence-cutting was fundamentally conceived. It was illegal action which led to illegal reaction, for fence-cutters in the beginning were concerned not so much with destroying barbed wire fences per se as with removing them from the free and unoccupied areas which belonged to the public and had been administered by the government as Open Range.

[158]

Fence-cutting generally was started by individuals or small groups of men with clear consciences—or very nearly so. Upright citizens, believing in their rights and accustomed to upholding them, were for some time the chief offenders in Texas and elsewhere. Barbed wire was too new, too unexpected; boundaries, too little known to Westerners. Unless or until they learned better how to live with the wire, men naturally tried to get it out of the way in the easiest manner possible, and in so doing they naturally clipped the wire and left it dangling from the posts. But by this simple action, they triggered more hostility and alarm than had been loosed upon the Texas grazing lands since the Mexican military forces under Santa Anna were sent scurrying homeward across the Río Grande. Fence-cutting in Texas flared into unofficial warfare almost overnight.

It has been said that the first fence cut in Texas was on the Hawkeye Cattle Company land in Frio County, and it has been intimated that the act was instigated by none other than W. A. A. "Big-Foot" Wallace, champion of the cowman's cause. It has been stated that Wallace's feeling on the subject was that "the men who whipped the Indians out of the country should have first choice of the range."[8] But whether this was an accurate report or not, whether Big-Foot was in any way responsible, or whether his name was linked with the affair entirely by circumstance, the fact is that Frio and Medina counties in the vicinity of Wallace's ranch constituted one of the main hot-spot centers of the fence wars in Texas. The other areas of greatest activity by fence-cutters were Clay County in the northern part of the state, Navarro and Limestone counties in the eastern part, and the central Texas counties of Brown and Coleman, though actions of men in these regions were repeated on a small scale throughout hundreds of miles of Texas range land.

Although the four centers of fence-cutting were located in different directions, they were contained within an area extend-

[8] Roy D. Holt, "The Introduction of Barbed Wire into Texas and the Fence Cutting War," *West Texas Historical Association Yearbook* (June, 1930), 74.

[159]

ing like a band through the middle of the state. It was a band of farm settlement bordering on grazing land. Neither far-east Texas nor the southernmost regions of the state saw as much actual conflict as the central regions, because the southern and eastern sections were generally accepted as agricultural areas. The Panhandle was the least affected of all because there were at the time mainly big cattle interests there. There was no line to mark range from grange, and on the edges of the plains cowmen still resisted pressure from advancing settlement and still expected to counteract it, but the Panhandle-plains proper was strictly cow country. It was where the two met, where some men farmed and some did not, that the trouble was worst. One man was killed just west of the one-hundredth meridian—Pat Warren at Sweetwater—and outside of Texas many men lost their lives in quarrels over Western fencing practices, but in the Texas fence-cutters war, most violence was concentrated where agriculture bordered the range.

Had the men engaged in fence-cutting continued to be only those who honestly needed to move their herds under stress of unusual circumstances, or men who honestly undertook to right the wrongs of unlawful fencing of unoccupied lands, their stand might have been exonerated on the basis of Western standards of their day and might eventually have been vindicated by history. But unfortunately another element joined the ranks. Bands of thieves and cattle rustlers along with other lawless groups saw the opportunity to cover up their wrongdoings by posing as protectors of the mistreated "little men," and they welcomed the chance to become the confederates of those wronged by the monopolistic cattle interests. The appearance of these irresponsible individuals in the midst of the conflict over fencing caused unnecessary bloodshed and violence. Their participation hastened and extended the spread of fighting, so that soon lawful as well as unlawful fencing fell under attack. In the wake of their heedless actions, fence-cutting flashed like a wildfire in the prairie grasslands, and it blackened the face of Texas ranges with shame.

One of the most unfortunate aspects of the fence wars was the formation of reckless gangs or "clubs," as they were some-

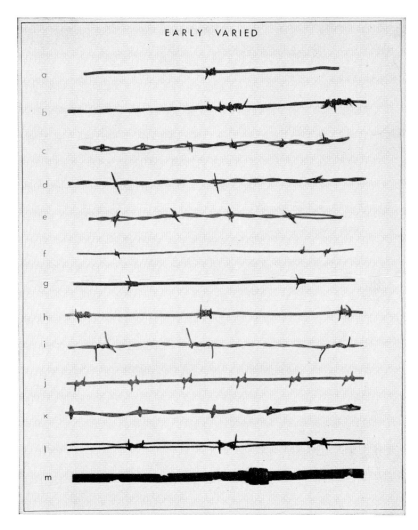

Early types of armored fencing usually controlled livestock by inflicting physical injury, and a wide variety of patterns resulted from the variety of concepts of this experimental trend. For example: *a,* Glidden's square wire; *b,* Glidden's "Twist Oval"; *c,* Glidden's "The Winner"; *d,* Kelly's "Thorny Fence"; *e,* Haish's "S"; *f,* Baker's single strand; *g,* Kennedy's three-point; *h,* Merrill's "Hold-Fast"; *i,* homemade two-point; *j,* Sunderland's "Kink"; *k,* "Corsicana Clip"; *l,* Nadelhoffer parallel; *m,* Harbrough's torn ribbon wire.

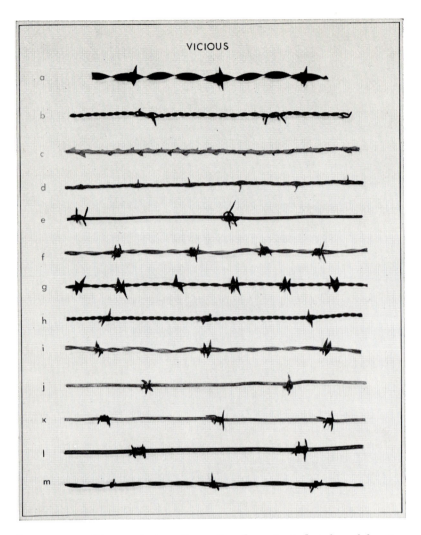

Inventors seeking variations from already patented styles of fencing often designed large and damaging barbs which inflicted injury on livestock. Some of these *vicious* styles were: *a*, "Brink Twist"; *b*, Mighell's two-point; *c*, "Wrap-Around" (as made by Cary's machine); *d*, "Tack-Underwood"; *e*, Reynolds' "Necktie"; *f*, Ross's four-point; *g*, "Arrow-Plate"; *h*, Scutt's "M/W"; *i*, "Scutt's Clip"; *j*, Wing's "Two-Staple"; *k*, Glidden reissue No. 6914; *l*, Merrill's "Buffalo Wire"; *m*, Brotherton (large).

times called, organized to co-ordinate the work of destroying fences. Such groups were generally composed almost entirely of the outlaw element, and even when made up mostly of serious-minded, responsible citizens, if there was one hardened, quick-on-the-trigger character in the lot, eventually the action of the whole group was likely to be colored by this one man's attitude. They stood more "against" everything than "for" anything, and they were very hard to come to terms with.

Although there were cases which sometimes could be settled amicably between individuals, there was seldom any easy solution in cases where gangs were involved. Whereas it was said that occasionally an individual stockman might agree to open his gates for his neighbor's cattle to come to water during drought, it was known that reconciliation was difficult with groups. The clubs sometimes retaliated against fence-builders not only by cutting the fence wires, but also by dragging away the fence posts and burning them.[9] It was not uncommon, in fact, for the same fences to be cut more than once by the same gangs, who would wait for the owner to complete repairs and then renew their attack. Under the circumstances, friendship and trust turned bitter to the taste, and all attempts at co-operation were summarily laid aside.

Gradually the rougher class took over most fence-cutting organizations, and with increased daring their clubs or so-called companies posted notes of warning signed with the company's name or mark. R. D. Holt tells that in Karnes County, Texas, a notice to "let your wire stay down" was signed with a drawing of a hatchet and the letters "Co.", representing Hatchet Company; and a farmer in Falls County received a notice saying, "We, the wire cutters, inform you not to fence no pasture land, for we will not suffer for it any longer. Don't spend any money to be wasted for we will cut it as fast as you can build it. This is a fair warning for all. [signed] 'Rolling Fence-Cutters' We do what we say." A certain "Mob No. 1" operated in central Texas, and fur-

---

[9] Wayne Gard, "The Fence-Cutters," *Southwestern Historical Quarterly* (July, 1947); Roy D. Holt, "The Saga of Barbed Wire in Tom Green County," *West Texas Historical Association Yearbook* (June, 1928), 32 ff.

ther to the south the "Blue Devils" and "Javelinas" struck out with vengeance against all enclosed pasture areas.[10]

Incidents compiled and retold by Wayne Gard in his article "The Fence-Cutters" include mention of the cutting of "every strand of wire" which Shanghai Pierce had strung around "about three leagues" of coastal land, of nineteen miles of fence cut "between each pair of posts" in some west Texas counties, of coffins left as warnings against the refencing of sections once cut, of burned pastures, of threats of poisoning, and of shootings. Gard says that "possession of a pair of nippers was a badge of membership in the resistance movement. Conversely, seeing a pair in a neighbor's pocket was ground for suspicion."[11]

Fence-cutters were hard to identify and harder to catch. They carried no loot, they worked mostly by night and often wore masks, they had no weapon (except in extreme cases) save nippers or pliers, left no trail except to the homes or ranch headquarters of friends and neighbors, and since these friends and neighbors also were antagonistic toward fencing, the trail of suspicion spread everywhere but settled nowhere in particular. The difficulty was, as Walter P. Webb described it, that "the fence-cutter carried no evidence of his deed. The horse thief was caught with the horse and the cow thief with the cow, but the fence-cutter rode away from the curling steel tendrils with no evidence upon him. He had to be caught on the job."[12] Written threats left tied to dangling wires were so worded as to throw some light on the identity of aggressor groups, but even with such a clue the fence-owner found it hard to pin the offense on individual members of the group. Also there was difficulty in gathering together a jury to convict fence-cutters, since many times the sympathies of the entire area would favor the fence-cutters.

There was needless provocation displayed by parties on both sides of the quarrel, and if there were only a few deaths recorded in connection with fence-cutting, there was plenty of shooting,

[10] Roy D. Holt, "The Fence-Cutters' War in Sign and Rhyme," *Dallas Morning News* (October 20, 1929).
[11] "The Fence-Cutters," *loc. cit.*
[12] *The Texas Rangers*, 426.

and plenty of cutting done under cover of drawn six-shooters which would have been fired if necessary. In Navarro County, disturbances continued for so long that special deputies were sent there in disguise. There was one killing each in Clay and Brown counties, and in the latter location cowmen once barricaded themselves in the courthouse facing farmers and small stockmen who had "holed up" in the opera house, both with guns loaded. At Brownwood, Walter Taber, at age ninety-one, had no personal recollections of this episode except to recall that it was settled without loss of life; but Mr. Taber still remembered well his own experiences as a boy sent on his horse in the dark of night to warn neighbors that fence-cutters were on the way. The urgency of his mission was impressed on him, he said, with the words, "Let no one stop you." As it happened, no one did. He met only one rider, and the two passed in the dark without incident; next day he discovered that the rider had been a boy of his own age, his friend, sent on the same kind of mission and with the same grave warning ringing in his ears.

Intimidation by threat led sometimes to outright murder, and there is no way to know how many killings in the long dry months of autumn were never recorded. It is clear that within the short period of time from drought to the beginning of snows, fence-cutting in Texas reached the proportions of open warfare, and although less than one year old, fence-cutting was regarded as a serious threat to orderly development of all Western settlements. In 1883, Governor John Ireland made a personal visit to Clay, Hunt, Denton, Wise, Tarrant, and Coleman counties. In October he called for a special session of the Texas legislature to deal with the problem. The legislature was not scheduled to meet for regular session until January, 1884, however, and in the meantime fence-cutting in Texas continued unabated. Property losses mounted. The value of Texas lands decreased, the demand for them dwindling into insignificance. Some recently arrived settlers fled, and few newcomers appeared to take their places. By the new year, Texas was in a foment of dissension. Progress in both farming and cattle-raising was thoroughly disrupted, and the state government was in a position of uncertainty with regard to both management of the public lands and rulings on private holdings.

The classic illustration of conditions at the time is the account of a Coleman County stockman's experience while in Chicago to arrange for a loan on his ranch property. He had lost sheepfolds, shepherd's houses, two thousand cedar posts, and his fences were cut. It was because he needed funds for repairs that H. R. Starkweather sought the loan. In the midst of negotiations, it was announced that a Chicago newspaper had come out with headlines, "HELL BREAKS LOOSE IN TEXAS," and with the news that wire-cutters had destroyed five hundred miles of fencing in Coleman County, the very place where the borrowed money was to be used. Mr. Starkweather plainly understood his position. He arose from the conference table without a word and left on the next train for Texas.[13]

Roy Bedichek, in his "come-alive" account of an experience recalled from his childhood, described conditions on his ranch:

> ... At sundown I saw stretching for miles across the gently rolling and virgin prairie a lately completed barbed-wire fence, four shining strands of galvanized Glidden held up by cedar posts peeled and weathered to the shade of old ivory and set solidly eight feet apart. It was the first real fence I had ever seen, and I had watched the workmen building it, wide-eyed with wonder. But at that it was an interest mingled with fear instilled by half-heard murmurs against fencing up the country. Men sitting around the general store on Saturday afternoons didn't like it a bit.
> During the night a frightful transformation had occurred. Each tightly stretched strand had been cut between each pair of posts, and the wire had curled up about them, giving the line as it led away into the sun a frizzled appearance, as of a vicious animal maddened so that every particular hair stood up on end. I was speechless. I couldn't for the moment call anyone to come and see what had happened.

[13] Starkweather later sold the ranch, but during the whole of his tenure there he was beset with fencing troubles. Charles W. Towne and Edward N. Wentworth, *Shepherd's Empire*, 138.

. . . [And yet I must confess that] every time a dog ran afoul of one of those cursed fences and split his noble back from neck to tail, my hatred flamed up against them. I sympathized with the fence cutters, no matter how much I heard them condemned by my elders.[14]

Despite sympathy, however, strong censure was recommended in the special session of the Texas Legislature. One proposal went so far as to make justifiable the shooting and killing of any man caught in the act of cutting fences. Another suggestion was to the effect that any man caught carrying pincers or wire-cutters should be charged on suspicion. The final bill passed by the legislature, however, appeared to be an attempt to meet the situation squarely and to prescribe reasonable measures for improving it. Regulations governing the specifications for the building of new fences were argued at length; then, due to the seriousness of the emergency, the new rulings were rushed through without the usual three readings.

It was finally decided that all public roads should be kept open, and a gate should be provided in every third mile of fencing which touched on public roads. It was declared a misdemeanor to fence without consent of landowners. A fifty-thousand-dollar appropriation was granted for the enforcement of the emergency acts covering "the wanton and willful cutting [throwing down or otherwise] injuring or destroying" of fencing. The Texas Rangers were called to police areas of danger, by authority of the state, and fence-cutting was summarily declared a felony, punishable by one to five years' imprisonment. The end of the trouble in Texas was then almost in sight. Some few cases dotted the court ledgers, especially during drought years, for nearly a decade; it could be said that in Texas the years from 1880 to 1890 were marred by such happenings. But thanks to the special legislation, the Texas fence-cutters' war was ended less than one year after it started.

The trouble in Texas was more concentrated and more precipitate than in other states and territories, and as a consequence

[14] *Adventures of a Texas Naturalist*, 5 f.

Texas was sooner rid of it. Since other states did not administer their public lands, they were not able to meet the problem with such dispatch. Federal action covering states other than the cattle-raising states required still further time for enactment. It was twelve to eighteen months after the Texas ruling of February, 1884, before new fencing laws were accepted nationally, and fence problems still dragged into the beginning of the new century. But in the state where barbed-wire fencing played the most havoc with the development of farms and ranches from open range, action of the special session of the Eighteenth Legislature still serves as a permanent deterrent to night-riders and fence-snippers. The law still stands; fence-cutting is still a felony in Texas.

CHAPTER 13

"IMPROVEMENTS" ON THE PUBLIC DOMAIN

THE END OF FENCE-CUTTING in Texas meant the end of free range for Texas cowmen, and they knew it. They had attempted to set back the clock by preventing the breaking up of open grasslands, and they had failed. If they were to continue in the range cattle business, they would be obliged to follow one of two courses: either they had to acquire rights to the land they were using, or they had to move on. Those men who could not or would not pay for owning or leasing ranges in Texas had but one alternative: to turn their herds toward what remained of Open Range on the public lands of other Western states and territories.

This was the course taken by W. B. Grimes when the Pierce brothers erected their circle of fencing to force him off the coastal plains. He had given up his brief experiment with the purchase of land, concluding that it was better to leave it than to own "a chunk of it." He had joined the exodus of landless lords of the cattle industry driving their Texas-bred stock to the plains of Colorado, Wyoming, Montana, and the Dakota Territory—which was, incidentally, the very region where Shanghai had meant that Grimes should go.

When he had threatened "to put Grimes on the Black Hills," Shanghai had not only meant that he wished to have his rival as far away as possible, but he had meant also to ruin him, for the Black Hills country was "a place in the cattleman's geography comparable to hell itself."[1] As it turned out, Grimes went only to

[1] Douglas, "Cattle Kings of Texas," *loc. cit.,* 13–16.

Indian Territory of present-day Oklahoma, and into parts of Kansas. Shanghai was denied the satisfaction of seeing his enemy pushed to the Dakota Badlands, but with Grimes established in the Cherokee Strip, Shanghai could claim to have sent him at least that far on the way.

Grimes combined interests with Major Andrew Drumm, a onetime California gold miner who had begun ranching operations on the Cherokee Strip in the years 1865 to 1870. Drumm had been one of the first cowmen in the area, and was instrumental in dealing with the Five Civilized Tribes holding title to the narrow two-hundred-mile strip of prairie along the northern boundary of Indian Territory.[2] Although the Indians owned the land, they had not the authority to lease it without approval from the United States government. They were empowered, though, to levy a tax on cattle driven through the Territory, and it had become the custom for cowmen to secure grazing permits from the Indians also. Some cowmen used the permits over extended periods, even to the point of maintaining permanent herds and erecting fences to guard them. Since the federal government did not recognize the grazing permits and had allowed only for collection on passage through the Territory, the "improvements" put up by cowmen were entirely unauthorized. As one cowman admitted, "Every man with enterprise enough to build a fence has the intelligence to know that we have no permanent rights in the Indian Territory."[3] Yet fencing continued because cowmen felt that as long as they paid tax tribute, they were justified in protecting their investment.

By the year 1882, when Grimes was taking part in the proceedings, federal authorities were receiving many complaints from the area. Cowmen were accused of erecting unusually large enclosures which broke into both range and trail. Bitterness was strong against all the cowmen fencing on Indian Territory, and

[2] The name "Cherokee Outlet" referred to that piece of land which had been granted to the Cherokee Nation as "perpetual outlet to the west" from whence came that all-important food for the Indians—buffalo.

[3] Letter of B. H. Campbell to Secretary of Interior, January 2, 1883. *Sen. Exec. Doc. No. 54*, 48 Cong., 1 sess., IV, 132.

the feeling was building to a climax. The Department of Interior which administered the lands undertook a study of the situation and verified the fact that illegal fencing in the Cherokee Strip definitely was "out of hand." Consequently, on December 2, 1882, the Commissioner of Indian Affairs directed the Indian Agent to notify stock owners who had "improvements of any character," or "materials upon the ground for the purpose," that all such improvements and materials should be removed from the lands "within *twenty days* . . . [or] the removal will be made by the military."[4]

The short time allotted for undoing a system of land usage which had been in the making for a matter of years proved to be untenable, and the threat of using soldiers was judged as hasty, to say the least. Letters, wires, petitions, pleas from legislators, and inquiries from attorneys poured into the Interior Department, and the War Department was worried about legal protection for troops that might be engaged in the matter. The strongest opposition came from cowmen of the Cherokee Strip who found themselves caught by surprise and in no way prepared to make so sudden a change. There seemed to be little prospect that they could arrange a quick substitute for the fences confining their herds. They could not even move the structures elsewhere, if that had been legal. "To remove means to destroy," as one cowman explained it, "for the fences torn down would not bear transportation to the nearest point in the State of Kansas."[5] Andrew Drumm echoed the plea, "respectfully requesting" a delay of action, and an extension of time was urged on the Department from all sides. As a result of the furor, the removal order was held in suspension while the government investigated further.

The Cherokee Strip Live Stock Association, with Drumm as one of the original directors, was formed to help smooth out difficulties. The Association signed an agreement with the Indian representative, Dennis W. Bushyhead, whereby the Association as a whole leased the Strip as a whole, and it was hoped that the

[4] H. Price to John Quincy Tufts, *ibid.*, 131.
[5] Campbell to Secretary of Interior, *ibid.*, 133.

federal government might sanction the arrangement. At this point, however, settlers and would-be homesteaders protested. This group pressed for the opening of Indian Territory to white settlement, and the old resentments between rancher and granger flared anew in an atmosphere now complicated by the Indian element.

United States Land Commissioner N. C. McFarland in 1883 published a reminder that cattlemen had no rights to fence federally controlled property, and he stated further that, when bona fide settlers were prevented "by barriers, threats, or force from lawfully acquiring lands," the settlers would be upheld in destroying fences.[6] President Grover Cleveland in 1885 issued a proclamation forbidding the construction of enclosures on any public land, and the next administration under President Benjamin Harrison continued with efforts to settle the problem. One of Shanghai Pierce's cronies who purchased "Matagorda Sea Lions" and pastured them on the Cherokee Strip wrote to Shanghai early in Harrison's administration: "Don't Let a Litle things [sic] Like Father Ben's order bother you"; but it was not long before the writer changed his tune. He began to bother himself considerably because he did not know where he would put his stock since soldiers were "hooping up the cattle off the Strip. [with] No foolishness this time."[7]

This time the government was in earnest. The cowmen would have to go. Finally in 1890 the cattlemen were driven out of Indian Territory, and three years later a portion of the Strip was opened to white settlers. But as long as the Indians retained parts of the Territory, they continued to make leases with cattlemen seeking grass.

In the meantime, government authorities were also busy with problems of fencing on other government-regulated properties. Because the Cherokee Strip had been assigned to the Indians and was merely administered by the government, provisions for its control were different from provisions pertaining to

[6] *Sen. Exec. Doc. No. 54*, 48 Cong., 1 sess., XXVIII, 30.
[7] Emmett, *Shanghai Pierce*, 230 f.

other areas; because Texas had retained supervision of its own public lands, its rules too were different. But outside Texas and Indian Territory, all public lands of the nation were under one set of rules upheld by the United States Department of Interior. To this arm of government fell the responsibility for preserving those vacant and unclaimed areas which constituted the public domain.[8]

Created initially from the cession of "land states," after the American Revolution, the United States public domain had been enlarged periodically by treaty, by further grants from states, by conquest, and by purchase.[9] Government policies for disposing of the lands had fluctuated across the years, becoming generally more strict as land became more scarce, but the general intent of government administration was rooted in the premise that upon proper application and minimum expenditure, a citizen might secure a portion of the land as personal property. The public domain was seen as land upon which a man could set up a home on his own quarter-section, and government rules of land distribution were designed accordingly.

The price of land varied but slightly from the normal $1.25 per acre. Since land was bought by the government for much less—Louisiana for $.036, Florida for $.17, the Gadsden Purchase for $.34, and Alaska for $.02 an acre—it would seem that the government tended to profiteer.[10] It is estimated, however, that the sale of lands actually did not amount to much in over-all profits. Many acres were sold at $1.25, but many more were given away free. "All the land sold in the 150-year period [of expansion] yielded less revenue to the federal government than the

[8] The General Land Office was first under the Treasury Department, but after 1849 it was operated by the Department of Interior.

[9] Arrell Morgan Gibson, "Utilization of the Public Domain of the Central and Northern Plains by the Range Cattle Industry, 1865–1900," MS in the University of Oklahoma Library, 2 ff. "There never was any public domain [federally owned] in the original thirteen states, nor Kentucky, Maine, Vermont, West Virginia, Texas, or Tennessee." Harry Kursh, *How to Get Land from Uncle Sam*, 17.

[10] William Atherton DePay, *Uncle Sam's Modern Miracles*, 129.

taxes on tobacco yield in an average six months period [of the twentieth century]."[11]

By the early 1880's a system of land disposal was well established, but it was a system which failed to take into account the special needs and necessities of that new segment of population which was attempting to settle the untested regions beyond the last frontiers. Government land policies at this point were not satisfactory to those people already occupying the West, and were not likely to attract others to the region. Farmers and cowmen alike decried the deficiencies in various provisions of federal land laws; and although the two factions continued to disagree on many issues, this was one subject upon which they could agree. There was one difficulty common to them both, for as occupants of the plains and prairie-plains regions, they shared a common need. They required more land.

West of the one-hundredth meridian the man who was dependent on forcing a livelihood from the untimbered and arid plains or even from the semiarid prairie-plains was in need of more liberal land laws. He could not operate with profit under the same amount of acreage allowable in Eastern areas. Whereas an 80-acre holding was considered satisfactory for an average family farming in the East, 360 acres or more were necessary for comparable families farming in the West. Where 10 to 15 acres of grassy meadow per animal would suffice in the uplands, on arid lands 25 to 100 acres would be needed. Land laws which had been set up on the basis of experience in older parts of the country had no application to the new regions; yet, with a few exceptions such as the situation in Texas, laws governing east and west, north and south, wet and dry, cold and hot were all the same. The historic Homestead Act—which has been called "the most important piece of land legislation ever passed by Congress"—signed by President Lincoln in 1862, had provided that in accordance with certain stipulations "each actual settler was to receive a farm of 160 acres without cost." But as settlement advanced farther onto the plains and as the range cattle business

[11] Gibson, "Utilization of the Public Domain," *loc. cit.*, 7 n.

[172]

increased, fewer and fewer settlers considered 160 acres as adequate. Moreover, in the arid and semiarid sections, water rights were involved, for whoever held the land upon which water was found held control of surrounding land also. Neither nesters nor cowmen could last much longer without legislation to remedy the situation.

Finally, at the end of the decade, two new laws were enacted specifically for the relief of Westerners. In actual application both laws fell far short of expectations, but since the main provision in each was to allow for the acquisition of additional land, they were moves in the right direction. The Desert Land Act of 1877 provided for a 320-acre claim, on the condition that the entry be made on arid land which the entryman would reclaim "by conducting water thereon within four years from the date of his application." The Timber and Stone Act of 1878 allowed for grants in areas where timber and/or stone made the land unfit for agriculture; but this Act limited the amount of acreage by stating that an applicant could not claim under this or under any other public land laws "any other lands which with the land for which he applies would aggregate more than 320 acres." In other words, one law was too hard and the other too limiting. Few settlers could be expected to supply the irrigation required for improving "desert" lands, and although 320 acres of "timber" land were not enough, most newcomers preferred farming this rough region to struggling with the unfamiliar plains country where they were not wanted anyhow. For the time being cattlemen were left pretty much to their own devices as farm families generally shunned the plains and prairies; and this being the case, cattlemen took into their own hands the laws which had been meant to aid their rivals, and turned the stipulations of each succeeding land act to their own advantage.

Since national legislation actually did not supply them with what was needed for developing the plains and prairies, cowmen began to feel that the region they sought, the vast range lands of the West, was of all sections of the nation the least understood and least attended. They were disappointed and discouraged.

Some gave up and moved again, still farther north into Canada where land laws already were being designed to attract the range cattle industry. But those who remained—despite everything—to occupy the great open areas in mid-continent America, to utilize the native grasslands as feeding grounds for the progeny of cows brought up from the Gulf Coast breeding grounds, these owners of large herds interpreted the laws to satisfy their own requirements. Where there was a local tax on "improvements," they turned it to their advantage by claiming "possession rights," and they pre-empted other properties under various pretexts. They set out to acquire land by one means or another; and, as matters stood, the Desert Land Act looked like the best means at hand. Because the act did not require claimants to establish residence within the bounds of the property filed on, cattle ranchers could easily lay claim to a number of plots simultaneously by filing individual entries under the names of ranch employees. And this they did, in violation of the intent but well within the letter of the law.

An influential cowman had only to pick out an area adjacent to that on which he himself held legal title, fence it in along with his rightful property, and then send his cowboys to file on the part needed to fill out the enclosure. After the entry was executed, the cowboys sold the land—with "improvements"— to the rancher for a nominal price, and the patent was deeded over to the cowman who had instigated the filing. In addition to these "ranch hands claims," sometimes men used fictitious names, or the names of illiterate newcomers and/or unknowing persons still residing "back in the old home counties" of Eastern states. Sometimes public lands were fenced inside privately owned areas. Occasionally the description of "desert" lands and the explanation of water provisions were deliberately falsified. And in the event a nester should be already occupying a portion of the land needed, sometimes he was forcibly ejected. Land was of such importance that in order to own and control it, cowmen were willing to file fraudulent claims and excuse themselves on the grounds that the inadequacies of the law justified such action. By deception and by force they consolidated extensive holdings, in direct defiance of the spirit of the Desert Land Act.

In fairness to the cowmen, however, it should be remembered that before taking the law into their own hands, they had tried to secure the land which they needed by good and legal processes. They petitioned for legislation. They proposed a lease system. They fought against the practices of overgrazing and overstocking of open lands. And they believed in their hearts—and by reason of their experience—that actually the land that they used was natural grazing land, unfit for cultivation and the plow. They insisted that in order to protect investments which they already had made, they were obliged to resort to force—and to fencing. So saying, they proceeded to enclose the areas that they meant to hold, including if necessary both privately owned plots and portions of the public domain.

Cases of illegal fencing crowded the ledgers of all plains and prairie states during the 1880's. Early in the decade, letters from indignant citizens poured into the General Land Office of the United States Department of Interior, indicating that the enclosure of public lands was widespread, and still spreading. In most cases the size of the enclosures was immense, and it was usually for this reason that private protests were made and inspectors were sent to investigate. In 1883 it was reported that fences 20 to 50 miles long were erected by one rancher in Nebraska. Another report stated that "bales of wire" were used to enclose "125,000 acres for the use of 6,000 head of cattle," and in this case the rancher was said to be "still fencing." Sheepmen wrote in from the Idaho Territory where sheep were being forced back "upon the bleak hills" while cattle ranged the good grasslands. A mail carrier obliged to cross fences on his route through public lands in Nebraska; small stock owners in Kansas; settlers in Wyoming, New Mexico, Utah—all complained to authorities. In Montana a rancher tried to evade trouble by leaving 1¼ miles unfenced in an enclosure many miles long. He claimed that because of this open strip he did not commit illegal enclosure, although he had cowboys patrolling the opening constantly. Some of the most serious reports came from Colorado. There one rancher was said to have enclosed both ends of a rather extensive canyon, Mancos Canyon; and a large cattle company was accused of illegal pre-emption "with posts and wire fences" to take in a total of 600,000 acres "or thirty townships of the public domain." In all there were probably 1,000,000 acres under enclosure in Colorado, and most of it was public property.

Fencing without authorization was as flagrant and as frequent as was the destruction of fences. Newspapers and farm journals reflecting conditions in Texas contended that "the stretching of barbed wire half across large counties inclosing lands that belong to the state, is, or should be, as great a crime against the state as fence cutting."[12] Barbed wire lent itself to construction as well as destruction; yet there was a difference. Whereas the unlawful taking down of fences was aimed mainly against private owners, the unlawful putting up of barbed wire on public lands was an offense against the United States government. Some illegal fences were drift fences, some were false claim enclosures, but most were cases of outright pre-emption of public lands. Some states attempted to check trouble by levying state taxes on fencing, but by this means the fence-builders gained the advantage of "possessory rights," and the state won no lands back for the federal government. Cowmen and farmers were contending against each other inadvertently in this matter, for most of the fence-building offenses actually were perpetrated not so much against rival individuals or rival groups as against the general public of the United States—whether by intent or not. It was land belonging to the United States citizenry which was being usurped in most cases, and therefore it was necessary that the United States government should take steps to end the abuses.

Much was made of the point that individuals all across the nation were affected. Propaganda suggested that future generations were being deprived of their rightful heritage, that "the children's grass" was being pre-empted by greedy cattle kings.

[12] *The Texas Farmer* (1883).

Since sympathies already were aligned with settlers—"permanent citizens," "dwellers on the soil," "the bone and sinew of the country"—there were outraged protests registered from all across the land. Most of these complaints were sent to the General Land Office, Department of the Interior, Washington; most regions continued to look toward federal authorities for prohibitory action.

By an old law of 1807 the President was empowered to direct the United States marshals to take down illegal fences, and many people thought that by this provision the wrongs of the late 1800's could be righted. But the problem was not so simple. It was not easy to prove fraud. The tricks of the trade were many and devious. Also, both factions in the fight for control of Western lands were guilty to some degree, since there were some instances where farm settlers also had to be charged with the same illegal enclosure practices which had been attributed to the cowmen. The fact that government inspectors were often fooled by makeshift improvements made matters worse. Where a habitable house was required as condition for claiming patent on a homestead, a log cabin on wheels sometimes was moved from place to place to create a pretense at occupancy of several claims. False descriptions of land claimed to be unfit for agriculture because of timber or stone, juggling of water rights on so-called desert lands, and similar misrepresentations of fact were not always promptly spotted. By and large, the federal government did little to end illegal acquisition of the public domain until the middle of the decade.

Finally Congress gave warning of things to come when on February 25, 1885, a statute was passed, directly stating that "construction and maintenance of inclosures on the public land" were forbidden. The new law, aiming straight at big cattlemen and big cattle companies, declared:

> No person, by force, threats, intimidation, or by any fencing or inclosing, or any other unlawful means, shall prevent or obstruct, or shall combine and confederate with others to prevent or obstruct, any person from peaceably entering upon or estab-

[177]

lishing a settlement or residence on any tract of public land subject to settlement or entry under the public land laws of the United
States, or shall prevent or obstruct free passage or transit over or
through public lands; provided, this section shall not be held to
affect the right or title of persons, who have gone upon, improved,
or occupied said lands under the land laws of the United States,
claiming title thereto, in good faith.[13]

On August 7 of the same year, by proclamation of the President, came the directive which had been in the offing since the
Commissioner of Indian Affairs issued his order of December 2,
1882. President Cleveland ordered all unlawful enclosures removed from public lands, and he "forbade any threats or intimi-
dations against actual settlers on the public domain."[14]

The federal government had given right of occupancy to
bona fide settlers and/or legal claimants; the federal government
did not intend to have the right nullified by private interests. The
President had spoken. The processes of government went into
high gear. It was clear at last that federal authority was to be
exercised in the administration of its land legacy.

Before government action could be undertaken on a wide
scale, individual interests were lined up as for battle. Farmers
shot cattle that roamed onto cultivated fields. Cowmen tore down
protective fences and burned crops. Settlers were accused of being the thieves who concealed straying cattle. Sometimes actual
thieves stole the few head of cattle belonging to settlers and small
ranchers, mixed them with animals rustled from big herds, and
in this way further sabotaged the usual identification processes.
Rustlers allied with legitimate landowners to destroy the fences
of big cattle owners; small cattlemen and well-meaning settlers
conspired to keep their own fences up; and cowmen, fighting a
losing fight in defense of the Open Range, tried to retaliate with
barbed wire—the same defensive weapon that farmers had used
against them. "Improving the country" was a two-way action,

[13] *United States Code*, Vol. IV, Title 43 (1946), Chap. 149, 3, 23, Stat.
322.
[14] *United States Statutes at Large*, XXIII, 321–22; XXIV, 1024. James
D. Richardson, ed., *Messages and Papers of the Presidents*, VII, 4893–94.

with one side and then the other crying vengeance on such "improvements."

There were proportionately fewer outbreaks of fence-cutting affecting United States public domain than on the public lands of Texas, but the murder and mayhem committed in battles waged throughout the West as a whole exceeded anything else which had affected the range cattle industry, short of Indian massacre. As had been the case in Texas, there were certain centers of trouble. There was violence in Nebraska where the Olive brothers wrought their ugly deeds, and there were "difficulties" also in Colorado and Montana, but the most notable outbreaks centering around fencing were in Lincoln County, New Mexico, and Johnson County, Wyoming. The New Mexico uprising predated the proclamations of the early eighties, and the dissension there was fairly well controlled once government policy was established; but in Wyoming there was outright rebellion against "law and order" as well as against rivals for the range land. The Johnson County war has been described in such superlatives as "The Crowning Infamy of the Ages."[15] It was known as a bloody range war, probably the worst, and the memory of it rankles still in the minds of many Westerners.

No less a figure than Billy the Kid made famous—or infamous—the New Mexico range war of 1878, but it was the issue of free range versus land enclosure which caused the fighting. Feuding was already developing into actual warfare before Billy decided which side he would favor with his support. Basically it was the fight of farm settlers and small ranchers struggling against the expanding mesh of wire fencing put up by John Chisum and his fellow cattlemen which developed into the Lincoln County war. Chisum took no part in the violence and meant to arouse none, but Billy the Kid hired out to one side and then the other; and in 1878 the needless murder of an Englishman who had befriended the young brigand aroused an awful thirst for revenge which drove him, literally, to his death.[16]

---

[15] This was the colorful subtitle to Asa S. Mercer's *Banditti of the Plains.*
[16] Ralph Emerson Twitchell, *Leading Facts of New Mexico History*, 1010.

William H. Bonney II (or Antrim or McCarty) was neither cowman nor farmer himself.[17] He was at this time pure outlaw, by profession as well as by reputation, but he attracted attention to both parties in the fight and to their conflicting philosophies. He clearly attracted attention of federal authorities to himself also, and as a result he became personally involved with their representative when President Hayes sent Lew Wallace to be governor of the Territory of New Mexico. Lawyer Wallace was then writing his great work *Ben Hur,* "scratch[ing] away at the book whenever and wherever he could, on trains, in hotels, in empty courtrooms, at home in the evenings."[18] But when he left the serenity of his surroundings in Indiana and came to the storied Spanish capital city of Santa Fe, Wallace found himself with a real Western gun fight on his hands. He was at once a very busy state official. At one point he undertook to have Billy the Kid turn state's witness; and though in the end nothing came of the matter, it was a tense moment when Governor Wallace and one companion rendezvoused with nineteen-year-old Billy, who was said to have come into Wallace's presence with "a Winchester in his right hand and a revolver in his left."[19] Billy was killed by Sheriff Pat Garrett in 1881—when *Ben Hur* was almost one year on its way to lasting success—and the excitement subsided. Gradually the issues at stake were smoothed out, without anyone at the time analyzing the question of whether the Lincoln County war made Billy a celebrity or vice versa.

The grasslands of New Mexico were not invaded by "armies of settlers . . . improving the country" in the same proportion as were neighboring regions. New Mexico cowmen were more successful than most in preserving the ranges, partly because they had from the beginning the advantage of the Spanish system of generous land grants, partly because of the remoteness and obvious aridity of the land, and partly because of constant vigilance

[17] James D. Horan and Paul Sann, *Pictorial History of the Wild West,* 59; Frazier Hunt, *The Tragic Days of Billy the Kid.*
[18] Robert Coughlan, "The General's Mighty Chariots," *Life* (November 16, 1959), 130.
[19] Horan and Sann, *Pictorial History of the Wild West,* 61.

on the part of livestock owners. This land across which both Coronado and Oñate had passed in search of Quivira, where buffalo once had grazed and where cattle were loosed on grasses so thick and so high that in many cases the rocky terrain beneath was not seen until after the building of fences was begun—this land was zealously guarded; because in due time the state designated such land as unfit for farming—"a fact for which the stockmen never ceased being grateful"—it was saved for cattle.[20] The fencing product which came close to ruining the New Mexico range played a part in preserving it, and the spot where the young outlaw of the Lincoln County war lay buried was—ironically— "protected from the curious" with a barbed-wire fence, "the only enclosure that ever held the Kid."[21]

In Wyoming, organized warfare broke out in 1892, more than a decade after Billy the Kid had fought his last fight, some years after fence-cutting in Texas had been squashed by severe legislation, and after the United States government had made all manner of rules against "unlawful inclosure," "obstructing settlement or transit," et cetera. Wyoming had been admitted as a state two years previous. Resentment and enmity still stirred the inner feelings of the two long-warring factions in the area, and the rights and privileges of each were not clearly defined in the minds of either. It had not been expected that settlers and cowmen would again engage in open fighting, but their rivalry was deep-seated, and the aggravation between them was constant and mutual wherever they came in contact. To the grasslands of Wyoming and other northern ranges had repaired men who still carried in their hearts the memory of early troubles, and when there was added to their traditional distrust the stimulus of organized planning—the appeal to "mob spirit"—crisis was inevitable. The result was bloodshed in Johnson County, Wyoming, in 1892.

On one side in this fight were the big cattle owners. On the

[20] *New Mexico, A Guide to the Colorful State*, 392.
[21] Horan and Sann, *Pictorial History of the Wild West*, 66.

[181]

other were the men who had evolved as a group from that strange alliance of homesteaders, rustlers, small cattle owners, and farmers—all enemies of big cattlemen. The members of this composite group owned their land, plowed a part of it, and fenced in the remainder for pasture. They were a new kind of settlers—ranchers —and on the average they were law-abiding and peaceful. However, there was within this group of well-meaning citizens an element which felt no compunction against the indiscriminate branding of cattle along with animals of their own. These men contended that a cow lost and strayed from a big outfit was fair prey for the little fellow, and some went so far as to approve the coaxing of mavericks from one side of the fence to the other. They were ranchers who rustled a little on the side, and rustlers who ranched a little, and it was sometimes hard to tell one from the other, as "they sought for themselves under the homestead laws the same opportunity pioneer cowmen" had enjoyed on the Open Range.[22] They claimed that cattlemen were usurping the land, monopolizing the cattle, and cornering the market generally. Fair-minded men as well as the prejudiced felt that it was incumbent upon the average cattleman to look out for his own interests, and as a result, the changing of brands came to be routine, the loss of livestock an ordinary occurrence.

There was a period during which it looked as if cattlemen actually were threatened with ruin because of the heavy losses incurred in this manner, and it was during this time that the powerful Wyoming Stock Growers' Association influenced the state inspectors to refuse certification of all cattle bearing the brands of certain suspected rustlers. By this action, many innocent farmers and honest small stockmen were accused of rustling, and unfortunately their sympathies were turned irrevocably against the Association. Rustling did not decrease. Cowmen were no better off. They were obliged to try some other means of putting a stop to petty thieving as well as to more serious offenses. But this time they went too far. They overplayed their hand when

[22] Mercer, *Banditti of the Plains*, xxvi, xxviii.

in the heat of organized planning, they brought in outsiders to do their dirty work for them.

The cattle barons personally attended to the hanging of Jim Averill and "Cattle Kate" in the summer of 1889—and it was said that by reason of inexperience they bungled the job somewhat. This incident the cowmen had intended as a lesson to rustlers who expected to enlarge their herds by branding, and to ranch settlers who expected to enlarge their pastures by fencing. They thought that by administering speedy punishment without waiting for explanation of the appearance of "missing" or stolen cattle in Kate's corral, they would put an end to trouble with rustlers. They had no thought of inciting more trouble. But they misjudged the effect which such highhanded action was to have on other men equally bent on punishment and revenge. Not many months after the double hanging there was a shooting, and then another, leading to a series of killings committed by one side and then the other. Meanwhile, thieving continued. After two years, cattlemen were not only sick of the sniping by settlers but were also worried because of mounting losses due to "disappearance" of cattle. They took the bold step. They mapped their strategy for cleaning out the most-suspected characters. They took the law into their own hands. And they arranged to equip bands of imported gunmen who would—for a price—show the people of Wyoming who was in command of the cow country.

The hirelings whom they chose were mostly from Texas, whether permanent residents there, or not. They were dispossessed cowpunchers or disappointed ranchers, along with a smattering of professional law-breakers and "law-makin', guntotin' marshals." Apparently many of these men did not at first understand the purpose for which they were being hired, but many others obviously understood from the beginning the meaning of "$5 a day wages . . . and $50 bounty to be paid to each hired man of the outfit for every man that was killed by the mob"; on this basis—if the reported facts be true—the members of the "invading army" were by and large nothing but paid killers.[23] At any

[23] *Ibid.*, 173.

rate, there were several bands of them, and they rode into Johnson County by special train out of Denver on April 5, 1892. They were engaged and encircled by the settlers. Eight days later they were routed by federal troops riding in with the dawn to the melodramatic sound of the bugler's "Boots and Saddles." The Johnson County war was over; but its memory lingered long afterward.

For their part in the affair, the Wyoming cattlemen have never been completely exonerated. Feeling against them has since been based on the premise that it was they who introduced the use of force into the dispute, but at the time of the outbreak of fighting, there was widespread resentment against all that was implied in the ugly word "monopoly." Hatred of big business of any kind was strong enough in the Western heart to override loyalty to cowmen and cow customs. Reminiscences of the fight strongly reflect such an attitude, and written versions recently brought to light contain the same thread of prejudice. The conclusions seemed to be that the cowmen and cattle corporations constituted a threat to freedom, and that by mob action they called down vengeance on their own heads. Individual interests as represented by the ranch settlers were winners in the end. Right or wrong, innocent or guilty of appropriating the cowman's property to make it his own, the man classified as settler was looked upon as rightful victor.

There was a question in many minds about the kind of "improvements" being built of barbed wire. It sometimes seemed that the old trail driver was right when he said, "Lord, forgive them for such improvements. . . . Fences, sir, are the curse of the country."[24]

[24] Louis Pelzer, *The Cattleman's Frontier*, 190.

CHAPTER 14

"TRAIL TO RAIL"[1]

Looking back at the range wars, it is plain to see that there were many circumstances which brought about these outbreaks of lawlessness and violence. R. D. Holt, in his study of the situation in Texas, lists ten basic causes for the fence-cutters' wars in that state, and each of the ten is applicable in some degree to the conditions in other regions.[2] Similar explanations are given in other writings on the subject, usually stressing, as does Holt, the effect of drought, "inconvenience to travel," unemployment of cowboys, cattle-rustling, the free grass controversy and the fight between labor and capital. The matter of injury to cattle also is sometimes designated as a basic cause of fighting, for it was unquestionably one of the underlying reasons for resentment against barbed wire, and a good excuse for the destruction of many of the earlier barbed-wire fence structures. Generally, though, the reasons given for outright war over fences could be summarized under the two main headings of extreme severity of weather and resistance to the passing of an era. The actions of both the upright and the unscrupulous men concerned with the fight to prevent

---

[1] Roy D. Holt, "From Trail to Rail in the Texas Cattle Industry," *The Cattleman* (March, 1932).

[2] A summary of Holt's lists covers the following points: severe drought, "desire for free grass and open range," "fear of monopolists," "inconvenience to travel," unemployment of cowboys, "the old conflict between the nester and the cowman," "the fight between capital and labor," opposition to "landless gentry," and "lastly, damage to stock." "The Introduction of Barbed Wire into Texas and The Fence Cutting War," *loc. cit.*, 70–74.

fencing of the West could be attributed ultimately to one or both of these conditions.

The weather was of course unaccountable. As on-the-spot reporter of the times John Clay explained it: "[Cattlemen] could not bet against God Almighty and a sub-arctic winter."[3] The weather they had always to contend with, but the determination of changes in a way of life was something else entirely. Trends sometimes could be foreseen and sometimes forestalled. It behooved those who in their own lives were formulating the basis for future life in the West to hold to their convictions; and this they intended to do.

Early Westerners more than most Americans were opposed to autocratic controls. At the very core of their tradition was the love of individual freedom, and basic to that freedom was fear of monopoly. Wherever they sensed the beginnings of autocracy in big business—whether in manufacture, land ownership, or the tyranny of "landless gentry"—Western interests rebelled. They would not compromise with the principles which lay planted deep in their philosophies. They objected to barbed wire first because they considered it a Yankee scheme for making money and extending the power of the industrial East. They held out against it later because they saw that fencing would negate the free and open use of range lands. Still later they continued to reject it in their minds even as they accepted it on the ground, because it had become by then the instrument of big cattle interests. Barbed wire appeared to them as tangible evidence of transformations which were taking place, and as visible warning of transitions still to come. It was a ready and reasonable target for resentment from the West, despite the ironic truth that its success had been made by and for the West.

In the fight against fencing there was more at stake, however, than the fate of barbed-wire fencing alone. The same conflicts which underlay this struggle were to be seen in other facets of Western living, and the consequences of one bout were reflected in others. There was hardly a development which was not

[3] Clay, *My Life on the Range,* 37.

affected in one way or another by the confusing attitude which on the one hand required economic advancement, industrial improvement, and sociological adaptation, but on the other hand was afraid of change. Yet change was everywhere, moving with inexorable force across the continent. From east to west and back again, from west to east and in reverse, with bold directness and with subtle repercussions, a host of innovations were pressed upon nineteenth-century Americans.

As both history and folklore have pointed out, advances were made the more sure and the more rapid by the introduction of the railroad, which was in itself epoch-making, and was in its aftergrowth revolutionary. The railroad was the tie that bound the nation together, the crux upon which recovery from civil war depended and the furtherance of prosperity could be attempted. The changes which it wrought in the West seemed to be without measure; the effects of its coming, without number. Once the fiery locomotive engine had made its way to a new terminus, the areas touched by its noisy progress were seldom ever the same again—and men who were the first to recognize its potential were never the same again either. The railroad, arriving on the American scene at the height of westward expansion, provided the foundation for new fortunes as well as the basis for new thinking, and men who promoted railroads soon attained financial stature far exceeding normal expectations of the times.

The agile mind of Jacob Haish, for one, showed some inkling of appreciation for the future of railroads when he filled his most extravagant advertisements of barbed wire with illustrations of railroad cars carrying the famous "S" barb westward. Barbed-wire salesmen in the Southwest where railroads were beginning to reach into the cow country—men like Sanborn and Gates who had grown rich on new fencing for the plains—found themselves in a position to invest in new transportation facilities for the region. Henry Sanborn learned quickly at Denison and Sherman in north Texas and near Rockport on the Texas coast that where the railroads came, business of many kinds abounded. He applied the lesson to good advantage in locating the city of Amarillo on

[187]

the Fort Worth & Denver City extension. Moreover, it was the railroad which brought John W. Gates's city of Port Arthur into being. When the town was established by railroad magnate Arthur E. Stilwell, between 1895 and 1899, as a water-front terminus for the Kansas City Southern Railway, "Bet-a-Million" Gates was dabbling in railroad stocks himself, and he managed to outwit Stilwell. By 1900, Gates had gained control of Stilwell's railroad and had taken possession of Port Arthur, the name of which, incidentally, Gates did not change despite the fact that the "Arthur" had been chosen in honor of Arthur Stilwell.

Meanwhile, cowmen—one after another—began to realize that their business was being completely revolutionized by the coming of railroads. They began to see that there was new wealth for them also, since cattle could be shipped by the thousands straight from the feeding grounds to market. And as the lines were extended farther into the plains and prairies, even the Pierce brothers in far south Texas had access to transportation by rail.

The story is told that in 1881, Shanghai jubilantly welcomed the New York, Texas & Mexican railroad (later a part of the Texas & New Orleans) to his land and named the new town built around the station "Pierce's" (or "Pierce Station"), for himself. In at least this one instance, however, Shanghai was outdone by his brother. Years later (1902) when the St. Louis, Brownsville & Mexican railroad joined the Texas & New Orleans near his rancho, Jonathan Pierce, who had worked long and hard to bring the railroads to the Tres Palacios waterways, was asked to name the new town created by the extension; and the name he chose was "Thank God"—because he was thankful to have the railroad at last. When railroad officials and postal authorities objected, Jonathan agreed to a compromise, and finally the town was named "Blessing"— because it was a blessing to have the railroad. The incident has been well remembered, and although there is still a siding at the place which is now called "Pierce" to mark the site of Shanghai's station, it was Jonathan's Blessing which came to be regarded as a sort of monument to the early days of railroads in the ranch country.[4]

The movement of livestock always had been a serious problem for cattlemen. In the regions where cattle were to be found native and in abundance, they were of little monetary value. From the moment they were rounded up on the coastal plains, there was need to move them, usually northward. South Texas cowmen had experimented in the early stages with water freight. The Pierces had sold sometimes $80,000 to $100,000 worth of steers to the Mathis interests at Rockport, where the steers were loaded for shipment by sea steamer.[5] Richard King had tried driving his first herds to seaports and to river docks. It was not uncommon just at the close of the Civil War to find herders trailing cattle to New Orleans, where there were ships bound for Atlantic seaboard markets.

Meanwhile, overland transportation of other goods was developed and gradually extended, but transportation of livestock was limited. Many times stockmen in the midwestern states sent a herder west with cattle to be grazed on the thinly populated prairie areas, and in the same way ranchers from the south sometimes sent herds to northern and northwestern feeding grounds. But the most important movement of cattle was the massive driving of herds over well-worn trails from Texas breeding grounds to railroads which connected directly with packing plants in Midwestern cities. The extension of a railroad to a new point on the map signaled the opening up of a new branch from the trail, the creation of a new market, and, as a by-product of the cattle industry, the establishment of new towns or growth of old ones. Six or eight major routes were used by drovers from Texas to Kansas, and many tens of thousands of great long-horned animals were taken over these trails in the years from 1866 to 1880. From south Texas pastures it was fifteen hundred miles or more, and the cattle walked all the long way. Their coming was like the coming of an army, sweeping aside all obstacles in the way of the march. Their passing left its mark. The trails which they wore into the

[4] Shanghai was responsible also for the choice of names for the Texas communities of Shanghai and Borden.

[5] James Cox, *Historical and Biographical Record of the Cattle Industry,* 617.

sod were graven into the annals of history, and "the sandy whis-
pers of [their] quick feet . . . Going north along earth's longest
street" still echo in men's memory.[6]

When trail-driving began, there had been practically no
fences along the routes which most herds traveled. But before the
end of trail-driving days, barbed-wire fences were crisscrossing
the plains and interrupting movement over the prairie. By 1880
there were enough fences markedly to affect cattle driving, and
when in addition to this complication there began to be more and
more railways reaching into the Western range lands, it was seen
that a new means for transporting cattle was inevitable. Drovers
sought new employment, and cowboys soon followed suit.

There were of course many reasons why the old should give
way to the new. Although other factors—notably the serious problem of controlling the so-called Texas fever—helped bring an end
to this particular phase of the Open Range era, still the effect of
new fences appearing in unexpected places throughout the country and sealing off the accustomed routes of transit cannot be
minimized. When Holt named "inconvenience of travel" as one
cause for the outbreak of fighting in the Texas fence wars, he not
only referred to human travel, but he indicated the fact that travel
of livestock was interrupted also. He pointed out, in other writings, that "barbed wire preceded both the plow and the railroad
and prepared the way for both" in West Texas, and that when
railroad rates were too high, cowmen threatened to return to the
trail, not only because it would be cheaper, but also because the
animals would be in better condition on arrival at market. Holt
indicated that fences as much as the railroads brought on the
end of trail-driving.[7] In addition to this, Wayne Gard, in *The
Chisholm Trail*, mentions barbed wire in the same breath with
railroads as explanation for the decline of trail-driving, and other
researchers refer to records of the times which name settlers and
their fences as the culprits responsible for the sad end of a grand

---

[6] Robert P. T. Coffin, "The Ghost-March," *Selected Poems*, 61.

[7] "The Saga of Barbed Wire in Tom Green County," *loc. cit.*, 32, and
"Barbed Wire," *loc. cit.*, 174–85.

tradition. Altogether it seems to be conceded that barbed wire, although never taking precedence over the railroads in over-all importance to even a limited area, surely was one of the major factors which contributed to fast-changing circumstances in the lives of nineteenth-century Westerners.

A quick comparison of events in chronological order pinpoints the influence of barbed wire on Western transportation. In 1873, when Glidden and Haish and Ellwood attended the De Kalb County Fair, 500,000 cattle went up the trail from Texas. Ten years later, when there was enough barbed wire in Texas to warrant the fence-cutters' war against it, 267,000 head of cattle passed over the trail and their drovers saw fences, cut and uncut, all along the way. In 1884 the pinch of drought and cold was felt, and when by special legislation fence-cutting was declared a felony in Texas, trail-driving was fast losing ground. This same year, when Joseph Glidden made his first visit to the Frying Pan ranch, drift fences banded the width of the Texas Panhandle, and the Colorado route to market was cut off "by homesteaders and their fences." Kansas and Missouri feared Texas cow-fever worse than Texans' vengeance and, as a result, the passage of Texas cattle through these states was banned by law. In case this strategy was not enough, the way was also blocked with barbed-wire fences and guarded with six-guns. Cattlemen continued to favor trail-driving, though, because as long as "grass was cheap, water plentiful, and the trail was broad and free," the rates charged by railroads seemed excessively high by comparison.

When the time came that fences could be easily and quickly constructed, however, fenced fields broke into the broad trail, water holes were enclosed, and grass sometimes was denied the hungry herds. Trail-driving obviously was expensive too. Cattlemen realized that "if the trails were abandoned, they'd be at the mercy of the railroads"; yet they could see that abandonment already was in sight.[8] Richard King at the National Stockmen's Convention in St. Louis, in November, 1884, proposed that cattlemen join together to purchase land for a national cattle trail, to

[8] Holt, "From Trail to Rail in the Texas Cattle Industry," *loc. cit.,* 50 f.

be bounded by barbed wire, and Shanghai Pierce supported the plan.[9] At the same time, there was agitation for a federally owned route; yet in so short a time as one more year, there were clear signs that trailing was finished. It was reported that in 1885, "Ford County [Kansas], of which Dodge City was the county seat, was checkered with fields . . . and numerous orchards many of which were enclosed by wire fences," where not long before had been the famous Cowtown, center of activity for the whole range cattle country.[10] In 1886 there were 50,000,000 acres in Colorado held as pastures, by virtue of barbed-wire fences, and there was dissatisfaction over the prospect of allowing even a handful of drovers to bring outsiders' herds across the edges of the State. With drought followed by blizzard in 1886, the year of disaster for the range cattle business was at hand. The great cattle drives were ended; the trail was reduced to "a crooked path."[11]

It was hinted that railroad interests were responsible for one of the strategic moves directed at closing off the Texas trails. An unknown corporation, claiming to be a cattle company, leased and fenced the Cheyenne-Arapahoe lands lying next to the Texas Panhandle, thus shutting off one more route out of Texas. It was believed that the company was not in the cattle business at all and had not any cattle with which to stock the area. It was intimated that the project was financed by a railroad company scheming to force Texas cattlemen to ship their beeves alive by rail. Each of these claims was disputed, however, and as a consequence it was not possible to tie direct blame for the incident on the railroads. Certainly it was to the railroads' interest to defeat the plan for a national trail, and they had the means for putting lobbyists to work in both federal and state capitols. Certainly the railroads wished for the day when more cattle would be shipped by rail than driven on the trail. But whether it was railroads which secured the Cheyenne-Arapahoe lease is difficult to ascertain. Certainly the railroads were not intending to ruin

[9] For a summary of the exciting events at convention, see Nordyke's *Great Roundup.*
[10] Pelzer, *The Cattleman's Frontier,* 69.
[11] *Ibid.,* 190.

the West, but saw in such action as they did take the possibility of bringing ultimate benefit to the populace as well as to railroading in the West. As long as there was a chance that railroad money was being used against them, however, cowmen were infuriated. Although in the long run they stood to gain from increased railroad facilities, they disliked dependence on this or any other industrialization. They were determined to oppose big-business tactics wherever such appeared and to stay free of outside manipulation for as long as possible.

Inevitably outsiders were having more and more to say about the cattle industry. Investment of European as well as Eastern capital had brought many of the large ranches into the hands of men who were both literally and figuratively "foreigners." Such related businesses as packing, shipping, marketing, and distributing beef, hides, dairy produce, and/or "cattle on the hoof" already were conducted by non-ranching interests, and were growing stronger. As more and more developments throughout the country affected the Western ranges, in the late 1880's the cause of the farmer as opposed to the rancher gained increasing sympathy and support across the nation generally.

In 1885 the distribution of public lands came under the direction of an administration which was much in favor of benefits for agricultural settlers, and the enactment of legislation on matters even indirectly affecting the homesteader was, for more than a decade, decidedly to his advantage. Furthermore, there were advances in industrial processes which benefited the farmer so that by the time he was able to consolidate his position as owner of land, he was able to improve his standing as user of land also.

Not the least of these advantages was, of course, the railroad. Not only did trains carry the settlers to their destinations, but equipment and provisions such as farmers never before had known were sped to the rescue of farmers hard put to cope with the hardships in the new lands. Where many times earlier he had been obliged to retreat because of inability to conquer Western elements, the farmer finally was able to return to the scene of his defeat and to take up his place again—thanks, many times, to im-

provements in plows, availability of building materials, and introduction of windmills and other water-supply equipment, to say
nothing of adaptability of new material for fencing—i.e., barbed
wire—delivered in steady supply by rail.

Since the migration of settlers was so dramatically increased
by this new form of transportation, the continued expansion of
railroad lines came to be a matter of importance to the prosperity
of the nation as a whole. This the government was quick to recognize. Where legislation concerning land disposal and other vital
matters affecting settlement many times was badly bungled and/
or disastrously delayed, provisions for the advancement of railroad interests generally were attended to with great dispatch,
and with an eye to mutual advantages. The United States government stood to gain from railroad-building and from the projects which its presence fostered. And railroads in turn stood to
gain from support given them in the form of ample portions of
Western lands granted from the public domain.

The assignment of public lands as subsidy for needed industrial developments was not new. In the line of transportation, this
type of public aid had been sought for the building of canals
very early in the century. It had been argued that by awarding
alternate sections of land in inaccessible areas, the value of sections retained by the government would be greatly enhanced
when reached by easy transportation. Even at the time of the construction of the Erie Canal the interests of railroads had been
affected by such arrangements, and one promoter had cam-
paigned vigorously for a line to be built across the state of New
York in lieu of the great canal. Finally in 1850 a bill was passed
in Washington providing that alternate sections of land in a strip
ten miles wide be given to those states wishing to use this means
of encouraging railroad-building in their respective regions. It
was twelve years before the bill was signed, by President Lincoln
in 1862, and the lands were assigned directly to the railroads. But
by this proviso, railroads had been allowed a four-hundred-foot
right of way, ten alternate sections for each mile of track, and permission to use timber, stone, and such materials as were required

for construction "from adjacent parts of the public domain."[12] Texas law allowed sixteen alternate odd-numbered sections per mile of railroad.[13] In 1864 twenty sections were allowed, instead of ten, and under certain provisions as much as forty sections might be granted in the territories. Also liberal loans were made available to the railway companies. In this manner the national government had provided what has been called by some "the legal equipment for the annihilation of the entire frontier between 1862 and 1871." Five new continental lines were started and although financial panic in 1873 caused a slack in activity, the projects were resumed in due time and extension of railways into the Pacific Northwest was at hand.[14] The great forests of the region were, as a consequence of legal provisions, parceled out to the rail companies.

By 1890 such strides had been made in transportation and in settlement that there remained no more "uninhabited frontier," no "unused West." A good part of it had been peopled through the efforts of railroad companies which sponsored settlement, and a good portion had been assigned to the railroads by legislation supporting expansion. How long it might have been before the outposts of settlement could have been consolidated without railroads, how long it might have been before the railroads could have expanded without the legislative support, is impossible to estimate. But the century of American progress which was nearly completed could not have been marked by the rapid growth which characterized it without the simultaneously rapid growth of the great "iron horse." America owed much to the railroads. America had paid with so handsome a share of Western property that railroads in the aggregate were among the biggest landowners in America, and by the end of the century, railroad holdings in the West far overshadowed the cattle barons and far outdistanced the farmers.

Against such power, the Westerner was bound to take of-

[12] The Act of 1862 and the amending Act of 1864. See Moody, *The Railroad Builders,* 133.

[13] Gammel, *Laws of the State of Texas,* VIII, 989.

[14] Frederick Logan Paxson, *The Last American Frontier,* 375.

fense. He went into all dealings with the railroad "carrying a chip on his shoulder," and his resentment was so ever present that it became necessary to have laws defining the railroad's rights and duties in even the most minute matters.

One of the chief sources of irritation was the adjustment of damages claimed by owners of livestock killed by the trains. All types of domestic animals wandered onto the tracks; they seemed actually to be attracted to the railroad right of way because it was usually higher and drier ground, and because sometimes the banks cut to make railroad beds were deep enough to furnish shelter from wind and cold. Occasionally cattle stampeded across tracks, thus endangering not only their own necks but also the lives of passengers and crews of approaching trains. As a rule, however, cattle, horses, mules, goats, hogs, etc., simply stood on the tracks and could not be frightened into moving. It was almost impossible for oncoming trains to avoid hitting them. As a result, losses in livestock were very high, and there was the constant threat of derailment and accident to human beings. The problem of who was responsible required specific legislation.

Laws varied, depending on local reaction and the age-old question of who should pay for erecting enclosures. The builders of fences still quarreled among themselves on this issue, and—as the courts declared—with the arrival of the railroad "a new element had been introduced," and an over-all agreement was needed. At this point it seemed more reasonable to require the comparatively few big companies controlling the railroads to fence the right of way than to expect the thousands of livestock owners all across the country to keep their animals behind fences. The final decision was left to the states, where, in most instances, the burden of responsibility was placed on the railroads. As a result, the railroads were in the market for suitable fencing materials.

The cost of enclosing right of way for the railroads was enormous. A legal fence was generally held to be "four and one-half to five feet high," and made of "rail, lumber, stone, or wire." Before the advent of barbed wire, board fences were most commonly used by railroads, but they were more and more expensive to build as lines pushed farther and farther beyond forested areas. Lumber was much too dear, even with transportation provided. The expense of wood-fence upkeep alone was exorbitant. When repair crews were sent to out-of-the-way places in the plains areas, they often found nothing left to repair because squatters had taken the fence timber for firewood. Boards were too easily removed by timber-hungry settlers eking out a living in a new land. Also wood fences were subject to destruction when fire swept the countryside in dry seasons, and in winter they caused snow to bank on the tracks. Stone fences were out of the question. Hedge fences were slow growing, unmanageable, required constant care and trimming, and acted as a hazard at crossings where visibility might easily be impaired. Barbed-wire fences were soon found to be the most economical as well as the best suited to the purposes of railroad enclosures.

Yet railroads hesitated before adopting so unconventional and so unpopular a product as barbed wire. They had enough trouble appeasing prejudices as it was, and they knew that if animals were injured by barbs of railroad fences, the damage would be charged against "that soulless corporation," the railroad company. As one present-day railroad official explains it: "The leanest, boniest, rangiest of cows immediately became a full-blood registered prize bull when hit by a Cotton Belt [St. Louis Southwestern Railway Company] train."[15] And it was believed that injury from barbs on the right-of-way fences would call forth the same sort of evaluation.

Shanghai Pierce had a number of characteristic run-ins with the railroads over provocations of this sort. In one instance, a Pierce-owned steer strayed onto the tracks and stayed there, causing a passenger-train wreck. The matter of reparations and responsibility was a touchy one, though not nearly so touchy as would have been the case if a passenger as well as the steer had been injured. Another time, Shanghai lost a horse because one of his men tried racing with the train—and Shanghai saw the

---

[15] W. H. Hudson, Jr., vice-president, St. Louis Southwestern Railway Company.

[197]

whole thing with his own eyes, yet he sought reparations from the railroad. Finally a steer was killed on a part of the track which had been left unfenced at Shanghai's insistence, and for this reason Shanghai said he would ask that only half the value of the steer be paid him. The railroad agent replied that since Colonel Pierce had "so liberally struck off one half the value of the animal, I [the railroad agent] shall be no less liberal and strike off the other half, hoping that there will be no more killing in the neutral ground."[16]

Pierce's main objection to the railroad fencing was that the proposed crossings over the tracks were too narrow for cattle-driving, and this was not an uncommon complaint. The rules had to be adjusted—and evidently were adjusted—to meet the needs of the time and place. It was said that in the Texas Pan-handle when ranch fences were about to be interfered with by the coming of railroads, long wire gates were made as extensions of the fence to reach across the tracks; and when the engineer slowed down at the sight of the obstacle, a member of the crew got off, opened the gate to let the train through, and signaled for the rear brakeman to close the gate behind them.[17] Obviously it was necessary to enact laws acceptable to both parties.

Some states made specific provisions for crossings. Texas law, for example, stated in 1887 that railroads—if requested by citizens—should make openings or crossings through their fences and over their roadbeds every one and one-half miles, said crossing to be thirty feet wide and kept in condition for horses, cattle, sheep, hogs, wagons, etc. to cross.[18] Colorado law of about the same period held the railroad responsible for damage to animals, but conceded that animals killed became the property of the railroad company "which might sell the same, but must keep the hide for . . . thirty days for inspection." In later rulings it became necessary to specify the responsibility assumed in the most minute detail, as in Washington state where in 1903 provisions were

[16] Emmett, *Shanghai Pierce,* 116.
[17] Hamner, *Short Grass and Longhorns,* 252.
[18] Gammel, *Laws of the State of Texas,* IX, Chap. 57, SSB #44.

made for occasions when fencing and/or cattle guards at crossings might be "ineffective because of snow."

Comparable situations occurred throughout the West, and
while in the East a different set of circumstances presented some
variations, the problem of enclosure of right of ways was basically the same all across the country. The need was for quick
erection of effective barriers at minimum cost. Barbed wire was
far and away the most economical, the most universally available,
and appeared to be the most adaptable. Fears and prejudices
stood in the way of its ready acceptance, but once barbed wire
was tried, the railroad companies were convinced of its advantages. The addition in later years of woven wire used with barbed
wire produced the best barricade of any yet tried to keep animals off the tracks, but the combination was expensive and in
most places the need for such close protection was not required.
Posts of various woods were used, depending on the locality, but
in many regions *bois d'arc* was the preferred material. Railroad
ties were made of *bois d'arc* too, and some of them which were
taken up sixty to seventy years later were found to be still in
good condition.

Apparently one of the men most active in persuading the railroads to give barbed wire a try was Isaac L. Ellwood. The Ellwood name appears on many transactions drawn in the late 1870's
and early 1880's, and, in fact, what seems to have been the first
barbed wire used by the railroads was bought from the Barb
Fence Company of De Kalb, Illinois—the partnership of Ellwood
and Glidden—in 1877. In this contract for fencing along "a mile of
the Chicago & Northwestern line," Ellwood agreed not only to
supply the wire but also to build the fence enclosing the right
of way and to remove it if not satisfactory.[19]

It was in this way that manufacturers of barbed wire went
into the business of building fences, sometimes organizing their
own separate construction companies for dealing with the rail-

[19] Earl W. Hayter, "Fencing of Western Railways," *Agricultural History*
(July, 1945), 166 n., quoting Agreement of Washburn & Moen Manufacturing
Company and Western Railway Association, Chicago, March 22, 1886, in
American Steel & Wire Museum, Worcester, Massachusetts.

roads. So reluctant were railroad officials to use a product which might prove to be more trouble than it was worth that stipulations such as Ellwood agreed to were often necessary in the early contracts. Even after such extreme precautions as these were eliminated in subsequent contracts, railroads still retained the right to delay payment on barbed wire until the fence was given a trial. When it became evident that patent rights were to be held up in the courts and threats against infringement frightened off farm customers, railroads grew cautious again. In 1881 the Washburn & Moen Manufacturing Company and I. L. Ellwood & Company made contract with the Western Railway Association of Chicago for the barbed-wire manufacturers to assume responsibility for all damages of infringement.[20] As late as June, 1895, the Ellwood firm was still constructing fences, and Ellwood himself signed bond for $1,000 on the understanding that "if the said I. L. Ellwood Mfg. Co. . . . shall keep the said St. Louis Southwestern Railway Company of Texas harmless and indemnified from and against all and every claim for material furnished and labor done in performing the terms of this contract, and remunerate the said Railway Company for all judgment, cost, fees and expenses of suit arising out of any such claims or liens, then this [bond] obligation shall be void."[21] The railroad, for its part, provided "free transportation of material to be used on this fencing contract."[22]

Ellwood's show of confidence in the Glidden product was well rewarded, of course, and the railroads, like the farmers and small stockmen who had begun to use barbed wire, kept coming back for more. By 1885 the Ellwood Company alone was selling to "over one hundred" railroads.[23] Although they had objected to the introduction of barbed wire partly because it would cut down on the railroad business of transporting lumber to the West, when the railroads themselves needed fencing for their Western properties, they bought barbed wire—hundred of miles of it. The rail-

[20] Ibid.
[21] Ellwood Family Papers, loc. cit.
[22] Letter from H. G. Kelley, resident engineer at Texarkana, Texas, to Agent M. K. Lott, Marietta, Indian Territory, June 24, 1895. Ibid.
[23] Glidden Barb Fence Journal (1885), 13.

roads' needs called for fencing material more reasonable in price, more durable, more available than standard fencing materials, and these needs Isaac Ellwood was prepared to meet. His barbed wire was effective, cheap, durable, portable, and of inexhaustible supply. The railroad became one of Ellwood's biggest customers, one of the chief consumers of all barbed wire manufactured in the 1880's and 1890's. How else the hundreds of miles of tracks spanning America at this early date could have been successfully enclosed is unanswerable.

CHAPTER 15

"ALAMBRE! ALAMBRE! ALAMBRE!"[1]

WHICH CAME FIRST TO THE WEST: the advance of railroads, fences, and towns in the face of the Law of Open Range,
or the weakening of the Law of Open Range in the face of railroads, fences, and towns? There is reason for argument over
which was cause and which was effect. But, in any case, it is
clear that the Open Range was doomed and a new order was
appearing in its place. New tools for the plains and prairies necessitated new rules—or vice versa—and the interdependence of the
two caused changes in all phases of life in the once-open, once-
unchartered cow country.

Colonel Charles Goodnight told a story which in a way explains the changes. It was an account of an incident which Goodnight had witnessed in 1878-79, at about the time of the founding
of "Saints' Roost," later named "Clarendon," in the Texas Panhandle.

Goodnight had heard that there was "a Christian Temper-
ance Colony" settling in the area, and one day it came to his
mind to "ride them by and look them over." He went alone in
the direction which had been told him, and when he came in
sight of the settlement, he could see that there was some excitement going on. The colonists had surrounded a group of Indians
on horseback and were questioning them. As Goodnight drew
closer, he could hear the "Saints" threatening to kill the Indians

[1] H. T. Burton, "A History of the JA Ranch," MS, University of Texas
Library, Austin.

unless the chief could give good reason for coming to the colony. As he listened, Goodnight began to understand what was happening. These were Pueblo Indians—"the most peaceful tribe"— under a chief whom Goodnight knew personally. The trouble was that the Pueblos were from New Mexico and spoke Spanish, but no English; and the Anglo settlers understood not one word of the old chief's talk. They thought that the Indians were Comanches—"who were killers"—and the whole colony was aroused for fear of being attacked.[2]

Approaching the tense group, Goodnight came up by a route where neither Indians nor colonists noticed him. He heard the chief trying to tell his captors in Spanish that he meant them no harm, that his was a peace-loving tribe, that he had friends among the white men, and that one who ranched near by—"the man with heap of cattle, heap of land and heap of everything," meaning Goodnight—surely would vouch for him if the settlers would send for the white man. At this point Goodnight rode up and spoke to the Indian in Spanish. "He recognized me instantly," said Goodnight. "I never saw anyone's face brighten up so much as this old chief's did."

After Goodnight explained about the Pueblos, the settlers released the Indians, and Goodnight questioned the chief to find out where the riders had been and where they were going. The chief said that they had gone to trade with Kiowas on the Oklahoma reservation and had decided to take a short route back to their homes in Taos, New Mexico. "Then," said Goodnight, "the old chief asked me a question that dumbfounded me.—'How do we get back to Taos?'"

For an Indian to put such a question to a white man was unheard of, and Goodnight could not understand the reason for it. "You surely know the way back to Taos," he countered. "Haven't you lived in this country all your life?" To this the chief answered sadly, "Alambre! Alambre! Alambre! todas partes!—wire! wire! wire! everywhere!"[3] And in this moment Goodnight realized

[2] Haley, *Charles Goodnight,* 322-23.
[3] Burton, "A History of the JA Ranch," *loc. cit.*

what barbed wire was doing to the Southwest, with new fences which cut up the terrain so that even native tribes of Indians could be confounded.

It was Goodnight's feeling that barbed wire and the Texas Rangers solved the Indian problem for Texans.[4] This was, of course, the Rangers' business, as they were expected to be protectors of legal settlement. Yet they were more successful than some other groups, perhaps, because they worked both independently and in collaboration with federal troops stationed at United States forts in Texas. As for the effect of fencing, Indians very much disliked the idea of enclosure even under peaceful conditions, and when they saw how barbed wire threatened to surround their camps and cut off their hunting grounds, they wanted no part of it. Furthermore, barbed wire completely disrupted the Indians' moonlight raids; their swift ponies went berserk when slashed by the vicious barbs, and the Indians' usual mode of warfare by sudden attack and close combat was made impossible. Some tribes attempted fence-cutting, but without much success. As more and more fences appeared and the ones which had been cut were replaced, there was little recourse left to the Indians except to move on to another area; they appeared less and less frequently in localities where settlers and their fences abounded.

Along with those cattlemen who refused to buy land and to enclose it, the Indians lost ground steadily as both field and pasture fences made a checkerboard of the rich grasslands which had been for so long the open grazing ground of first buffalo, and then cattle. Finally Indians, cattlemen, cowboys, sheepherders, trail-drivers, homesteaders, and land-grabbers—all realized that the principle of unrestricted grazing and uninterrupted passage was ended and must give way to a new concept favoring enclosure. Fencing, Westerners were forced to acknowledge, was "here to stay," thanks in most part to the development of barbed wire. And, as time went on, the question ceased to be whether there should be barbed-wire fences; the question was, who should build them—farmers or stockmen?

4 A newspaper interview of 1886, quoted by Holt in "Barbed Wire," *loc. cit,* 174–85.

[204]

In Eastern states which were composed largely of closely-knit farm communities, farmers had been the dominant influence for a long time, and the principle of Herd Law, a custom requiring livestock owners to fence in their stock, had long prevailed. In this region there were no large herds, however, nor affluent stockmen whose fortunes were dependent on the welfare of cattle. Many times, even where the Herd Law was in effect, farmers found that to be practical they themselves should enclose "fields where the most valuable crops were grown." In Western states, farmers had come into an area where Range Law was well established and cattle traditionally had been allowed to run at large. Farmers were the late-comers and the minority; if they wanted the protection of fences, in the beginning at least, they had to supply it for themselves. Generally the fixing of responsibility of fence-building was a matter of local determination by whichever faction was in power. Where cowmen held sway, they would say to the farmer, "Fence your fields"; where farmers were in control, "they would turn on the stockman and say, 'Herd your cattle.' "[5]

Many times, however, there was in reality no such well-defined delineation of responsibility, for throughout each succeeding period of American settlement in both East and West, there were continually recurring complications which prevented reduction of the problem to basic issues. Moreover, there came a gradual shift in policy as the granting of public lands to homesteaders and the leasing of Western ranges altered the circumstances. Despite a Territorial Herd Law which had been on the books for two decades in Colorado, for example, "during the wet years of the middle eighties," settlers having trouble with range cattle began to put up "black-painted barbed wire" rather than depend on stockmen to fence.[6] California, "having been one of the best ranges for stock," was at this same period "by degrees turning everywhere except in the mountains, into an agri-

[5] Major W. Shepherd, *Prairie Experiences in Handling Cattle and Sheep,* 124.

[6] Millard F. Vance, "Pioneering at Akron, Colorado," *The Colorado Magazine* (September, 1931), 175; also Dick Goff, "Guardian of the Grass Country," *The Denver Westerners Roundup* (November, 1958), 13.

cultural state."[7] Farmers felt that early Range Law worked a hardship against them; cattlemen, "seeing more and more fields put into grain, [and finding] cattle unable to range wide areas and change location with season," were brought to the acceptance of ownership and enclosure practices; and the availability of barbed wire in the 1880's reinforced the resolve of both parties.[8] Meanwhile, in Texas, Colonel Goodnight put up his first fence in 1882, and the trend toward buying and leasing and fencing in that area was set. Even though Goodnight fenced more as protection against other cowmen than in acquiescence to farmers, the effect was largely the same.

In the earliest days of settlement in the Southwest, sentiment had been with the agriculturist. In 1550 the Spanish crown had ruled in favor of Indians whose unfenced fields were molested by Spanish cattle. But when certain Canary Islanders settled in Mexico's province of Texas in 1732, a common stockade had been built around a common field as protection from the common herd, and although such action did not discriminate against either the agricultural or the stock-raising element of the society, the advantage lay with the latter.[9] One hundred years later, benefits to cattlemen in Texas were even greater. In the far reaches of this region, as well as in adjacent regions which extended deeper into the Western plains where farm settlers were nearly nonexistent, owners of great herds of Texas cattle pushed on to whatever locations they wanted. But when the West was opened up for agricultural settlement after the Civil War and pressure was applied to break the hold of the range laws, it became apparent that because it *was* range, the West could never be wholly converted to farm laws. There had to be a mingling and merging of interests, even as there was and had been a combining of influences.

Fencing remained a problem of protection. Fundamentally, fencing was, as someone put it, "an attempt to separate the cattle

[7] Shepherd, *Prairie Experiences.*
[8] Clara M. Love, "History of the Cattle Industry," *loc. cit.*, 376 ff.
[9] Malcolm D. McLean, "Don't Fence Me In," *Southwestern Historical Quarterly* (January, 1948), 225.

from the corn," or to keep "the pigs from the posies," and where
it was the farmer who wanted the separating, it had been historically his task to see it done. The farmer was—as always—on
the defensive. But when the time came that big cattlemen of the
West, like small stockmen of the East, saw that they could profit
from having their animals confined, it was no longer incumbent
on the planter of corn to assume full responsibility for keeping
cattle separate. More and more it became the responsibility of
the stockman—or, at least the responsibility was more evenly divided than it had been before the advent of barbed wire, and
the subsequent development of purebred cattle. Gradually the
fencing of the West became the business of the cattleman as well
as of the farmer, and to some degree the cattleman was to blame
for the change. To some degree he had brought it on himself.
Not that he had failed loudly to protest and manfully to oppose
the change, not that he had weakened his own position knowing-
ly, but in the course of events his own course of action inevitably
was changed.

The cowman's viewpoint was modified partly because he became interested in breeding stock, but mainly because he found
it expedient to grow supplementary feed for the stock. In one
instance after another, the cowman pointed the way for planters
as he turned part-planter himself. He planted not corn, perhaps,
but hay and other feed crops which he harvested with such success and in such abundance as to indicate clearly the agricultural
potential of heretofore unpopulated and mostly uncultivated
areas. In an undulating belt reaching to the Sierra and Cascade
Mountains, he planted in spring so that before winter he had
great surpluses of hay in stacks like giant loaves of bread at the
foot of each hillock and at the edge of each meadow. Both he and
his livestock were well provisioned; but by the very success of his
program the cowman-planter was at the same time inviting the
"annoyance"—as Goodnight termed it—of farm settlers who would
learn from him how great were the agricultural possibilities of
these regions, and would move in to become his neighbors.

In some instances it was the stockmen who initiated irrigation also, and thereby made the prospects for farming even more promising. In southern Wyoming, for example, irrigation was begun very early in the valley of the Laramie River, before the influx of settlers reached the Territory; and in New Mexico, both river and well water were put to use on the John Chisum range where Billy the Kid rode herd for first one faction and then the other.[10] Reports of 1879–80 show that in Montana a cowman of Gallatin County had been turning small streams to irrigation "for 15 years," well ahead of the arrival of the hated "honyak."[11] Stockmen knew better than anybody the need for utilizing life-giving water anywhere that it might be found west of the one-hundredth meridian. They knew that over a period of years normal rainfall would not suffice for small farming tracts, and that protection of all sources of flowing water was essential. They knew that by cutting off such sources they could force many homesteaders out of the plains region—and in some cases they went so far as to employ these tactics.[12] In their opinion, "the range country . . . was never intended for raising farm-truck."

"Where you allow a settler to take up 640 acres," the cowmen said, "and he disturbs the grazing of 6,400, where is the gain?"[13] They contended that the plains and prairies were meant to be range land forever. From the Sand Hills of Nebraska and the gumbo lands of South Dakota to Texas' Llano Estacado, the land itself had turned back many a settler, yet by their own action cattlemen unthinkingly disclosed the potentials which tempted farmers to keep coming in spite of threats and warnings, and, once arrived, to stay.

[10] Clyde Meehan Owens, "Studies in the Settlement and Economic Development of Wyoming," *Annals of Wyoming* (July, 1931), 52; and George A. Wallis, *Cattle Kings of the Staked Plains*, 60 ff.

[11] Testimony of C. Edwards, Bozeman, Montana, 1879, 46th Cong. 2 sess., *H.R. Exec. Doc. No. 51*, 348–49.

[12] Pelzer, *The Cattleman's Frontier*, 181–88. It was said that in some places, two weeks after the President's proclamation ordering removal of fences which many times enclosed water holes or blocked passage of stock to water, irrigation projects were begun by "companies" proposing to divert streams and change the natural drainage in order to make adjacent properties unfit for settlement, and thus substituting dams and ditches for the illegal fences which had been ordered down.

[13] *Ibid.*, 191.

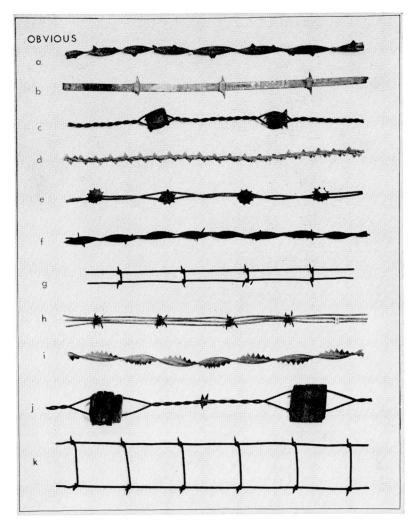

In an effort to prevent undue injury to wild and unsuspecting cattle, to give warning to horses, and to counteract objections on humanitarian grounds, manufacturers turned to easy-to-see styles of *obvious* barbed wire. For example: *a*, "Buckthorn"; *b*, "Brink Flat"; *c*, "Stubbe Plate" (small); *d*, Crandal's "Champion"; *e*, Hodges' "Spur Rowel"; *f*, "Brink-Martelle"; *g*, Decker's parallel wire; *h*, Cline's "Rail"; *i*, "Sawtooth"; *j*, Scutt's wooden block with barb; *k*, Decker's two-inch parallel.

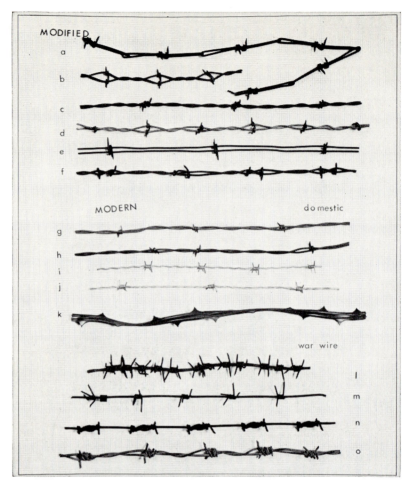

Barbed-wire designs were gradually modified so that they were practical for manufacture as well as for control of domesticated livestock. Modified designs were later improved. Modern patterns, for the most part, reverted to simple styling made of improved materials, but war wire for use against man was even more vicious and cruel than the early styles used against untamed animals. Some examples of *modified* to *modern* wire are above: *a*, "Chain Link"; *b*, Decker's "Spread"; *c*, Brotherton (small); *d*, "Spread Reverse"; *e*, Frye's parallel; *f*, Nadelhoffer's "Twist"; *g*, modern Glidden, *h*, Baker "Perfect"; *i*, four-point corrugated strand type; *j*, high-tensile "Reverse Twist"; *k*, plastic ribbon; *l*, German square wire (World War I); *m*, United States concertina; *n*, Australian four-point; *o*, heavy four-point wire from the Korean front.

Settlers soon learned that successful farming in arid regions was not possible with the small acreage allotted under the original homestead laws. They learned that to survive on the plains and prairies, they must have access to more extensive areas. They learned that in order to prosper under conditions prevalent in the West, they had best raise some livestock, and in order to graze the stock, the owner must control areas more nearly the size of those which early cowmen had commandeered. In the same way as the cowman began to raise crops on his dwindling domain, the farmer began to raise cows on his expanding properties. Each man fenced his fields and, ultimately, his ranges and pastures too. Each became settled—the cowman almost part-sedentary farmer, and the farmer almost converted to an understanding of traditional range customs. Unwillingly and unwittingly, each participated in the gradual development of a new, composite figure—a Western man called "rancher." And in the process, farmer and cowman both took unto themselves that which they already had begun to demonstrate to each other, the new set of tools and the new set of rules for ranchers.

The merging of activities was more important as more settlers came to the cow country, and the numbers coming increased as railroads advanced westward. Cowmen were resentful. Many felt as Colonel Goodnight felt when the Fort Worth & Denver City Railway was extended into the Texas Panhandle in 1887, that as a result, settlers would move in "by the hundreds" and "annoy us so we cannot make money in our business."[14] As their first objection to railroads had sprung from basic resentment toward monopolistic enterprise, the second stemmed from traditional resentment toward agricultural settlement. It was true: settlers were an annoyance on the range, and settlers did come in increasing numbers once this new miracle of transportation was available. Furthermore, their numbers were increased a hundredfold by a system of land promotion undertaken by the railroads.

In order to finance their westward expansion, rail companies

---

[14] Haley, *Charles Goodnight,* 329, quoting a letter from Goodnight to Mrs. Adair, December 10, 1886.

offered for sale the vast holdings which they had acquired from state and federal governments. They entered into land-speculation business on a large scale, with fanfare. They were enormously successful, and handsomely repaid. Furthermore, they spurred the rapid settlement of vacant lands which normally would not have been occupied for a long time to come.

Normally settlers moved slowly. To be sure, they had moved in great waves, migrating by the thousands in nineteenth-century America. They had populated the better part of a continent in record time. But they had gone cautiously, nonetheless, usually proceeding by small steps into the unknown. As they had reached into new lands, the locations which they chose had been, as a rule, the arable regions closest to their old homes. They had followed generally the age-old pattern of occupying the grounds contiguous to home ground. But when they had reached the forbidding expanse of the plains country, they had been confronted with the necessity either to wait, banked along the edges of plains and prairies, or to pass over to the far side. As a consequence, they had crowded both flanks of the arid mid-sector of the continent, unable to fill the arid short-grass region until such time as they could produce the tools and formulate the rules for a new way of life. It was not until then—near the close of one century and the opening of another—that the railroads were able to induce the overflow of settlers onto the plains, and to bring, from all parts of the nation and from other lands as well, newcomers equipped to remain on land from which heretofore only the Indian had wrested a living.

Railway companies offered Western land on very attractive terms. They provided it in town blocks, in single lots, in small farms, in whole colonies. They developed elaborate advertising schemes. They organized excursion trips to show the properties, or arranged for buying "sight unseen." They brought immigrants —within thirty days—from their homes in foreign lands to farms in the undeveloped territories, and even set down whole colonies of Europeans on the open prairie. Whole communities of settlers from Eastern seaboard states also were deposited in ready-made townsites on the high, dry, windy plains. And families from worn-out farm lands of other sectors were set upon virgin sod in the heartland of America.

Traces of the wholesale migration of the widely divergent groups are still to be seen throughout the West—in Yankee names for Oregon cities, in colonial architecture of Texas hamlets, in Scandinavian farms in the heart of Kansas, in Russian celebrations still observed in southeastern Montana, and in many other characteristics which give evidence of the variety of cultures which went into the making of twentieth-century Westerners and their twentieth-century ways.

It was a colony of Swedish farmers settled on El Rancho Grande that named Jonathan Pierce "King Jon," and a group of "snow-shovelers" from Northern states that took up the rest of his lands. Despite his brother Shanghai's insistence that the coastal lands would remain open prairie "for as long as water runs and grass will grow," Jonathan always had envisioned the breaking up of open range into enclosed ranches. He had worked tirelessly toward bringing the railroad to his lands because he saw that as surely as railroads would transport cattle and produce to the East, they would transport newcomers and their belongings to the West—and he was prepared to profit from both ventures, with cattle ready on the loading platform, and land partitioned into lots for sale.

In time the two viewpoints were blended; both brothers, justified. In the Tres Palacios area, as in other sections where both farm settlers and stockmen could be accommodated, big holdings gradually were pared away. Big men walked with less bravado. Bustling cattle-shipping centers, townships such as Jonathon's Blessing, subsided into insignificance. The bounty of the land still was harvested, the proceeds still provided good living for the settlement, but more and more it was divided between moderately prosperous farmers and generally well-to-do stockmen, or ranchers who represented a combination of the two.

And it was the same elsewhere. Many towns grew and flourished during the period of intensive expansion when railroads not only brought the "honyockers" and their families from far places, but also stimulated the advance of "movers" waiting on the edges of settlement. Some towns later faded and disappeared, but others continued to be average Western communities servicing wide areas of ranch country throughout the West. The story of Douglas, Wyoming, for example, closely parallels the history of many settlements.

In June, 1886, the story goes, location of a railway station and townsite was announced, and immediately a near-by "Tent Town" was put on wheels and moved—"in three days"—to the Fremont, Elkhorn & Missouri Valley Railway. Provisions were ordered to be delivered by rail, and plans were made for receiving the strangers who would be brought by the railroad to the new town, named in honor of Stephen A. Douglas.

> On August 29, the first passenger train arrived, loaded with people, and the sale of lots began. The first lot sold for $760. Erection of buildings began at once, and, for the next 60 days, hammers pounded from daylight until dark. Five brick buildings were constructed of hand-made brick; the streets were lined out in broad, orderly avenues, and trees were planted. . . . In 1887, an election was held at Douglas to determine the location of the county seat. . . . Douglas won the election. In those early-day informal affairs, maverick votes in the election booth were as common as mavericks on the range. In the Converse County election, a Captain O'Brien was one of the judges; when the names of 69 O'Briens had been counted for votes, the Captain shouted, "No more O'Briens today." There were only 16 O'Briens in the county.
>
> The region around Douglas was attractive to livestock men, because of its abundance of water and its fine native grasses. . . . In the early 1880s many big outfits ran cattle in the vicinity, and, during the fall of 1886, great numbers of cattle were driven in from Texas. The range was soon very much overstocked. . . . [Then came the storms of 1886–87, and the story was the same as elsewhere] . . . from a settlement of 1,500 or more, Douglas dwindled to less than 400.
>
> Although many large cattle ranches and sheep outfits remained

in the vicinity, gradually the lands were taken up as homesteads, and fences forced the cattle kings to find more open range. Homesteading was slow . . . [but] with the establishment of the Federal Land Office at Douglas in 1890, filings were made immediately, and agriculture began to take the place of extensive cattle business.

Douglas was the goal of settlers intent upon helping to open up the new "Fetterman Country," and speedy agricultural development brought stability to the town. Permanent buildings and fine homes gradually replaced the first crude shacks. Among the early residents were some of Wyoming's most distinguished citizens, including DeForest Richards, who served the State as the fourth governor, and Dr. A. W. Barber, acting governor during the historic Johnson County Invasion. . . .

In 1936 Douglas celebrated its 50th anniversary. Population 1940,—2,205.[15]

Douglas, Wyoming, was typical. Settlements throughout the old cowcountry saw that "speedy agricultural development brought stability" to a town and to an area. Where Colonel Goodnight had seen that "The only way a farmer can do well here [on the Western plains] is to combine stock-raising with farming," his successors saw that by the same token stockmen might benefit from combination of activities also.[16] The face of the West was altered. Even the "Saints' Roost" showed similarities to Douglas and Blessing—and to countless others.

"Saints' Roost" was moved to the Fort Worth & Denver City tracks, and the name "Clarendon" was made official. Eventually the serving of intoxicating beverages was permitted as the temper of the times changed also. Ranchers, in need of a more cheerful reception than the original colonists had offered, saw to it that a number of changes were made. But the farm settler was not dismissed from the scene; he was merely absorbed. There was produced, as a net result, a figure not all cowman, still less farmer, yet like each of these, blazing a new trail. His predecessors in

[15] Agnes Wright Spring, *Wyoming, A Guide to Its History, Highways, and People*, 284–86.
[16] Haley, *Charles Goodnight*, 383.

each case had struggled not so much to be better, as just to be; he could dare to do better.

The West was a new world peopled with new men, and those who clung to the ways of the past were lost, their obvious frustration the more regrettable because it was inevitable. The end of an era had come, and the future was for the rancher. Loved and hated, glorified and maligned, "cussed and discussed," he appeared as both hero and villain; but he remained as more than a symbol, as the embodiment of all that was left of the great American West. The rest was gone. The rooting nester and the old cowpuncher were vanished. Like the Indian before them, they were surrounded by obstructions. "Alambre todas partes" was only the beginning of their confusion. And their plaint must surely be one of the most poignant cries in our history, when it concludes with unmistakable finality that the old range life has disappeared never to return, and the cowman confesses, "if I knew a country where it would, I'd go there if I had to go in a canoe."[17]

[17] Pelzer, *The Cattleman's Frontier*, 248.

CHAPTER 16

A NINETEENTH-CENTURY ALLEGORY

THE STORY OF THREE MEN present at an Illinois county fair in the early 1870's, although it is the only authoritative story of the origin of barbed-wire fencing, was not the only one to find its way into journals and periodicals printed since that time. There have been other versions, most of them easily disproved by research. But those most baffling, most difficult either to verify or to nullify, are those which have been reduced by time to the happy state of folklore.

In a London publication of 1888, an English gentleman, discussing the hazards of the English hunt with respect to fencing, declared that "we never have had much doubt" about who was the inventor of barbed wire or from what unholy place it first had sprung, "still sizzling hot!"[1] In the New World also the names of Satan and of his abode figured prominently in the conversation of Western cowmen and settlers confronting each other across barbed-wire fences. They too were inclined to ascribe the development of such an "inhuman" contrivance to the nether world. But the main body of legend preserved in both oral and written form was more realistic. It dealt not with demons and their devices but with an average man, his typical pioneer wife, and their life together on the American frontier.

Started as a ready explanation for the emergence of a practical product for use by farmers and stockmen, the barbed-wire

[1] "Wire," *The Saturday Review of Politics, Literature, Science, and Art* (January 7, 1888), 14.

legend grew as naturally as the grass roots from which it had come; and in the growing it acquired something of the ring of truth, the sound of history. It was never more than a story, yet it persisted and gained significance for two reasons: because of the possibility that it might have been true, and because of the fact that it was representative of what was true. The characters of the story served as symbols representing the two dominant factions of westward movement, and their actions typified the actions of farmers and ranchers contending against each other. Their story—almost too plain and unromantic to be termed a legend—developed over the course of years and gained momentum as it spread, until it finally assumed the proportions of an apologue, a nineteenth-century allegory.

According to some accounts, the man in the story was a rustic, with cows; others sometimes called him a blacksmith, with pigs; still others claimed that he was a more affluent gentleman, with hunting dogs. In every case, however, it was said that the man had a wife who grew a garden; and what cows, pigs, and/or hunting dogs did to the garden brought on a deal of trouble, until the wife insisted that something drastic be done to protect her plants from livestock. She goaded the man into making a barrier of wire with sharpened nails twisted between the strands, and together they put it up around the garden. Pigs and such soon rooted elsewhere—and this, it has been said, was the beginning of barbed wire.

Occasionally this pigs-in-the-posies version has been given as prelude to the "folksy" Glidden episode of the converted coffee-grinder, and in this way the name of the real-life inventor has become associated with the legend.[2] Inevitably it was concluded that Joseph Farwell Glidden and his wife Lucinda were the originals of the man-and-wife characters of the legend, though such

[2] Probably the first person to associate Glidden's name with the flower-bed episode was John Lambert, Joliet business associate of Gates. There is no direct quotation from Mr. Lambert, however, and the account of his words gives the impression that he was speaking on this subject extemporaneously—and expansively. Warren, "History of the Manufacture of Barbed Wire Fencing," 26, AS&W Records, *loc. cit.*

a conclusion has never been substantiated by research.[3] There has been found no evidence either of identification with the Iowa blacksmith who bent horseshoe nails into the form of fence barbs, or with any other experimenter with defenses. The fictitious couple has necessarily remained fictitious.

The man in the story simply personified cowmen and other livestock owners of the West; the woman represented landowners determined to protect their interests from depredation. Trouble between them was the same on the edge of the woman's garden as on the margin of agricultural settlement. The aggravation between them was the conflict between advocates of free range and of defensive barriers. He was an unnamed hero, and she was his green-thumbed wife. No more need be known, for it is fitting that they should be remembered as the prototypes of two groups of pioneers struggling for self-assertion and self-preservation in a new land.

[3] An amusing story from the *American Lumberman*, though typical, must be minimized. The Glidden kinsman telling the story was evidently very distantly related, and must have been strongly influenced by hearsay.

"It happened the other day that I heard the story of the invention of barbed wire. I was waiting for an interurban car near the Country Club of De Kalb, Ill., when a middle-aged watchman approached. It was his task to guard a crossing nearby during certain hours and he was then on his way home. We fell into conversation and I finally asked him if De Kalb had not been the home of Joseph Glidden, the inventor of barbed wire. He said this was true and that Glidden had been distantly related to him. Then he told me the story of the first barbed wire.

"It seems that before he made his invention, Glidden had not been so wealthy. He got along the way the rest of us do when we are not born with silver spoons in our mouths, and among other ways he had of making ends meet was the keeping of a cow. Fortunately for Glidden, as it afterward proved, this cow was breachy. She took a morbid delight in going through any kind of a fence Glidden could fix up. Nothing seemed high enough or strong enough when she set her mind, with a singleness of purpose worthy of a better ambition, to the task of getting out of the pasture. Glidden was provoked and about at the end of his resources. It occurred to him that if thorns on a hedge will command bovine respect, perhaps thorns on a fence would do the same; so his first move in that direction was to drive nails through the fence boards so that bossy would encounter the sharp ends when she engaged in the gentle exercise of smashing the fence down. . . ." "Realm of the Retailer," *American Lumberman* (October 26, 1918), 40 f.

PART THREE
Types of Barbed Wire

CHAPTER 17

MODERN TRENDS

I N SEPTEMBER, 1910, Isaac L. Ellwood died in De Kalb, Illinois. Among the passengers on the special train "provided to take guests to and from the funeral" was John W. Gates, coming back to De Kalb to pay his respects to Colonel Ike. Gates received newspaper reporters in the smoking car of the train and reviewed with them the barbed-wire business as he and Ellwood had known it. Gates, "reminiscently blowing on the lighted end of his cigar," concluded the interview by saying: "They never made any wire that was an improvement on that first attempt [by Glidden and Ellwood]." Or, at least, Gates was so quoted in the *Chicago Tribune*.[1]

This was, perhaps, too much to say; but Gates was known for making broad claims, and this one was typical of him. For once, however, he was very nearly correct, for although his statement was colored by imagination and tinged with prophecy, it was based on truth.

From the time when Joe Glidden first made barbs for his neighbors, the Glidden wire was a commodity of exchange. From the moment when Ike Ellwood and his wife first saw the Glidden fence, it was recognized as an important invention. From the day when Gates strung the Glidden product in the dusty plaza at old San Antonio, it was a success. Of all the kinds of barbed wire manufactured before and since that time, only one—"Baker Perfect"—came close to the record of production, sale, and long usage

[1] Brush, "Workers' Magazine," *Chicago Tribune* (September 18, 1910).

set by Glidden's patent No. 157124, "The Winner." Since Baker's wire probably was a "moonshine" product, statistics on it are incomplete and accurate comparisons are not possible, but "Baker Perfect" seems to have run a very close race with "The Winner" throughout the years.[2]

It was after the last sad decade of Gates's life and after his death on August 9, 1911—less than a year after he had attended Isaac Ellwood's funeral—that the peacetime invention which these two had fostered came to be widely known as an instrument of war. By 1914 the industry which Ellwood had prodded into being and the companies which Gates had pushed into prominence were in a position to take the lead in producing wire especially designed for use by America and her allies in the defense of democracy. The American Steel & Wire Division of United States Steel Corporation, along with other important manufacturers, supplied the front lines in Europe with a new kind of protective weapon in the form of barbed-wire entanglements.

Barbed wire had been created in the beginning as a means of protection. Its origin was rooted in the principle of defense, and it was armed for just such purposes. As a weapon of war it continued in this tradition. Its war record could be traced back to the time before wire had barbs, to an era when small amounts of smooth wire sometimes were staked in front of fortifications as an extra precaution against attack.

In 1898 the firing of the battleship *Maine* in Havana Harbor and the ensuing war with Spain had the effect of stimulating steel manufacture in the United States. Little use was made of barbed wire in the fighting, done mostly at sea, but the subsequent increase in steel production for war had an ultimate influence on wire-making. In the South African War of 1899–1902 barbed wire was used around prison compounds by the Boers, who already were familiar with it as a fencing material. But it

___

[2] It must be assumed that the Baker wire was manufactured under the patent granted George C. Baker for a machine to make barbed wire of this type, and under another patent (No. 273219) for a flat two-point barb wire.

[222]

was during the Russo-Japanese War of 1904–1905, when wire entanglements were used in the defense of Port Arthur (Manchuria), that wire with barbs made its debut as a weapon of war. Ten years later its place in the front lines was well defined. Publications as early as December, 1914, discussed not only the use of barbed-wire entanglements but also the various devices being suggested at the time as ways to circumvent the awful effectiveness of such barricades.

The part which barbed wire played in two world conflicts was of greater significance than is usually supposed. In World War I miles of it were strung, bales of it were scattered, rolls of it were tangled across the battlefields of Europe. Ground troops found it impossible to make their way through the matted web of wire which was so sharply barbed that soldiers could not take hold of it to cut it. "Gauntlets and gaiters" made of specially treated fabric were tried against the wire, as were various cutters, explosives, and small one-man tanks. Some attempt was made to surmount the entanglements with ladders, planks, or bags filled with straw, but without success. It was said that barbed wire was "the most formidable obstacle a modern infantry attack [had] to contend with," and as an outgrowth of this situation the motorized tank which could pass through or over the wire was developed by the British in an effort to control or counteract the use of barbed-wire entanglements.[3] In 1939, when the hope of world peace again was shattered, the industry was ready with protection, in the form of improved war wire for battle barricades.

In World War II the Japanese sank carloads of barbed wire into the sea in an effort to block their ports from the approach of submarines. To overcome this strategy, a new kind of military personnel was evolved—the "frogmen," who were trained and outfitted for underwater work in clearing the way for ships' propellers and for submarines. During the action in Korea, great whorls of concertina wire were used by United Nations forces confronting the enemy's light tanks and trucks. A concertina-like

[3] *The Scientific American* (December 5, 1914; April 14, 1917; June 22, 1918); and *The Weekly Journal of Practical Information* (February 24, 1917).

product had been made in 1914–18 with sharper-than-usual and longer-than-usual barbs on highly ductile steel wire. At mid-century it was made of spring steel with tensile strength rated at 200,000 p.s.i., and was put together in bales made up of twenty-eight units of wire compressed into one. At a plant contracted to manufacture concertina wire for the government, in Protection, Kansas, the strands were made to hold together in such a way that upon the loosening of a clip, the roll of wire stretched out like an accordian, or concertina. The wire might then extend fifty-six feet in length and forty inches in height, and after use, the whole could be compressed again into one tight roll.[4] Armored tanks attempting to open a path through the whorls of hard, drawn, spring-steel were slowed down or stopped as the wire was pushed rather than crushed, and the ends invariably sprang back behind the tank in mounting whorls which prevented the passage of troops intending to follow the tanks. At the close of fighting in Korea, the use of concertina wire was continued in defense operations, and it still is shipped in large quantities to military installations all over the world. In its present form it is a wire almost as vicious as could be devised, having four-point sharpened barbs three-quarters of an inch long, fourteen thousand to a roll.

Barbed wire made specifically for war use is different from the ordinary commodity. It is often of heavier gauge, usually has heavier barbs of almost twice the normal length and spaced close together. There is little variation in pattern as the design of barbs that do injury to livestock will do injury to human flesh also, but the four-point barbs on war wire are made stronger and longer, more wicked and more vicious, and this type is used for compounds as well as for combat. Such is "man's inhumanity to man" that he has contrived the most cruel wire of all for confining his fellow being. Even in the unhappy role of a war weapon, however, barbed wire still remains an instrument of defense only. Never has barbed-wire fencing been armored for offense.

4 *Kansas* (July–August, 1958).

A World War I soldier wields wire clippers in a barbed-wire entangle-
ment.

Barbed wire in No Man's Land, 1918.

Galvanized and/or high-tensile barbed wire for fences is taken for granted in the twentieth-century. During the years when plain smooth wire was being tried, however, people struggling with the problems of westward expansion in America had no assurance of having serviceable fencing. They knew that wire would stretch or tighten in accordance with the weather, but also would be attacked by oxidation to the point of rusting and eventually breaking. They were obliged to find some sort of protective coating which would preserve its usefulness.

Various means were tried, each having some advantage over untreated wire. Jacob Haish, at an early date, attempted the use of paint as a covering. Also the Thorn Wire Hedge Company, manufacturing Michael Kelly's invention, advertised a "Rust Proof Paint," saying, "We were the first to use red paint . . . others have tried with poor success to appropriate the discovery. They got the red color, but have not yet discovered the secret of the manufacture of the genuine rust proof metallic enamel." A later advertisement, put out by the Trenton Iron Company, "Makers of Iron & Steel Since 1847," offered "bright, annealed, coppered, tinned, galvanized" finishes. William A. Root of New York City in 1881 patented a type of barbed wire "galvanized at every point which is liable to damage by rust," i.e., "a new fence-wire . . . already galvanized" (patent No. 237130). And the *American Agriculturist* of January, 1882, noted "the Japanning of common articles of tinware," and explained that "Japan or Japan Drier" was made with "Linseed oil, Litharge umber and sometimes other ingredients."

Today there are many known additives for retarding or preventing oxidation of standard wire, and there are non-rust products made of materials such as plastic and aluminum. In the past, manufacturers were dependent on simple coating until chemical and mechanical difficulties could be overcome. Protective finishes, in addition to lime coating affixed in manufacture, included the following: paint, varnish, anneal, copper, tin, japan, bright, galvanized, galvannealed, chromium, cadmium, and zinc.

[225]

Barbed wire was for a long time essentially an American product. Although first patented in France and later manufactured in many countries, by far the greatest percentage was made and used in the United States. Barbed wire was, as historian Webb described it, "a child of the [American] prairies and plains."[5] Barbed wire was born in the shadow of an old-world tradition of providing protection for fields and vineyards, but it grew up in the light of a new-world philosophy of confining the aggressive animal rather than enclosing the inert plant rows. It was tested in pitched battles dignified with the names of Lincoln County war, Johnson County war, and fence-cutters' wars. It was matured in the struggle for control of one of earth's five great natural grazing grounds, and found its destiny at last in its natural habitat on "the boundless plains of America."[6]

In addition to its role as war material, barbed wire was exported to war-torn countries attempting to build up agriculture and stock-raising after the fighting. Farm fencing as well as combat wire used throughout the world was predominantly American-made until recent times. Then, shortly before 1950, manufacture in Europe began to increase, and within a few years foreign wire was offered for sale in the United States at prices below American levels and the import rate rose rapidly. German and Belgian wire companies in particular cut into the American market by supplying wire manufactured in Europe, shipped across the ocean, "freighted to Cleveland by rail and hauled from the warehouse by truck," for approximately forty dollars per ton less to the jobber than the price of a comparable product made in Cleveland. In 1957 "some 64,000 tons" and in 1958 "almost fifty per cent of the total [American] market" was imported into the United States.[7]

In an effort to overcome this disadvantage, a number of firms revised production to put improved wire on the market. Ameri-

<hr />

[5] *The Great Plains*, 296.
[6] Great expanses in Central Asia, South Africa, South America, and Australia are also counted as natural grazing grounds of the world by James S. Brisbin, *Beef Bonanza*, 23.
[7] *United States Steel Quarterly* (February, 1959), 5.

can Steel & Wire Division of United States Steel Corporation gave its new product a new name, "American Ranger," and the Sheffield Division of Armco Corporation called its new version "Sheffield 100 Wire." Using superior wire, both products could provide "twenty per cent greater tensile strength in comparison with the standard 12½ gauge wire" which had been rated at approximately 75,000 pounds per square inch. The "Ranger" advertised its 13½-gauge strands at a tensile strength of 90,000 to 105,000 pounds per square inch, and "Sheffield 100" advertised "husky 13½ gauge wire with full gauge barbs ... combining high strength with ductility."[8] Both admittedly were meant to be countermeasures to the high quality of foreign competition.

Development of these high-grade products was widely acclaimed by the wire industry. The great increase in ductility and in tensile strength far outdistanced the brightest dreams of early-day manufacturers, and even the modern world was impressed. The changes in quality of material were hailed as great innovations, and were pronounced by some as the first improvements in barbed-wire fencing in seventy-five years. In view of the number of patents issued and variations improvised during the seventy-five-year period, such a statement seems unacceptable. But a look at the facts, and at the style of barb on the "Ranger" and the "Sheffield 100," gives cause for thought. Both designs follow closely the same designs used on early products; modern improvements in material certainly were much more significant than alterations of design. Beside the lighter weight and greater strength, the chief change in design for high-tensile wire is the reverse twist of strand wires, alternating the direction of twist between each two barbs because of torque in the high-tensile strand wires.[9] Furthermore, an even more recent product of plastic barbed fencing made in Odeborg, Sweden, is not appreciably changed

[8] *The Sheffield Fence Rider* (Sheffield Division of Armco Corporation, Houston, Texas), Vol. XXI, No. 3; Vol. XXII, No. 4; Vol. XXIV, Nos. 2 and 4.
[9] The reverse twist was an invention of the Belgian Trefileries Leon Bekaert, whose founder, Leon Bekaert, coincidentally was using an inverted wheel barrow for twisting strand wires in the 1870's when Glidden, half a world away, was experimenting with a grindstone.

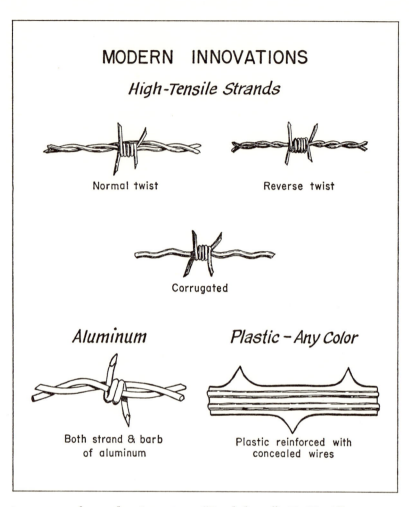

MODERN INNOVATIONS

High-Tensile Strands

Normal twist

Reverse twist

Corrugated

Aluminum

Both strand & barb
of aluminum

Plastic – Any Color

Plastic reinforced with
concealed wires

in pattern from the American "Buckthorn"—T. V. Allis patent No. 244726, July, 1881. Material, again, is the element most changed in barbed-wire fencing, for the reason that the early inventions already were basic.

Most of the applications for patent on barbed wire were made in quick succession, mostly in the seventeen-year period before the original patents expired in 1892. Most of them purported to be improvements on the Glidden Wire, but actually

[228]

most of them were not. The "Baker Perfect" was simpler than all others, with only one wrap of the flat barb around one of the double-strand wire cables. Many other patents were granted, however, even though most had only inconsequential differences in cut or twist of barb or strand. Variations were not necessarily advancements. The principles introduced in the first few inventions proved to be so fundamental that there was little room left for deviation from the original intent and purpose, little possibility for variations in basic structure, little chance for real improvement. Only by improvising some slight changes were twentieth-century inventors able to come up with new patents. Basic designs already were simplified, and basic combinations of materials already explored.

By August, 1871, two years before Henry Rose's fence was displayed at the De Kalb fair, the first four United States patents on barbed-wire fencing—not including Dabb's invention, which was no more than an attachment—had been granted; and these four had incorporated most of the features which were to be used in the future for securing the hundreds of additional sets of patent specifications. Patents on single-strand (Hunt, 1867), double-strand (Kelly, 1868), and ribbon-strip (Judson, 1871) wire covered the chief variations in strand-wire design. Patents on wire points (Smith, 1867), spur-rowel (Hunt, 1867), sheet-metal points (Kelly, 1868), and points torn out of a ribbon strip (Judson, 1871) covered most possibilities for variations in barb points. Thus, the basic features already were accounted for before Joseph Glidden worked out his practical barnyard fencing, and before the host of would-be inventors who took notice of Glidden's success ever began to "improve" on his handiwork. Had the first inventors lived in the prairie or the plains regions instead of in New York and Ohio, had the pre-Glidden barbs been produced by factories comparable to the Washburn & Moen Company, had Gates's type of publicity been practiced earlier, the date of discovery of barbed wire might now be known as 1867–68 rather than 1873–74.

This is not to say that Glidden's wire should be regarded as anything less than the leading barbed-wire invention. This is not to belittle the importance of developments at De Kalb, or to underestimate the men who made a success of barbed wire. But it must be emphasized, again and again, that environment was an important factor in determining their success. It was not only the few intervening years that made the difference in acceptance of barbed wire for fencing; it was locality also. And it was something else, for it must be understood that despite the basic requirements already hit upon in pre-Glidden designs, there were two main features still unused before 1873. It was Glidden and his contemporaries who perfected or brought into practical focus two-point and four-point wire barbs, and two-, three-, four-, and multiple-point sheet-metal barbs.

Nearly all wire barbs manufactured at the present time are either two-point or four-point barbs. Of the dozen or so four-point styles once made, only a small number now are in production, though earlier types ofttimes may be found still in use in one way or another. During the heat of competition in the 1880's there was less co-operation between firms, whereas today each of the steel companies which deals in barbed-wire manufacture makes two styles of two-point and of four-point barbs, each on double, twisted, longitudinal strand wires.

Ultimately the most important group of commercially acceptable barbed-wire designs was the two-point wire barb group headed by Glidden's "Winner" and "Baker Perfect"; the next most important, the four-point wire barb; and next, the four-point sheet-metal barb. During the years of the opening up of the American West, Glidden's was the main barbed wire used, and in the years that have followed, there has been little added to it. Woven wire has taken the place of barbed wire in many instances, supplemented it in others. But for the industry as a whole, the barbed wire conceived as "a child of the prairies and Plains" has continued in substantially unchanged form. Present-day factories, using lighter, more ductile steel for both strand wire and wire barbs, now manufacture more efficiently and in greater quantities. They make barbs shorter and in smaller gauge than "vicious" types, but still sharp and often styled according to Joseph Glidden's specifications for the simple twist patented in 1874. Other styles have come and gone, serving a purpose for a limited time, but most of them passing, with the passing of time, into history. The "Winner" continues. No other product is known to have brought more over-all profit, directly or indirectly, to the barbedwire industry than the Glidden fence.

For once, John W. Gates was almost right. The exaggerated statement made in the last year of a lifetime full of exaggerations came close to fact. It was very nearly true that, as he said, "They never made any wire that was an improvement on that first attempt."

CHAPTER 18

CLASSIFICATION

SAMPLES of barbed wire do not always fit neatly into categories. They do not fall easily into chronological order because of discrepancies between dates of discovery, application for patent, issuance of patent, and beginning of manufacture. Moreover, the style of design alone does not provide for arrangement of all types of barbed wire into groups. Both chronology and design must be taken into account, for both serve as parts of the basis for classification. Whereas chronological order is only general and grouping by design is only a partial classification, the *reason* for the inventor's choice of design to be used at a given period provides the best criterion of all. Most samples fall almost naturally into categories reflecting the purposes for which the wire was designed.

On this basis, four natural groupings can be set up, with approximate dates and appropriate titles, as follows: "early varied" types of wire fencing which, as the name implies, were the first, unco-ordinated attempts at patentable inventions; "vicious" types of wire fencing intended to inflict injury to livestock, on the theory that in this way animals would be taught to stay away from fences; "obvious" types of wire fencing which were meant to add visibility to the fence to warn livestock, and thereby to counteract the danger of injury; "modified" types of wire fencing which incorporated modified forms of some of the helpful features of the other three types. Though there is an overlapping of dates, these general categories serve as a foundation for understanding what took place in nineteenth-century fence-making activity across the breadth of America.

EARLY VARIED (1868–77)

The wire which Glidden and Ellwood together manufactured in the early days of their association, the product which they first sent for sale in the cattle country, was armed with sharp wire barbs. It was manufactured for the purpose of stopping cattle. It was meant to pierce but not necessarily to injure. Some of the barbs were almost blunt in comparison with the barbs that could—and later would—be made. The first small factory at De Kalb was not equipped to produce uniformly, even though some uniformity was achieved. Glidden's barb was a type which could be made more sharp and more threatening if need be, but it was not originally conceived to do harm of a kind which would offend prospective customers, among either cattlemen or the farm faction. The "Winner," as made by The Barb Fence Company from 1874 to 1876, was simple, practical, and effective against livestock, without being extreme.

Much the same could be said of Haish's "Famous 'S' Barb." Although not as simple or as versatile as Glidden's wire, the "S" barb was only moderately damaging to livestock, and it too could be made somewhat more or less dangerous if need be. Insofar as his early factory at De Kalb was able to maintain uniformity, Haish must have produced his wire with barbs of medium length and sharpness.

This was not the case with other wires introduced during the same period, however. There were many whose basic characteristics were neither blatantly vicious nor clearly obvious, but whose barbs had the effect of one extreme or another. Ellwood's invention, which ran concurrently with the better-known patents by Glidden and Haish, and Kelly's invention, which came earlier, are good examples. Both must be called "early" types because of the dates on their patents; yet Kelly's wire actually was equipped with barbs sharp enough and strong enough to be termed "vicious" barbs, and Ellwood's was made of material conspicuous enough to make it an "obvious" type. But the lesson to be learned from the success of more moderate types over these two extremes went unheeded or unseen, and a wide range of variations and exaggerations continued to appear. In some cases the variants proved to be forerunners of new trends, but most of the differences did not represent definite styles. The first early patterns were in reality only experiments, and they were as divergent and as unrefined as experiments are bound to be. Kelly's was a piercing barb, Haish's was a strong one, Ellwood's was an easy-to-see variety, and Glidden's was as near a norm as ever would be made. Under the circumstances, "early varied" seems a proper title for the group of them.

Vicious (1876–80)

If, in the beginning, inventors had not concentrated on sharpness of prongs, when barbed wire first went into actual production, there were manufacturers who did. It was thought that the success of the fencing depended on punishing cattle that violated boundaries. Some manufacturers believed that barbs must be long and strong as well as sharp. Some barbs were made keen-edged enough to cut a cow's hide, some big enough and long enough to penetrate a half-inch through the hide into the flesh of young steers charging hard against a fence. In the enthusiasm over the new business, inventors and manufacturers carried the principle of vicious design to an extreme. Only in later years were the long, sharp, sometimes heavy barbs seen as deserving of the title "vicious." Though the threat which these cruel barbs posed to the cattle industry was later understood and loudly lamented, for a period in the late 1870's anything which effectively stopped or turned cattle was acclaimed as successful.

It was during this phase of development that barbs with four points instead of two were emphasized, both wire barbs and sheet-metal barbs being influenced by the change. The use of sheet metal for four-point barbs proved to be immediately popular, for a number of small factories made rapid sales in such products as the "Arrow Plate," "Split-Diamond," and "Scutt's Clip" fencing.

Hiram B. Scutt was a moving spirit in the activity at Joliet during the unsettled period of litigation when many newcomers entered the field of barbed-wire manufacture. He had become interested in 1873 when he first heard of wooden strips armed with wire points, and, according to a onetime employee, "he thought of using small bamboo poles similar to ordinary fish poles" as substitutes for the one-inch wooden strips. He made a trip to Louisiana for bamboo, and "arranged to drill holes through the poles and drive through small lengths of wire cut diagonally to form points." When he found this method too costly, "his next idea was to utilize a half-round iron strip weighing about 4 pounds to the rod." But in 1875, Scutt visited De Kalb, saw the Glidden barb, and "realized at once that his strip, weighing 4 pounds per rod, could not compete with the Glidden, weighing between 1 and 2 pounds per rod, and after associating himself with . . . two farmers . . . [Scutt] entered the manufacture of barbed wire, using sheet metal barbs."[1] Subsequently he was granted eight patents on barbed wire or barbed-wire machines, all widely diversified and reasonably successful. Most of his patents originated at an early date, but they touched on all four main classifications of barbed-wire types. He was thrown from a horse and died in 1889 as a result of the accident. Had it not been for his untimely death, Hiram Scutt might have produced still more usable fencing, particularly of the four-point metal-plate type of barb, for he was of an adaptable turn of mind and he kept apace with the developments of his time.

Obvious (1879–84)

Effective though the many kinds of "vicious" wire proved to be, they were at the same time dangerous and destructive. As livestock losses due to injury by barbed wire mounted, humanitarian arguments against it increased. Sentiment was strong and

1 Gedge and Boley, "History," I, 66–67.

gaining evidence against the evils of the newfangled fencing. What for a while had been a promising young industry was suddenly threatened with extinction. Manufacturers had to act fast. Inventors who never had given up the search for variations on the early patents were encouraged to take a new look at the fencing problem, and they came up with scores of patterns based on a new concept of easy visibility. In 1879 the trend toward "obvious" wire was started in earnest, and during the early 1880's it was in full swing.

Meanwhile, consumers were experimenting with barbed wire all over again. Cowmen sometimes would cut flaps of tin to hang as warning signs, for cattle as well as for horsemen, to stay away from barbed fences; and such devices were produced commercially also. Washburn & Moen Company's and Ellwood's enemy, E. M. Crandal, was granted patent No. 220912, on October 28, 1879, for a treated wooden block called an "Indicator" for use as "a warning to cattle." It was described as being lighter than most warning signals and, because it had been water-treated, less likely than some to be stolen for kindling wood. Patents were issued for similar gadgets variously described as "tags," "guards," and "signals" made of various materials, and apparently they were considered to be worth while. An occasional patent was issued during the decade from 1879 through 1889 for warning attachments which could be used on fences already erected.

When ranchers hung out these warning flags for their stock to see, they were in a sense putting up warnings for the barbed-wire people also. The tags served as a sort of prelude to the development of "obvious" types of barbed wire. Sheet metal such as the ranchers used to make their tags became one of the chief materials for commercial experimentation. Where it was feared that double- or triple-strand wire might not readily be seen, broad flat strips of hoop or band iron were substituted, and many times big eye-catching barbs were cut from sheet metal. E. M. Crandal's "Indicator," for example, was followed by his sheet-metal barbs on effective fencing known as "Champion," and other producers developed large, heavy strand fencing with barbs less vicious and/or more obvious than ever.

Galvanizing processes appearing at this time were helpful in resolving some of the manufacturing difficulties. However, most of the "obvious" styles were manufactured for only that period during which the search for successors to "vicious" wire was most pressing. Some were hardly manufactured at all, and only a few were developed into successful, standard types.

One of the main innovations occurring in "obvious" wire was a sheet-metal strand cut to form broad, flat, so-called ribbon wire. This type of strand wire had been patented before. Michael Kelly as early as November, 1868, had received patent No. 84062 (not the "Thorny Fence") on the first wire fencing of this type. Kelly's was followed by Lyman P. Judson's patent No. 118135, Jacob Haish's patent No. 147634 (not the "S" barb), and I. L. Ellwood's patent No. 147756. However, none of these were successful, and it was not until the trend toward visibility took hold that ribbon wire became really popular. Once adopted, it flourished, and ribbon wire was used in perhaps 50 per cent of the "obvious" types of the early 1880's. Thereafter it remained for a long time one of the best-selling fence materials. It was easy to manufacture, easy to see, strong, and sturdy. In some early cases the ribbon was cut with jagged edges to serve in the place of barbs, and in the styles which had barbs attached in the usual way, the barbs did not slip on the ribbon; once clamped on and galvanized, they stayed in place better than on other varieties of single-strand barbed wire. This feature alone accounted for the development of several "obvious" ribbon-wire patents.

Modified (1884–92)

As full-scale production of barbed wire was resumed after the scare at the close of the 1870's, barbed-wire manufacturers who were in the business on a long-term basis apparently turned their sights on the future. What they saw must have caused them some concern, for the manufacture of "obvious" types of wire was soon curtailed, and still another trend in design was begun.

[237]

A good deal of metal went into the making of intricate and extreme designs of "obvious" wire, and the patterns necessitated also the addition of new machinery for cutting the new barbs. Costs of manufacture and shipping had gone up steadily during the period of "obvious" wire manufacture, and profits had gone down. Though different styling had brought more sales, the sales were not in proportion to the increase in investment. The demand did not warrant the mounting expense, and it was clear that another change was needed, this time in the direction of moderation.

By 1884 the requirements for good fencing had changed. Cattle had become less wild and more accustomed to enclosure. On the part of stockmen, there was less need for stressing visibility of either barbs or strand wires; on the part of the manufacturers, there was more need for practical styling. Whereas formerly it had been the owners of cattle and horses who had precipitated the change from "vicious" wire to something less damaging, this time is was the manufacturers who led the way from "obvious" wire to something less expensive. They began to search out the best features of "early varied," "vicious," and "obvious" wire, to blend them where possible, and to convert the extremes in each category to modified forms.

Most of the barbed wire made after 1885 and continuing into modern times can be classified as "modified" wire, but the classification includes also some types which appeared much earlier. The "modified" grouping probably is more extended in scope than the other classifications. For example, the success of the three best sellers of all—Glidden's "Winner," "Baker Perfect," and the "Brotherton Barb"—should be attributed in large part to their simple modified character. They were carried over from the general era of "early varied" inventions, past the turn of the century, and up to modern times, yet their styling remained virtually unchanged through the years because it was essentially moderate from the beginning.

If the happy medium settled upon before the close of the nineteenth-century is to be improved upon in the twentieth century, the improvement is not likely to open up a new category of design. It may bring a change in material, or the technique of production may be further streamlined. But modern barbed wire is likely to maintain the characteristics of "modified" styling. Indications are that the simple, moderate designs will continue to prevail. The "Winner" is winner still, having, in general, outranked, outlasted, and outsold all other types and styles in all four categories of barbed-wire fencing.

CHAPTER 19

IDENTIFICATION

Exactly how many different kinds of barbed wire have been made since issuance of the first United States patents in 1867 is not known for certain. Arthur G. Warren in his "Barbed Wire—Who Invented It?" used the number two hundred as an estimate, but he evidently did not hold with this estimate for very long. Copies of his article, reprinted from *The Iron Age* of June 24, 1936, show that Warren struck out the printed number "200" and wrote in with ink, initialed in his own handwriting, the words "more than 400." Since then, this accounting has been generally accepted, even though there is only limited information on what four hundred or more varieties Warren had in mind, and no way of knowing what percentage of this number were patented, manufactured, and used.

During the first frantic decade of invention and the legal involvements which followed, three classes of barbed wire were produced, and Warren had knowledge of all three—i.e., standard products with approved patents, "moonshine" wire manufactured deliberately without patent, and wire which was made with patent pending. It is clear that he did not limit his count to patented products. It is known that some of the wire with which he was familiar was never granted patent, and some was never meant to be. Furthermore, there is difficulty with patent numbers because of early reissues which originally were allowed as a means to account for slight alteration or amplification of patents already secured. Yet, in the main, records of the United

States Patent Office fairly well corroborate the Warren estimate. The list of barbed-wire patents compiled by Arthur Hecht of the National Archives Administration in 1958 names 364 registered patents on barbed wire, and these do not cover a number of known types of early wire—evidently not patented—or some barbing machines, the patents on which could have served as permits for manufacture of wire without patent.

A set of original bynames has been devised for use in the following pages, which identify thirty-six prominent types of barbed wire. Formation of the bynames has been based mainly on expressions from papers pertaining to the barbed-wire business, or on characteristics of design and circumstances of discovery of a sample. In each case the choice has been made with the hope that the name will give some clue to the history of a particular pattern, or to its relation to the barbed-wire story as a whole.

MERIWETHER IMPROVED FENCE (Early Varied—
smooth wire)

Patented on November 8, 1853, by William H. Meriwether of New Braunfels, Texas. Patent No. 10211.

This early smooth-wire-and-board type of fencing incorporated several important points which should be noted. Cast-iron posts were pictured, in the patent papers, alongside the regularly accepted wooden posts for fences. Also the patent specifications provided for four strands of wire with "one rail of wood about three or four feet from the ground next below the top wire." The board was expected to perform several services, such as keeping small cattle from going under and large cattle from going over the fence, keeping the wire stretched and "elastic," helping to lighten the effects of both external pressure and internal reactions to heat and cold, and defining "the position [of the fence] to cattle, when from distance the wire is invisible." In other words, the Meriwether design, though made of smooth wire and a wood rail, foreshadowed at an early date a number of features which were incorporated in "obvious" wire of a quarter-century later.

It is not known if this particular pattern was used beyond the sphere of Mr. Meriwether's personal influence, but presumably it was not. Where the invention was prescient in some ways, it was impractical in others, and probably was not accepted commercially.

THORNY FENCE (Early varied)

Patented on February 11, 1868, by Michael Kelly of New York, New York. Patent No. 74379.

This double-strand wire has a two-point elongate diamond or parallelogram shape barb which is perforated in the center so that one of the strands may be threaded through the hole. Although actually a very early patent, the wire was vicious and did great damage to unknowing cattle and horses. Only after the second generation of "penned in" cattle became accustomed to wire fences did they manage to escape injury when contacting the "Thorny Fence" wire.

This was the earliest effective barbed-wire patent in the United States. Inventor Kelly was the very first patentee to use two strands in making barbed wire, and although this extra strand served three main purposes, Kelly stated only that it was to give added strength to the wire. His neglect in stating also that the second strand helped to hold the barbs in place cost him untold thousands of dollars in royalties.

The Kelly patent was involved for some time in the eighteen-year litigation with owners of the famed Glidden patent for "The Winner." Kelly wire was awarded the decision in lower court, but the decision of the higher court was in favor of Glidden because of the stated purpose of a second strand-wire.

ELLWOOD RIBBON (Early varied)

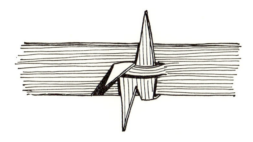

Patented on February 24, 1874, by Isaac L. Ellwood of De Kalb, Illinois. Patent No. 147756.

This is the only barbed-wire patent obtained by I. L. Ellwood, probably because he recognized the superiority of Glidden's "The Winner" at an early date and chose to buy half-interest from Glidden, even while applying for patent on his own wire.

The fence consisted of two smooth wires supplemented with a wide ribbon strip having four-point sheet-metal barbs. It would belong to the "obvious" class had it not been invented so early and evidently discontinued before the need for and purpose of "obvious" design was recognized.

Probably little, if any, of the Ellwood wire ever was made.

KENNEDY BARBS (Early varied—separate barbs)

Patented on August 11, 1874, by Charles Kennedy of Aurora, Illinois. Patent No. 153965.

This patent was concerned primarily with a three-point barb, although notice was given in the publicity that on request four- or five- or six-point barbs were available. These were separate barbs meant to be applied to single-strand wire already in use.

THE WINNER (Early varied)

Patented on November 24, 1874, by Joseph F. Glidden of De Kalb, Illinois. Patent No. 157124.

This simple wire barb twisted onto double-strand wire was known even in the nineteenth century as "The Winner." It was winner in the long litigation over priorities, and was winner too in sales competition. Modern styles of domestic barbs differ little from the Glidden invention.

CORSICANA CLIP (Early varied—separate barbs)

Patented on June 29, 1875, by Daniel C. Stover of Freeport, Illinois. Patent No. 164947.

[244]

This is the most unusual of the separate barbs group. It is described in the specifications as a twisted double-strand type of wire upon which the barb may be secured either before or after the fence is in place.

These barbs were cut with dies and were to be heated before being applied to fences already in use. If the application was to be made at the factory, the wire was to be heated instead of the barbs.

HAISH's "S" (Early varied)

Patented on August 31, 1875, by Jacob Haish of De Kalb, Illinois. Patent No. 167240.

In an earlier patent on a less satisfactory type of barbed wire, Haish maintained that his double-strand wire had overcome the seasonal effects of expansion and contraction that gave so much trouble with the iron fence wire of that early day. It is presumed that he expected the same advantage to hold for the double-strand "S" barb wire also, and in addition the strong, S-shaped wire barb was expected to be effective in use as well as practical for manufacture. As a matter of record, it may be seen that these expectations were not in vain.

This was the fifth and most important patent granted Jacob Haish. It was a successful wire and may have equaled the sales of Glidden's and Ellwood's product, "The Winner," in the first few years of manufacture.

It was largely because of the success of this wire and the Stevens machine for making it, plus the tenaciousness of Jacob Haish, that the owners of the Glidden patent could not establish a complete monopoly of the barbed-wire industry.

SPLIT DIAMOND (Early varied or obvious)

Patented on December 14, 1875, by Henry N. Frentress of Dunleith, Illinois. Patent No. 171008.

The diamond-shaped barb is split, according to patent specifications, "from the acute angles nearly to the center, and prongs bent at each end at an angle with each other to adapt them to be twisted into a two-strand wire cable." Comparable barbs had been tried on ribbon fencing twenty-two months before the Frentress patent was issued, but the "Split Diamond" probably was the earliest successful patent to utilize four-point sheet-metal barbs applied directly to double-strand wire fencing.

At first glance, it is difficult to distinguish this barb from the "Arrow Plate," which was by far the most important type of four-point sheet-metal barb. More of the "Arrow Plate" wire has been found in more places than all the remainder of the four-point sheet-metal barbs put together, and patents are available on two machines that appear to have been designed for making this barb, yet the inventor of the barb design is not positively known.

The Frentress "Split Diamond" patented in 1875 seems to have been almost as effective and practical to manufacture as the "Arrow Plate" made in 1880. The "Split Diamond" has been found in many places in the Southwest, notably in a drift fence put up by General Winfield Scott near Robert Lee, Coke County, Texas, and also in a half-buried fence around the old cemetery at Washington-on-the-Brazos, first capital of Texas.

JAYNE-HILL (Early varied)

Patented on April 11, 1876, by William H. Jayne and James H. Hill of Boone, Iowa. Patent No. 176120.

The simple four-point wire barbs of this patent were applied to single strands "in such a way that the [U] bend of each piece . . . [locked] between the arms of the other piece . . . clamping each other firmly and securely to the said fence wire, and leaving four points projecting in opposite directions."

Although the barb points shown on the patent papers appear tapered and very sharp and long, samples include also barbs with blunt, dull points. Otherwise, the patent papers description is appropriate. The barbs do in fact lock tight to each other and to the single strand upon which they are placed. Apparently these barbs had to be applied at the factory rather than clamped on fences already in use, as was done with many two- or three-point barbs of an earlier date.

TWIST OVAL (Early varied)

Patented on August 22, 1876, by Joseph F. Glidden of De Kalb, Illinois. Patent No. 181433.

The barb used in this product was the same simple wire attachment designed for "The Winner," but in this case it was used on a single- instead of double-strand wire. Furthermore, the strand was specified as an oval wire twisted to form crimps or bumps along the strand, in the hope that these two features would prevent slipping and cause the barbs to stay in place. The oval shape of the wire was intended to overcome rotary action, and the crimp, to prevent lateral motion. However, the barbs seemed to slip and gang up as on other single-strand types, and for this reason the product was not particularly successful.

This was Glidden's attempt to meet the competition of other single-strand products which were lighter in weight and consequently cheaper in price than double-strand wire.

"Twist Oval" is found in a number of states, including Kansas, Colorado, and the Texas counties of Caldwell and Childress.

POOLER-JONES (Early varied—separate barbs)

Patented on August 29, 1876, by Rheubin H. Pooler and William T. Jones of Serena, Illinois. Patent No. 181537.

Although the date of this patent is not as early as that for Kennedy barbs (above), it is thought that Pooler and Jones might have been making their separate barbs and marketing them before applying for patent. Pooler claimed that in 1874 he made and sold loose barbs, "3–10 to the pound," for fifteen to twenty-five cents per pound, and pincers for one dollar each, to farmers who wished to clamp barbs onto plain #8 or #9 wire fences. He said further that the patent on these barbs, along with rights to the pincers, he sold to Washburn & Moen Company after he was sued for infringement on the Glidden patent.[1]

In applying for patent, Pooler and Jones described their barbs as "made of wrought-steel, and with three points, somewhat resembling the tines and tang of a two-tine fork," but their

[1] Warren, *Barbed Wire—Whose Invention,* 39.

[248]

drawing showed that all three points of the barb would be exposed to use on the fence wire.

Lazy Plate (Early varied)

Patented on November 21, 1876, by William Watkins of Joliet, Illinois. Patent No. 184486.

This four-point sheet-metal barb is placed between the wires and twisted lengthwise to conform to the two strands. The barb is arranged so that a crotch is formed, and into the crotch the strand wires fit closely enough to prevent movement of the barbs. The byname "Lazy" is meant to designate the longitudinal or lying-down position of the barbs.

This is one of a series of seven or more sheet-metal barbs which evolved as a result of attempts to circumvent patents already issued. From analysis of patent developments in the years 1875 to 1878, it appears that the "Lazy Plate" may have been the third patent in the series, the first being, presumably, Frentress' "Split Diamond," with Scutt's "M/W" second.

Watkins' "Lazy Plate" has been found in Kansas, and in Bell, Kaufman, and Navarro counties of Texas.

Crandal's Link (Early varied)

Patented on November 28, 1876, by Edward M. Crandal of Chicago, Illinois. Patent No. 184844.

This old type of link wire, rather primitive in appearance, possibly may be a homemade variety. The links are five inches long, the barb one and one-half inches over all. There is no ring (or eye) in the end of the link, as the patent papers suggest there might be, apparently because it was found from experience that the wire could be handled better without the ring.

A second type with barbs only one-half inch in length is apparently an improvement over patent No. 184844, since no papers were found on this variation.

KNICKERBOCKER (Early varied—separate barbs)

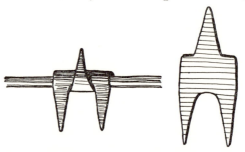

Patented on December 12, 1876, by Millis Knickerbocker of New Lenox, Illinois. Patent No. 185333.

This was another patent for three-point barbs in the bulk.

HOLD-FAST OR MERRILL TWIRL (Early varied)

Patented on December 26, 1876, by John C. Merrill of Turkey River, Iowa. Patent No. 185688.

This wire is one of the earliest successful four-point double-strand types having a wire barb. The barb design has been found in both single- and double-strand varieties. The barb was of the kind which could cause serious injury to cattle, and was among those types which initiated the era of "vicious" barbed-wire manufacture, dating generally from 1876 to 1880. The heavy-gauge variety was sometimes called "buffalo wire" by old-timers, presumably because it was so strong that it would even hold back buffalo.

The two-piece wire barbs are twisted together around the wire, and then wrapped "two around" on the strand or strands, as the case might be.

Heavy-gauge single-strand wire of this type has been found near Jayton, county seat of Kent County in West Texas. The small-gauge double-strand style has been found in Anderson and Navarro counties, both in East Texas.

BURNELL'S FOUR-POINT (Vicious)

Patented on June 19, 1877, by Arthur S. Burnell of Marshalltown, Iowa. Patent No. 192225.

Probably this is the most successful of the four-point, double-strand varieties of barbed wire. Each of the barbs "passes over a strand of the cable, thence between its strands . . . wherefrom the points of the wires project as from a center." This wire might be referred to as "four-point—two around, two between and opposite."

The wire was made by the "Iowa Barb Wire Company," sometimes called "Iowa Barb Fence Company," and sometimes also "The Iowa Barb Steel Wire Company." Home office was in Marshalltown, Iowa, and branch offices were in Johnstown, Pennsylvania, and New York City. In the two-year span between December 1, 1878, and December 17, 1880, the company had 31

[251]

machines making 2,000 pounds each in twenty hours, totaling 7,705,338 pounds.

Advertisements claimed: "It is the chapest fence made; the most durable,—is not affected by fire, wind or flood; does not cause snow drifts, takes fewer fence posts; stock can not push it down; it protects itself—acts on the defensive; it takes but little room; you can cultivate close to it. . . ."

The wire has been found in the prairie states of Kansas, Missouri, Colorado, and Texas.

NECKTIE (Vicious)

Patented on May 14, 1878, by Hiram Reynolds of Marshalltown, Iowa. Patent No. 203779.

This weird four-point barb on single-strand wire typifies the period from 1876 to 1880 when most new barbed-wire inventions were of the "vicious" type, this being one of extreme viciousness. Not only was this pattern made of single, thin strands which were harder than most to see, but the ends of the knotted barbs must have drawn blood on slightest contact.

The material was used in the Dakotas.

SCUTT'S CLIP (Vicious)

Patented on June 18, 1878, by Hiram B. Scutt of Joliet, Illinois. Patent No. 205000.

[252]

This so-called tongued barb is one of the earliest of Scutt's several patents. It is a four-point sheet-metal barb, having a central tongue or clip which grips one of the horizontal strands of wire and prevents the barb from slipping out of place. The barbs and clip together are cut from sheet-metal strips without waste.

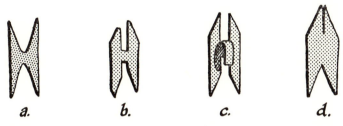

a.   *b.*   *c.*   *d.*

Pictured above are four variations of Scutt's patents: *a*, Scutt's "M/W"; *b*, Scutt's "H-Plate"; *c*, Scutt's "Clip"; *d*, "Arrow-Plate," probably Scutt's.

"Scutt's Clip" has been found in Freestone, Hill, Navarro, and Smith counties of Texas.

BILLINGS SIMPLE (Vicious)

Patented on June 25, 1878, by Frank Billings of Cleveland, Ohio. Patent No. 205234.

This is one of the least important of the four-point double-strand types of barbed wire. Relatively little of it was used, even though the simple wrap of the barbs would seem to make it one of the more effective of the four-point group. The two wires forming the barbs are short and sharp; one wire is twisted around one strand, the other around both strands, in such a way that the barbs lock themselves and the two strands together.

[253]

The wire was made and sold by the Ohio Steel Barb Fence Company of Cleveland, Ohio. It was advertised as "The lightest four-point barbed wire on the market. Therefore the cheapest." It has been found in Hill County, Texas.

TACK-UNDERWOOD (Vicious)

Patented on August 6, 1878, by Henry M. Underwood of Kenosha, Wisconsin. Patent No. 206754.

There were at least three other patents involving the use of tacks for barbs. Each of these concerns a ribbon strand rather than a wire cable, as in the case of the patent at hand. Michael Kelly's early patent No. 84062 (1868) concerned tacks driven through ribbon strips; A. J. Upham's patent No. 239892 (1881) involved rolling the sheet metal into a tubular shape; and George C. Baker's patent No. 256535 (1882) held the tacks by folding the edges of a longitudinal ribbon strip over the head of tacks. In each case, the points were left extending as barbs.

This patent is a three- or four-strand wire twisted together as a cable: three strands to hold one tack in place, four strands if two tacks are placed together back-to-back.

It has been found in Denton County, northwest of Dallas, Texas.

BROTHERTON BARB (Modified or Early Varied)

Patented on September 3, 1878, by Jacob Brotherton of Ames, Iowa. Patent No. 207710.

This easy-to-make, two-point, double-strand design, with

one end of the barb first placed between strands to separate them and next wrapped around both strands to lock them, varies only slightly from several other patents; yet it was this simple, improved version which overcame all slipping and turning of the barbs. For this reason it deserved—and achieved—considerable success. The wrap of the barb was advantageous also as a check to keep the wires from unraveling in case the strands were broken.

The Brotherton design was in close competition in two-point barbed-wire sales, if not in all types of barbed wire, until around the turn of the century.

Samples have been found in most of the prairie-plains states, including Kansas, Nebraska, Iowa, South Dakota, Illinois, Colorado, and Texas.

BRINK-TWIST (Vicious)

Patented on April 8, 1879, by Jacob Brinkerhoff of Auburn, New York. Patent No. 214095.

This patent represents Jacob Brinkerhoff's third attempt to develop a successful metal or ribbon-strip barbed fence. The strip is twisted to take care of expansion or contraction due to changes of temperature. Because the ribbon is twisted, the barbs are set on different planes and thus are in position to tag or tear anything that scrapes against the wire.

Although the ribbon is easy to see and is therefore considered as an "obvious" type of wire, the effectiveness of the barb in taking hold of passers-by outranks all other considerations and places the invention in the "vicious" category. The barb is 1.2 inches in length over all, though only .4 inches on either side of the ribbon can penetrate.

This "Brink Twist" patent on twisted barbed ribbon should be compared with the "Brink Flat" barb on flat ribbon patented by Jacob and Warren M. Brinkerhoff in 1881. The two patents are almost identical except for the one feature of a straight flat or a twisted ribbon strand. Where the ribbon strand was not twisted, the barbs did not prick or tear an animal that merely brushed against it; the animal had to try to get through or between the fence strands before the barbs could make contact enough to pierce the hide. This one slight difference places the two types of wire in separate categories: "Brink Twist" was "vicious" wire; "Brink Flat" was "obvious."

Ross's Four-Point (Vicious)

Patented on June 10, 1879, by Noble G. Ross of Chicago, Illinois. Patent No. 216294.

This is one of the six best patents granted for double-strand four-point wire. With the exception of one point, the barbs are twisted around the outside of the two-strand wires; the remaining point extends between the strands, serving as a binder or lock for the four-point barb. It might be identified as a "three around, one between" type of twist.

The wire was made by the Lyman Manufacturing Company of Grand Crossing, Illinois. Probably this is the most common of the older patents concerning four-point wire barbs, having been found in all of the prairie-plains states.

Champion or Zigzag (Obvious)

Patented November 4, 1879, by Edward M. Crandal of Chicago, Illinois. Patent No. 221158.

This wire consists of a zigzag strip of sheet metal twisted between two strands of plain wire. The points of the strip form the barbs. The wire is one of the earliest of the "obvious" types specifically designed to counteract cowmen's claims that cattle were being injured by running against fences made of the earlier "vicious" types of barbed wire. Crandal claimed that the points of his wire would deter livestock but would not injure animals that pressed against his wire accidentally. It was advertised as "the most visible and effective and the least dangerous barb wire known." It was named "The Champion."

Crandal invented eight types of barbed wire or machines for making barbed wire. His "Champion," sometimes called "Zigzag," was one of the most widely prized of "obvious" types.

Quantities of Crandal's "Champion" wire have been found east of Red Bluff, California, on the road to Lassen National Park, as well as in Refugio, Navarro, and Live Oak counties of Texas, and near the old Santa Fe Trail where it crossed the Oklahoma Panhandle. This crossing of the Trail is now marked with a historical monument reading "Traffic on the Trail finally came to an end in the 1880s as homesteaders fenced the prairies and railroads pushed west."

Shinn's Four-Point (Vicious)

Patented on March 1, 1881, by Milton C. Shinn of Burlington, Iowa. Patent No. 238447.

This type of wire has its four-point wire barb twisted regularly around one of the two strand wires, leaving the barbs pointing in four directions. The last twist of the barb is fixed in place by the four-points of the barb crossing each other and locking on one of the strands, as "two around, two between and tie."

BRINK FLAT (Obvious)

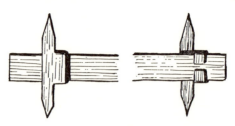

Patented on May 17, 1881, by Jacob and Warren M. Brinker-hoff of Auburn, New York. Patent No. 241601.

This three-eighths-inch ribbon strip of flat galvanized metal has two-point sheet-metal barbs clamped on vertically at four- to six-inch intervals. The design is considered an improvement over the "Brink Twist" patent of 1879, although the only difference is that in the earlier patent the ribbon strand is twisted, whereas it remains upright in the later style. The change was made because of the realization that cattle could be cut if they merely brushed against barbs on the twisted ribbon, and it was seen that with the straight strands cattle would be cut only if they tried to break through or reach out between the strands.

"Brink Flat" was the most successful of the several types of ribbon strip patented by the Brinkerhoffs, and it was probably second only to "Buckthorn" in demand of all types of ribbon wire manufactured. It was the "Brink Flat" which was used in the 1880's by the Capitol Syndicate in fencing much of the extensive northern division of the three-million-acre XIT ranch of the Texas Panhandle. In all probability the "flat wire with barbs" which Shanghai Pierce chose was this same product, for in the Pierce part of the Texas coastal plains. "Brink Flat" has been seen on the Duncan ranch, Wharton County, and in the little Northington Museum at Egypt, Texas, and was described by Louis Luco who helped lay off land with a rope to put in telephone poles in old Matagorda County. Mr. Luco, of Wharton, Texas, recalls the early wire fencing as being "like a tape measure, galvanized, with barbs set to the wire."

[258]

Some years ago, when all remaining barbed wire was being removed from the famed King Ranch of south Texas, it was the observation of a member of the Kleberg family (descendants of Captain King) that this wire—"Brink Flat"—appeared to be in better condition after fifteen years in use on the ranch than some wire is when first put up. This was unusually high praise because of the location of the King property near the Gulf of Mexico, where the wire was subjected to the highly corrosive effects of salt air blowing in from the Gulf. This heavily galvanized Brinkerhoff product had stood the test, however, and was removed only because of the damage it might do to unknowing cattle who encountered it. As a rule, the King Ranch stressed the use of smooth wire for this very reason.

The "Brink Flat" has been seen from northern Colorado eastward into Kansas, and into south Texas; and regardless of locality, it was found always to be in excellent condition, due to its heavy coat of galvanizing.

BUCKTHORN (Obvious)

Patented on July 26, 1881, by T. V. Allis of New York City. Patent No. 244726.

This twisted ribbon strip of galvanized metal has dull prongs or lances spaced at one-inch intervals on one side of the ribbon only. It was advertised not as a wire but as a solid ribbed strip of steel, being "very strong" and "presenting the largest possible surface to view." Also, it was said to be "effective, safe and strong, handsome, lasting and cheap." It was known as a good fence material for sheepmen, not only because it could be seen plainly but also because the lance-shape of the barbs caused the sheep wool to slip off the barb without being pulled out.

Although this was probably the most popular of all ribbon types of fencing and was patented in the United States, Great

Britain, and other principal industrial countries in Europe, it was expensive to make and never offered serious competition to the less expensive two- or four-point double-strand wire. It was off the market before 1900.

DODGE AND WASHBURN (Modified)

Patented on January 24, 1882, by Thomas H. Dodge and Charles G. Washburn of Worcester, Massachusetts. Patent No. 252746.

Each of the two wires of the four-point barb of this patent is twisted one and one-half times around one of the two strand wires, or "four around one." It is a simple four-point wire.

BAKER PERFECT (Modified)

Next to "The Winner" in sales was a product designed by George C. Baker of Des Moines, Iowa. This was the most popular of the products manufactured outside the jurisdiction of the Washburn & Moen Company. Except for a period of curtailed or canceled production, sales on this wire continued strong throughout the period of legal controversies—and beyond. The Baker factory, located in successive order at Des Moines, Lockport, (Illinois), and Joliet, was an important center of the barbed-wire industry. Its over-all output in all probability was as great as any manufactory other than the Washburn & Moen Company. The different steel companies later taking up the manufacture of Baker wire gave it various commercial names incorporating the term "Perfect." However, there is only limited information on this wire in records of the industry, and there are no known positive patent papers for "Baker Perfect."

"Baker Perfect" wire is a flat, two-point barb on double-strand wire. Since authoritative patent papers are lacking, identification must be based on practical knowledge and experience. George C. Baker did receive a number of patents, four or more on barbed-wire designs and three or more on machines for making barbed wire, but none at hand definitely covers the "Perfect" wire. The machine granted patent No. 295513 was probably the one used to make "Perfect" wire, and the two-point flat, notched barb granted patent No. 273219 may have been the design from which the "Perfect" wire evolved since the two are the same except for the notches in the earlier barbs.

The Baker name crops up in many places throughout the history of the development of the barbed-wire industry. It is thought that a Baker machine was used by John W. Gates to begin his "moonshine" operations; in the midst of the Iowa Protective Farmers' Association fight was the Des Moines factory; and when the Columbia Patent Company bought out the important Washburn & Moen wireworks, it was agreed that the "Baker Perfect" wire was not to be produced by Washburn & Moen Company and Ellwood "until after February 27, 1894."[2] But the product continued in popularity despite complications.

The fact that large amounts of it are still to be found on fences all across the nation indicates that this wire was second only to "The Winner" in sales, service, and general satisfaction. Samples of it have been found in twenty-odd states stretching from coast to coast.

[2] Gedge and Boley, "History," II, 84.

STUBBE PLATE (Obvious)

Patented on October 23, 1883, by John Stubbe of Pittsburgh, Pennsylvania. Patent No. 287337.

This unusual type of barbed wire was designed so that cattle might easily see a fence made of the wire, and avoid contact with it. The barbs were fashioned so that if contact was made, the points would scratch or prick rather than cut the animal.

"Stubbe Plate" was manufactured in two sizes, one having a one-inch metal plate and the other a one-and-five-eighths-inch plate (the ultimate in visibility for double-strand wires) attached at regular intervals along the strand wires. Both plates have diagonal slits cut at the four corners, permitting the sides of the plate to be curved, and making eight points on each plate—the equal of an eight-point barb. The curving sides also provide a space for horizontal strands to fit and hold the wire tightly.

Both sizes of "Stubbe Plate" have been found in Texas, the large plate in Llano, Fannin, and Parker counties, and the small plate in Bastrop County.

CHAIN-LINK (Modified)

The wire was made by a machine patented on January 22, 1884, by Frank P. Cady of Chicago, Illinois. Machine Patent No. 292408.

This wire, built like a chain, also sagged like a chain.

DECKER SPREAD (Modified)

Patented on June 3, 1884, by Alexander C. Decker of Bushnell, Illinois. Patent No. 299916.

This double-strand wire features longer-than-usual barbs placed at regular intervals between twists "to spread the strands apart," and coiled around the separated strands to extend in two-point wire barbs.

Alexander Decker, in partnership with James Ayers, a wagonmaker, was among the first to be sued as an infringer against Washburn & Moen Company after the 1880 court decision. However, the Ayers-Decker combine with a partner named John McNeill continued operations under another name at a new location in Keokuk, Iowa, until 1894.

Actually Decker was granted several patents on barbed wire, beginning in 1876 (No. 178605) when he and Ayers set up a handmachine in a back room of Ayers' wagon shop. Decker's patent No. 186716, granted early the following year, however, was the one most responsible for the legal entanglements. In this case one-half of the rights were assigned to John McNeill; one-third of one-half went to Ayers; then McNeill's half went to Ayers; and Ayers' rights were finally transferred to Washburn & Moen Company in December, 1878—though not without a fight. The lawsuit filed against Ayers and Decker was tried before the United States Circuit Court for the Southern District of Illinois, with the defendants claiming that barbed wire was not new even at the time of the Kelly patent in 1868, and citing patents such as Meriwether's (smooth wire), Gale's and Clinger's inventions, along with the usual undocumented pre-Glidden experiments of

Hair, Hibbard, Cook, and Beers. In the end, the complainants won the suit, but not without bringing in many of the important personalities of the barbed-wire world, and not until these special witnesses had given lengthy evidence.[3] The Ayers-Decker-McNeill firm received license from Washburn & Moen and Ellwood in 1881 and 1882, and was re-licensed by the Columbia Patent Company in 1885—this time, presumably, to manufacture under the 1884 patent for the popular "Decker Spread" design.

Being neither "vicious" nor "obvious," this wire represents the "modified" group, despite the fact that the spread of the strand wires serves to make this kind of wire more noticeable than most.

This wire has been found in Kansas, Missouri, and Texas.

"SUNDERLAND KINK" (Early varied or modified)

Patented on August 12, 1884, by L. E. Sunderland of Joliet, Illinois. Patent No. 303406.

In contrast to most older varieties of single-strand barbed wire, this type employs a kink in the wire strand, with the two-point wire barb wrapped on either side. Because of this feature, and the characteristic wrap of the barb, the barbs do not slip on this strand wire as they do on most single-strand types.

Three earlier patents—Emerson's No. 176523, Rose's No. 198688, and Orwig's No. 201890—may have led to the perfection of "Sunderland Kink." Also, the machine for making it seems to have been patented on February 12, 1884; application for patent on Sunderland's wire was filed in May and granted in August of the same year.

[3] Depositions in the case of Washburn & Moen Manufacturing Company and Isaac L. Ellwood vs. James Ayers and Alexander C. Decker, U.S. Circuit Court, Southern District of Illinois, 1877; AS&W Records, *loc. cit.*

The wire usually is found nowadays in good condition in spite of its age and in spite of the fact that there are no indications of its having been galvanized. Its widespread use indicates that it was the most common single-strand type of barbed-wire fencing. Samples have been found in many places, notably in Kansas and in a number of east Texas counties, including Navarro County, where the wire was cut repeatedly during the fence wars of the 1880's.

WAUKEGAN WIRE (Modified)

This two-point half-round, wire barb design still is a leading product of the American Steel & Wire Division of United States Steel Company, and the plant established at Waukegan, Illinois, in 1890 and rebuilt in 1899 is still known as an important manufactory.

BRINK-MARTELLE (Obvious)

Patented on August 11, 1885, by John J. Brinkerhoff of Auburn, New York. Patent No. 324221.

This rare patent calls for both ribbon and round wire to be stretched longitudinally together to form a fence strand. The inventor, another Brinkerhoff (and probably kin to Jacob and Warren Brinkerhoff, also of Auburn, New York) goes into detail to explain and picture the advantages of ribbon and round wire twisted together. Despite three pages of pictures and over two full pages of closely printed explanation, however, it is difficult to understand what the advantages may be. This must have been the feeling of other people also, for one full sheet of the patent papers had been crossed out with an X before reprinting, as though to indicate that the wording meant nothing. A cautious employee of the Patent Office evidently tried in vain to erase the X-mark, and then lettered "Print This" across the page so that it would be reproduced—as indeed it was—and furnished with all copies of the original patent. The only other patent for this combination of ribbon with round wire (No. 163955) was as futile a variation as this one.

SPUR-ROWEL (Modified obvious)

Patented on August 2, 1887, by Chester A. Hodge of Beloit, Wisconsin. Patent No. 367398.

In contrast to the apparent ease with which one man came upon and perfected the dominant Glidden style of barbed wire, many inventors worked for years in developing satisfactory forms of some other designs. The spur-rowel, spur-wheel or roulette-shaped metal barb on a double-strand wire was one of those which, although tried at an early date, was not perfected until thirteen men with separate patents had labored over a period of twenty years.

The rowel design was first conceived by William D. Hunt of Scott, New York, and was granted patent No. 67117, which figured prominently in barbed-wire litigation. The Hunt patent, besides advancing the concept of armored fencing, also stirred up interest in the use of a rotating rowel which would be visible, yet would not damage livestock. In other words, his invention anticipated objections which later were to arise from the use of barbs which were too sharp and not easily seen. But in spite of the fact that the Hunt design had desirable qualities, its performance was disappointing because the rowel, which was intended to turn, usually remained rigid enough to tear the hides of animals contacting it.

Thirteen other inventors received patent on variations of the same principle, each patentee expecting to overcome the difficulty which had kept the Hunt patent from being satisfactory. Finally, in 1887, Chester A. Hodge of Beloit, Wisconsin, received patent for a successful spur-wheel with axle that worked properly, but after twenty years of experimentation, the product did not prove to be as usable as had been expected. The simpler, modified barbs of other styles had become more popular, livestock had adjusted to them, and manufacturers were mass producing them. Thus, the spur-rowel design was never to compare with any of the other leading styles, and certainly was not used in comparable quantities. Though William D. Hunt was accorded a place in the annals of the industry, his design was never produced on a large scale, under either his patent or others. Little of the spur-rowel of Hunt or of his successors ever was made; little or none of it is to be found today.

1. MANUSCRIPTS

American Steel & Wire Company. Interior Views. "Collection of Photographs from the Industrial Museum of American Steel & Iron Company, founded 1908, Interior Views Marking 15 Years of Growth, 1908–1923." 2 vols. Baker Library, Harvard University.

———. Records. American Steel & Wire Company of New Jersey. [Records in the Baker Library, Harvard University, contain AS&W history, including court records and unpublished briefs. There is also a three-volume set of books showing specimens of early barbed wire from the Industrial Museum. Many other materials in this large collection are invaluable to a study of barbed wire.]

Burton, H. T. "A History of the JA Ranch." University of Texas Library, Austin.

Ellwood Family Papers. University of Wyoming, Laramie; family library, Colorado City, Texas.

Gedge, John, and William Boley. "History of the Manufacture of Barbed Wire." Compiled by G. L. Meaker and L. C. Bailey for the American Steel & Wire Company of New Jersey, 1913. Baker Library, Harvard University.

Gibson, Arrell Morgan. "Utilization of the Public Domain of the Central and Northern Plains by the Range Cattle Industry, 1865–1900." University of Oklahoma Library, 1948.

Haish, Jacob. "A Reminiscent Chapter from the Unwritten History of Barb Wire Prior to and Immediately Following the Celebrated Decision of Judge Blodgett, December 15, 1881." Ellwood Family Papers, University of Wyoming, Laramie.

Hayter Collection. University of Wyoming, Laramie.

Peterson, Ben. The Peterson Scrapbook. Property of Mrs. Ben Peterson, Everson, Washington.

Sanborn, H. B. The Sanborn Scrapbook. Amarillo City Library, Amarillo, Texas.

Tracy, Fred. "Reminiscences of No-Man's Land." University of Oklahoma Library.

Wallis, George A. "Cattle Kings of the Staked Plains." University of Wyoming Library.

Webb, Walter Prescott. "Hypothesis and History." 1960. Mimeographed copy in authors' files.

2. GOVERNMENT DOCUMENTS

Annual Report of the United States Commissioner of General Land Office, 1882, 1883, 1885, 1890.

Annual Report of the United States Department of Agriculture, 1869.

Richardson, James D., editor. *A Compilation of the Messages and Papers of the Presidents, 1789–1897.* 10 vols. Washington, Government Printing Office, 1896–99.

Subject Matter Index of Patents for Inventions Issued by the U.S. Patent Office from 1790 to 1873, Inclusive. M. D. Leggett, Commissioner of Patents, comp., 1874. 3 vols. Washington, Government Printing Office, 1874. . . . 1790 to 1956, Robert C. Watson, Commissioner of Patents, comp. Washington, Government Printing office, 1956.

United States Code, Vol. IV, Title 43, 1946.

United States Congress, House. *H.R. Exec. Doc. No. 51,* 46 Cong., 2 sess., 1880.

———. *H.R. Exec. Doc. No. 47,* 46 Cong., 3 sess., 1881.

———. *H.R. Exec. Doc. No. 1,* 47 Cong., 2 sess., 1882.

———. *H.R. Exec. Doc. No. 72,* 47 Cong., 2 sess., 1883.

———. *H.R. Exec. Doc. 232,* 50 Cong., 1 sess., 1888.

United States Congress, Senate. *Sen. Exec. Doc. No. 54,* 48 Cong., 1 sess., 1883.

———. *Sen. Rep. No. 1278,* 49 Cong., 1 sess., 1885.

United States Statutes at Large. II, Boston, 1856; XXIII, Washington, n.d.; XXIV, Washington, n.d.

3. NEWSPAPERS

Austin American Statesman, June 13, 1937.

Chicago Tribune, September 18, 1910.

Dallas Morning News, October 20, 1929.

De Kalb Daily Chronicle, June 24, 1920; April 18, 1958.

De Kalb Review, April 15, 1915; November 23, 1916.

Des Moines Register, January 21, 1940.

Fort Worth Star Telegram, May 26, 1912.

Houston Post, September 17, 1957.

Industrial World, The (Chicago), December 23, 1880.

Texas Siftings (Austin), July 22, 1882.

Waco Tribune Herald, April 3, 1955.

Wharton (Texas) *Spectator,* September 2, 1898; June 30, 1884.

4. BOOKS AND PAMPHLETS

Adams, Ramon F. *Western Words.* Norman, University of Oklahoma Press, 1944.

Bedichek, Roy. *Adventures of a Texas Naturalist.* Garden City, N.Y., Doubleday Company, 1947.

Billington, Ray Allen. *Westward Expansion.* New York, The Macmillan Company, 1949.

The Biographical Record of De Kalb County, Illinois. Chicago, S. J. Clark Company, 1898.

Bishop, Curtis. *This Day in Texas.* San Angelo, Standard Times, 1948.

Bracht, Viktor. *Texas in 1848.* Translated from the German by Charles Frank Schmidt. San Antonio, Naylor, 1931.

Briggs, Harold E. *Frontiers of the Northwest*. New York, Appleton Century Company, 1940.

Brisbin, James S. *Beef Bonanza*. Philadelphia, J. B. Lippincott, 1882.

Burroughs, John R. *Where the Old West Stayed Young*. New York, Morrow & Company, 1962.

Call, Hughie. *The Golden Fleece*. Boston, Houghton Mifflin, 1942.

Clark, Ira G. *Then Came the Railroads*. Norman, University of Oklahoma Press, 1958.

Clay, John. *My Life on the Range*. Chicago, privately printed, [1924].

Coffin, Robert P. T. *Selected Poems*. New York, The Macmillan Company, 1955.

Cox, James. *Historical and Biographical Record of the Cattle Industry and the Cattlemen of Texas and Adjacent Territory*. St. Louis, Stock Growers Association, 1895.

Dale, Edward Everett. *Cow Country*. Norman, University of Oklahoma Press, 1942.

———. *The Range Cattle Industry*. Norman, University of Oklahoma Press, 1930.

Debo, Angie, editor. *The Cowman's Southwest, Being the Reminiscences of Oliver Nelson*. Glendale, Arthur H. Clark Company, 1953.

DePay, William Atherton. *Uncle Sam's Modern Miracles*. New York, Frederick A. Stokes Company, 1914.

DeShields, James T. *They Sat in High Places*. San Antonio, Naylor, 1940.

Dobie, J. Frank. *The Longhorns*. Boston, Little, Brown, 1941.

———. *A Vaquero of the Brush Country*. Dallas, Southwest Press, 1929.

Emmett, Chris. *Shanghai Pierce*. Norman, University of Oklahoma Press, 1953.

Faulkner, Virginia, compiler. *Roundup: A Nebraska Reader*. Lincoln, University of Nebraska Press, 1957.

Fisher, Douglas A. *Steel Serves the Nation.* N.p., United States Steel Corporation, 1951.

Gammel, H.P.N. *Laws of the State of Texas.* 10 vols. Austin, The Gammel Book Company, 1898.

Gard, Wayne. *The Chisholm Trail.* Norman, University of Oklahoma Press, 1954.

Giese, Henry. *Farm Fence Handbook.* Cleveland, Republic Steel Corporation, 1942.

Gross, Lewis M. *Past and Present of De Kalb County, Illinois.* 2 vols. N.p., 1907.

Haley, J. Evetts. *Charles Goodnight.* Norman, University of Oklahoma Press, 1949.

———. *The XIT Ranch of Texas.* Norman, University of Oklahoma Press, 1953.

Hamner, Laura V. *Light'n Hitch.* Dallas, American Guild Press. 1958.

———. *Short Grass and Longhorns.* Norman, University of Oklahoma Press, 1943.

Harrington, W. P. *History of Gove County, Kansas; Organized in 1886.* Gove City, Republican Gazette Press, 1920.

Hart, John A. *Pioneer Days in the Southwest.* Guthrie, Oklahoma, State Capitol Company, 1909.

Horan, James D., and Paul Sann. *Pictorial History of the Wild West.* New York, Crown Publishers, Inc., 1954.

Hunt, Frazier. *The Tragic Days of Billy the Kid.* New York, Hastings House, 1956.

Jackson, W. Turrentine, *et al. When Grass Was King.* Boulder, University of Colorado Press, 1956.

Kogan, Herman, and Lloyd Wendt. *Bet-A-Million: The Story of John W. Gates.* New York, Bobbs-Merrill, 1948.

Kupper, Winifred. *The Golden Hoof.* New York, Alfred A. Knopf, 1945.

Kursh, Harry. *How to Get Land from Uncle Sam.* New York, W. W. Norton and Company, Incorporated, 1955.

McCoy, Joseph G. *Historic Sketches of the Cattle Trade of the*

West and Southwest. Washington, D. C., The Rare Book Shop, 1932.

Marsh, C. W., compiler. *The De Kalb County Manufacturer*. De Kalb, Chronicle Press and Bindery, n.d.

Mercer, Asa S. *The Banditti of the Plains*. Norman, University of Oklahoma Press, 1954.

Miller, Joseph, editor. *New Mexico: A Guide to the Colorful State*. New York, Hastings House, 1940.

Moody, John. *The Railroad Builders*. New Haven, Yale University Press, 1919.

Nordyke, Lewis. *Cattle Empire*. New York, William Morrow and Company, 1949.

———. *Great Roundup*. New York, William Morrow and Company, 1955.

Osgood, Ernest Staples. *The Day of the Cattleman*. Chicago, University of Chicago Press, 1929.

Otis Steel Company. *The Story of the First Steel Company*. Cleveland, Pioneer Press, n.d.

Paddock, B. B. *A Twentieth-Century Historical and Biographical Record of North and West Texas*. Chicago, Lewis Publishing Company, 1906.

Paxson, Frederick Logan. *The Last American Frontier*. New York, The Macmillan Company, 1915.

Pelzer, Louis. *The Cattleman's Frontier*. Glendale, The Arthur H. Clark Company, 1936.

Pennybacker, Anna J. H. *A History of Texas*. N.p., Pennybacker, 1895.

Preece, Harold. *Lone Star Man, Ira Aten, Last of the Old Texas Rangers*. New York, Hastings House, 1960.

Schaefer, Joseph. *A History of the Pacific Northwest*. New York, The Macmillan Company, 1921.

Shepherd, Major W. *Prairie Experiences in Handling Cattle and Sheep*. London, Chapman & Hall, Ltd., 1884.

Steen, Ralph W., and Frances Donecker. *Texas, Our Heritage*. Austin, The Steck Company, 1962.

Towne, Charles W., and Edward N. Wentworth. *Shepherd's Empire*. Norman, University of Oklahoma Press, 1945.

Twitchell, Ralph Emerson. *Leading Facts of New Mexico History*. 5 vols. Cedar Rapids, The Torch Press, 1911–17.

Turner, Frederick Jackson. *The Frontier in American History*. New York, Henry Holt and Company, 1920.

Vestal, Stanley. *Short Grass Country*. New York, Duell, Sloan and Pearce, 1941.

Von Richthofen, Walter Baron. *Cattle-Raising on the Plains of North America*. New York, D. Appleton and Company, 1885.

Wallis, George A. *Cattle Kings of the Staked Plains*. Dallas, American Guild Press, 1957.

Warren, Arthur G. *Barbed Wire—Whose Invention*. Worcester, American Steel & Wire Company, 1926.

Wellman, Paul I. *The Trampling Herd*. New York, Carrick and Evans, Incorporated, [1939].

Warshow, Robert I. *Bet-A-Million Gates: The Story of a Plunger*. New York, Greenberry Publishers, 1932.

Webb, Walter Prescott. *The Great Frontier*. Boston, Houghton Mifflin Company, 1952.

———. *The Great Plains*. Boston, Ginn and Company, 1931.

———. *The Texas Rangers*. Boston, Houghton Mifflin Company, 1935.

Wilbarger, J. W. *Indian Depredations in Texas*. Austin, The Steck Company, 1935.

Winkler, Louis H. *Mordia Memorial Lecture of 1942*. N.p., Bethlehem Steel Company, 1942.

Wortham, Louis J. *A History of Texas*. Fort Worth, Wortham-Mollyneaux Company, n.d.

W.P.A. Writer's Program. *Wyoming, A Guide to Its History, Highways, and People*. New York, Oxford University Press, 1941.

5. Periodicals

Anon. "The Barbed Wire Story," *Wireco Life* (1956).

——. "John W. Bet-a-Million Gates," *Wireco Life* (1956).

——. "New England Fences," *Scribner's Monthly* (February, 1880).

——. "A One Man Tank for the Barbed Wire Cutter," *Scientific American* (April 14, 1917).

——. "Realm of the Retailer," *American Lumberman* (October 26, 1918).

——. "Wire," *The Saturday Review of Politics, Literature, Science, and Art* (January 7, 1888).

Aten, Ira. As Told to Harold Preece. "Born to Bust Barb," *Wireco Life* (1956).

Carmichael, Joe M. "The Thorny Fence," *The Cattleman* (January, 1949).

Clapp, G. P. "The Manufacture of Wire," *Scientific American* (1892).

Conger, Roger N. "Fencing in McLennan County, Texas," *Southwestern Historical Quarterly* (October, 1955).

Coughlan, Robert. "The General's Mighty Chariots," *Life* (November 16, 1959).

Dale, Edward Everett. "Cow Country in Transition," *Mississippi Valley Historical Review* (June, 1937).

Douglas, C. L. "Cattle Kings of Texas," *The Cattleman* (December, 1935; January, 1936).

Douglass, William Boone. "How Inventor Kelly Lost His Millions," *Professional Engineer* (October, 1928).

Gard, Wayne. "The Fence Cutters," *Southwestern Historical Quarterly* (July, 1947).

Goff, Dick. "Guardian of the Grass Country," *The Denver Westerners Roundup* (November, 1958).

Goodnight, Charles. "Managing a Trail Herd," *Frontier Times* (September, 1949).

Haley, J. Evetts. "And Then Came Barbed Wire to Change History's Course," *The Cattleman* (March, 1927).

Hayter, Earl W. "Barbed Wire Fencing—A Prairie Invention," *Agricultural History* (October, 1939).

——. "Fencing of Western Railways," *Agricultural History* (July, 1945).

——. "An Iowa Farmer's Protective Association," *Iowa Journal of History and Politics* (October, 1939).

Holt, Roy D. "Barbed Wire," *The Texas Monthly* (September, 1929).

——. "Barbed Wire Drift Fences," *The Cattleman* (March, 1935).

——. "From Trail to Rail in the Texas Cattle Industry," *The Cattleman* (March, 1932).

——. "Introducing Barbed Wire to Texas Stockmen," *The Cattleman* (July, 1930).

——. "The Introduction of Barbed Wire into Texas and the Fence Cutting War," *West Texas Historical Association Yearbook* (June, 1930).

——. "Net-Wire Fences Changed Sheep Raising," *The Sheep and Goat Raiser* (March, 1951).

——. "The Saga of Barbed Wire in Tom Green County," *West Texas Historical Association Yearbook* (June, 1928).

Hubert, Harry. "The First Barbed Wire in Coleman County," *Frontier Times* (July, August, September, 1953).

Hunter, J. Marvin, Sr. "When Barbed Wire Came to Coleman County," *Frontier Times* (August, 1951).

Latta, Adrian C. "Evolution of the Barbed Wire Fence," *Scientific American* (November 2, 1907).

Love, Clara M. "History of the Cattle Industry," *Southwestern Historical Quarterly* (April, 1916).

McClure, C. Boone, editor. "History of the Manufacture of Barbed Wire," *Panhandle-Plains Historical Review* (1958).

McLean, Malcolm D. "Don't Fence Me In," *Southwestern Historical Quarterly* (January, 1948).

MacIntosh, P. J. R. "Barbed Wire in Texas," *The Texas Weekly* (May 23, 1936).

Mirrielees, Lucia B., editor. "Pioneer Ranching in Central Montana from Letters of Otto Maerdian, Written in 1882–1883," *The Frontier* (1930).

Mooar, Wright. "First Buffalo Hunting in the Panhandle," *West Texas Historical Association Yearbook* (June, 1930).

————. "Some Observations on the Cattle Industry," *West Texas Historical Association Yearbook* (June, 1929).

Moses, Tad. "Development of the Cattle Business in Texas," *Texas Almanac* (1949).

Owens, Clyde Meehan. "Studies in the Settlement and Economic Development of Wyoming," *Annals of Wyoming* (July, 1931; October, 1931).

Pooley, William V. "The Settlement of Illinois from 1830 to 1850," University of Wisconsin *Bulletin No. 220* (May, 1908).

Records, Ralph H. "A Cowhand's Recollections," *The Cattleman* (June, 1943).

Robinson, Rowland C. "New England Fences," *Scribner's Monthly* (February, 1880).

Sheffy, L. F. "Old Mobeetie—The Capital of the Panhandle," *West Texas Historical Association Yearbook* (June, 1930).

Tanner, A. M. "A French Patent of the Year 1860 for a Barbed Wire Fence," *Scientific American* (November 12, 1892).

Vance, Millard F. "Pioneering at Akron, Colorado," *The Colorado Magazine* (September, 1931).

Vandeburg, C. M. "Barbed Wire," *Wire* (February, 1936).

Warren, Arthur G. "Barbed Wire—Who Invented It?" *The Iron Age* (June 24, 1926).

Webb, Walter Prescott. "From Split Rails to Barbed Wire," *True West* (1960).

————. "The West and the Desert," *Montana* (January, 1958).

Woodhull, Frost. "Ranch Remedies," *Texas Folklore Society* (1930).